REPRISE

An Irish church musician looks back

Harry Grindle

Author: Harry Grindle
Published by: Harry Grindle
©2009 Harry Grindle
ISBN 978-0-956378-00-2

Available through:
The Good Book Shop,
61-67 Donegall Street,
BELFAST
BT1 2QH
Tel: 028 9024 4825
E-mail: sales@goodbookshop.com

Designed by April Sky Design, Newtownards
Printed by W&G Baird, Antrim

April Sky Design (part of the Colourpoint Group)
Colourpoint House
Jubilee Business Park
Jubilee Road
NEWTOWNARDS
County Down
Northern Ireland
BT23 4YH
Tel: 028 9182 7195
Fax: 028 9182 1900
E-mail: info@aprilsky.co.uk
Web site: www.aprilsky.co.uk

In memory of my parents

Harry Edward and Agnes Jean Grindle

and of my brother

David

CONTENTS

Illustrations ix

Foreword by the Rt Revd Lord Eames OM of Armagh xi

Author's preface and acknowledgements xiii

Abbreviations xv

Bibliography xvii

Discography xviii

1. 1935-53 Childhood, Bangor Abbey, Regent House School 1

2. 1953-61 University, school-teaching and first organist posts 23

3. 1961-62 Further study and school-teaching in London 38

4. 1962-64 Bangor Parish Church 50

5. 1964-65 Belfast Cathedral 66

6. 1965-67 Belfast Cathedral, The Cathedral Consort 81

7. 1968-70 Belfast Cathedral, Dean Samuel Crooks 98

8. 1971-72 Belfast Cathedral, St Louis Sisters' Choir 114

9. 1972-74 Belfast Cathedral, Choir's first commercial recording 128

10. 1975-76 Belfast Cathedral, rebuilt Organ, first Cathedral Festival 143

11. 1975-85 Stranmillis College, further studies 163

12. 1986-2008 Stranmillis College, The Priory Singers, Retirement 180

Index 208

Illustrations

West front of Belfast Cathedral. (Line drawing by James Drennan) fontispiece

Harry's father and mother with Stanley Heyburn (message-boy) outside the shop in Church Street, Bangor c1940 p 3

Three generations – Harry with his father and grandfather c1937 p 6

Harry and his brother, David – choristers at Bangor Abbey c1946 p 9

Bertram L Jones (aged 91) MA (h.c.), Queen's University, Belfast 1988 p17

Ernest H Emery at the organ of Bangor Parish Church c1959 p17

Form VI Latin Class at Regent House School, Newtownards, 1953 p19

Edred M Chaundy c1908 p21

Members of the Choir of Willowfield Parish Church, Belfast c1960 p28

Sir Adrian Boult's conducting course, Bromley, Kent, August, 1960 p35

The Grindle family c1960 p37

The Choir of Friern Barnet Grammar School, London, December 1961 p47

Programme of FBGS Summer Concert, July 1962 p47

Harry at the organ of Bangor Parish Church, 1963 p50

The Choir of Bangor Parish Church, 1962 p52

The Clergy of Bangor Parish Church, 1963 p58

Harry at the organ of Belfast Cathedral in 1965 p67

Captain C J Brennan at the organ of Belfast Cathedral on the day of his retirement in June 1964 p70

Belfast Cathedral Choir outing to Newcastle, Co. Down mid-1960s p71

Programme of recital by the Choir of Belfast Cathedral in May 1965 p79

Cover picture of May-September, 1966 issue of the *Oxford Music Bulletin* p83

The Cathedral Consort in 1969 p85

H F Selwood Lindsay with his father, Canon Herbert Lindsay, outside their home at Stranmillis p90

Harry and Heather on their wedding day, 6 August 1968, with their parents p102

Dean Crooks and the Revd John Nolan with Harry and some of the choristers p109

The St Louis Sisters' Choir in February1973 p120

Belfast Cathedral Choir at Westminster Abbey, August 1973 p131

Hannah (aged six) p143

Rachel (aged three) with Heather p143

Cearbhall Ó Dálaigh, President of the Republic of Ireland, with some of those participating in the opening concert of the 1975 Dublin Arts Festival at St Patrick's Cathedral p146

Henry and Kenneth James with Harry at the console of the rebuilt organ at Belfast Cathedral, 1975 p149

Professor Gerard Gillen p150

Letter from Herbert Howells, January 1976 p157

Harry rehearsing the Stranmillis College Choir c1997 p165

Hugh Alexander Boyd and his wife, Pearl, with Harry in the early 1980s p175

Commencements (i.e. graduation) at Trinity College, Dublin, July 1985. From left: Harry's sister, Norma, his mother, Professor Brian Boydell, Harry, and Joseph Groocock. p179

President of the USOC (1986-87) p184

A group of officials of the USOC with Donald Hunt, Organist of Worcester Cathedral, at the Society's annual dinner in October 1986 p185

Shauna Hoey being presented with the RSCM's Young Organist's Certificate by Archbishop Eames in 1996 p187

Harry with the Rt Hon. Michael Foot MP at the Swift Seminar at Celbridge Abbey in July 1991 p192

Practice organ at 37 Cairnburn Crescent, Belfast p197

The Priory Singers in 2006 p203

Harry with Archbishop Rowan Williams at Lambeth Palace, 6 June 2005 p204

Harry with his sisters, Margaret and Norma, July 2009 p205

Harry and Heather with their daughters, Hannah and Rachel at Buckingham Palace, June 2009 p206

Foreword

by

The Right Reverend Lord Eames OM of Armagh

Memory is one of life's most subtle yet invaluable attributes.

Our recollection of the past is a myriad of images, impressions and experiences which blend into the contrasting happiness or sorrow of our life. We recall easily those happy periods which we tried to hold on to just as we prefer to forget the failures or unfulfilled dreams. But whether happy or sad, memory can make us what we are – and dictate what we will become.

Harry Grindle shares so many pictures of the past in these pages. It is a real privilege to be allowed to live again with him people, events, places and, of course, music. For Harry will be for many of us inseparable from the musical life of Northern Ireland. From parish church to cathedral, from individual teaching to conducting large choirs, from broadcasting and recording to writing his own scores Harry has lived, breathed and been all that is best in music in the Province.

It has been my privilege to count him as a friend since 1963 when we both served at Bangor Parish Church (St Comgall's), he as the organist and I as the new curate.

Through the years since our paths have taken us far from 'the Bangor days' but I have seen Harry develop his God-given talents to the benefit of countless numbers of people. He has become a household name for perfection in preparation and production of choral work which has brought great beauty to congregations and audiences.

This book allows us to share much of a very special life.

In return we all say 'Thank you, Harry, for giving us so much of yourself and your music.'

† *Robin Eames*

Author's preface and acknowledgements

Although statistics would suggest that attendance at church services is in decline there would appear to be conversely a lively and fairly general interest in church music of various sorts. While some parish church choirs struggle to survive, many of those in cathedrals and university college chapels as well as certain élite independent choirs consistently achieve very high standards of performance. Specialist recording companies continue to issue a steady stream of excellent CDs and DVDs of church music of all periods to meet the demand which evidently exists.

A further development in recent years has been the publication of autobiographies by a number of well-known English church musicians with one man's story extending to a second volume. Both informative and entertaining, these writings introduce the reader to a way of life which can be at once very demanding and profoundly satisfying. Music that is aptly chosen, thoroughly prepared and performed to the greater glory of God has the power to enhance the worship of the Church and to give the faithful a glimpse of a better world. Those whose calling it is to direct this music not only bear a considerable responsibility but enjoy a special privilege.

The core of the present book deals with the eleven years from the mid-1960s when I was in charge of the music at St Anne's Cathedral, Belfast. During the second half of this period, i.e. in the early 1970s, Northern Ireland's notorious 'Troubles' were, of course, at their height. Although I have been engaged at other times primarily in education, church music has remained something of an *idée fixe* throughout my life and I have always been involved in its promotion.

I should like to express my deep sense of gratitude to all those who have assisted me in various ways over the past year while I have been working on the text and preparing it for publication.

The Right Reverend Lord Eames OM of Armagh, formerly Primate of the Church of Ireland and a friend for over forty years, kindly agreed to write the foreword.

The key role of editor was undertaken by Mr Wesley McCann. A published author himself, Wesley brought to the task a wealth of professional experience as a librarian, a wide knowledge of literary matters and an enthusiastic commitment. I have been very fortunate to have had such a guide.

April Sky Design of Newtownards, Co. Down provides a highly efficient service for self-publishers. Dr Wesley Johnston, who deals with customer relations and technical matters at the firm, did everything possible to ensure that the end product fulfilled our expectations.

Mr Alan Boyd, the Hon. Librarian at Belfast Cathedral, showed a keen interest in the project from the outset, assisting me with my researches and giving me access to his personal collection of orders of service and concert programmes. Alan also checked the final draft of the text with great care.

Mr Jonathan Clark was unfailingly patient and obliging whenever his uncle's rudimentary computer skills proved to be inadequate.

The water-colour of Bangor Abbey which adorns the cover of the book is by my wife, Heather, who was always supportive of her preoccupied husband.

I should also like to record my thanks to the following for their prompt and helpful responses to my requests for information:

Messrs Tom Agnew, Billy Adair, Michael Baguley and Andrew Beal, Dr George Beale, The Revd Canon John and Mrs Carole Bell, Mr Noel Beattie, Mr Gordon and Mrs Brenda Claney, Mr Fred and Mrs Margaret Clark, Mr Vernon Clegg, Mrs Gwynneth Cockcroft, Mrs Dorothy Collie, Messrs Mervyn Collins, David Craig and Andrew Crockart, Bishop Edward Darling, Dr Donald Davison, Mr Ronnie Drury, Mrs Susan Feldstein, Miss Janet Ferguson, Dr Eamon Phoenix, the Revd Stephen Fielding, Mr Jack Gamble, Professor Gerard Gillen, Messrs Brian Gordon and Edwin Gray, Dr Norma Grindle, the Revd Dr George Grindle, Messrs Stephen Hamill, Uel Hardy, Michael Harris and Peter Harris, the Revd Paul Hoey, the Venerable R G Hoey, Archdeacon of Armagh, Mr Peter and Mrs Rosemary Hunter, Miss Valerie Ireland, Miss Joan Irwin, Mr Paul Irwin, Mr Christopher and Mrs Carole Jenkins, Mrs Caroline Jones, Messrs Paul Knutson, John Lyttle, William McCay and Aubrey McClintock, the Very Revd Dr R S J H McKelvey, Dean of Belfast, Messrs Hugh Mackey and Roger Martin, Dr Roy Massey, Mr Earl Moffitt, Mrs Pauline Mortimer, Mr Michael Murray, the Revd Canon Ronnie Nesbitt, Rector of Bangor Abbey, Mr Barry Niblock, Dr Gertrude Patterson, Dr Eamonn Phoenix, Mrs Gwen Preece, Mr Leonard Pugh, Dr Keith Ramsay, Mr Jonathan Rea, Dr Raymond Refaussé, the Sisters of the St Louis Order, Mr Clive Scoular, Mr Barry Simmons and Ms Lorna Rutter, Mr David Smart, Ms Janette Simpson, Mrs May Smith, Miss Margaret Smyth, Mr Roderick Smyth, the Revd Dr Bert Tosh, Professor Raymond Warren, Mrs Shauna White and Mr Richard White.

Abbreviations

ACCU	Armagh Church Choir Union
ACNI	Arts Council of Northern Ireland
ARCM	Associate of the Royal College of Music
ARCO	Associate of the Royal College of Organists
BMus or MusB	Bachelor of Music
CHM	Choir-training diploma awarded by the Royal College of Organists
CMICF	Church Music International Choral Festival (Limerick)
DMus or MusD	Doctor of Music
FBC	Friends of Belfast Cathedral
FBGS	Friern Barnet Grammar School
FRCO	Fellow of the Royal College of Organists
FTCL	Fellow of Trinity College of Music, London
LTCL	Licentiate of Trinity College of Music, London
h.c.	(honoris causa - 'for the sake of honour') This indicates an honorary award.
IAO	Incorporated Association of Organists
PGCE	Postgraduate Certificate in Education
RAM	Royal Academy of Music
RCM	Royal College of Music
RCO	Royal College of Organists
RIAM	Royal Irish Academy of Music
RSCM	Royal School of Church Music
RTÉ	Radio Telefís Éireann. Irish Public Service Broadcaster.
SATB	Soprano, Alto, Tenor, Bass.
SPMU	Society of Professional Musicians in Ulster
TCL	Trinity College of Music, London
UCMC	Ulster Church Music Centre
USOC	Ulster Society of Organists and Choirmasters

Bibliography

Author: (i) *Irish Cathedral Music* (Institute of Irish Studies, Queen's University, Belfast, 1989)

(ii) *'…and organs and singing' The Organ and Music of St Patrick's Cathedral, Dublin* (No.2 in St Patrick's Cathedral 800 Series of monographs, 1991)

Various articles in *The Blackwell Companion to Modern Irish Culture* ed. W J McCormick (Oxford,1999) and in the *Encyclopaedia of Music in Ireland* (University College Dublin Press, publication pending).

Editor: (i) *Sing and Pray. Hymns, Songs and Prayers for Children.* (The Sunday School Society for Ireland, Dublin,1990)

(ii) *The Armagh Service Book Volume 1* (Armagh, 1999)

Hymn-tunes and arrangements by the author are included in such collections as the *St Paul's Cathedral Hymnal* and the *Church Hymnal (Fifth Edition).*

PUBLISHED COMPOSITIONS

Choral: *Preces and Responses,* SATB *a cappella* (Encore)

A Baby is born, SSSAAA *a cappella* (Encore)

Heaven Song, SATB and organ. An arrangement of the melody, *In the Gloaming* by Lady Arthur Hill.(Encore)

Jesu, the very thought of Thee, SATB *a cappella* (Encore)

Let my prayer come up, SATB *a cappella* (Encore)

Love came down at Christmas, SATB *a cappella.* An arrangement of the Irish traditional melody, *Gartan.(Encore)*

Peace be to this congregation, SATB *a cappella.* An arrangement of the hymn- tune, *Ellen,* by Alison Cadden (Encore)

We believe in God the Father, SATB and organ *(Encore)*

What is that light? SATB and organ *(Roberton)*

Organ: *Prelude on the tune 'University'* in *The Cathedral Organist* (J B Cramer & Co., London, 1976)

Discography

LP: *Christmas Music from Belfast Cathedral*
The Cathedral Choir / Director and Solo Organist: Harry Grindle
Assistant Organist: EdwinGray
        (New Irish Record Co., Dublin......NIR 005 Stereo. 1973)

CDs: (i) *Twenty Favourite Hymns*
     The Priory Singers/ Director:Harry Grindle
     with David Drinkell (Organ)
     (Emerald Records, Ballyclare, Co.Antrim..GESCD 1247   1993)

     (ii) *'Beside the Waters of Comfort'.*
     The Glorious Psalms of David.
     The Priory Singers/ Director: Harry Grindle
     with Donald Davison (Organ)
     (Priory Records, Leighton Buzzard, Beds., PRCD 808   2003)

     (iii) *Let Christians all with joyful Mirth.*
     Christmas Music from Northern Ireland
     The Priory Singers/ Director: Harry Grindle
     with Philip Stopford (Organ)
     (Priory Records   PRCD 856   2005)

     (iv) *Hymns of Love, Hope and Joy*
     The Priory Singers/ Director: Harry Grindle
     with Philip Stopford (Organ)
     (Priory Records   PRCD 873 2006)

CHAPTER ONE

1935-53 | CHILDHOOD, BANGOR ABBEY, REGENT HOUSE SCHOOL

Our family name seems to be of English origin and may be spelt in various ways e.g. Grindle, Grindall, Grindal, Grundle, Grundal, Grindel, Grindell, etc. Grindles are to be found throughout Great Britain with the greatest current concentration being in South Yorkshire. The Irish branch of the line can probably be traced back to the brothers Henry and Ralph Grindall who, in the early 17th century, at the time of the Plantation, bought land from a certain John Hamilton in Counties Armagh and Monaghan.

My parents were both from farming stock. My father, Harry Edward Grindle, the eldest of a family of six (three boys and three girls), was born in 1900 at Drumcaul, Rockcorry, near Newbliss in Co. Monaghan. My mother, Agnes Jean Atkinson, the third of a family of five, and the only daughter, was born in 1905 at Ballyshiel near Tandragee, Co. Armagh. My father's mother died when he was in his teens. In fact, he was called in from the field where he was ploughing with horses to be at his mother's side as she passed away. His father lived to a ripe old age. My mother's father died of diabetes in his early fifties. A farmyard accident resulted in the amputation of one of my maternal grandmother's legs in middle age and she was housebound for the rest of her life.

Two of my father's siblings, Aunt Annie and Uncle Charlie, were school teachers, the latter serving as Vice-Principal of the Ulster Institution for the Deaf, Dumb and Blind on the Lisburn Road in Belfast. He was held in very high esteem by all connected with the Institution and when it relocated to a site at Jordanstown (as the 'Jordanstown Schools for the Education of the Deaf and Blind') one of the new buildings was named after him. George, the eldest of Uncle Charlie's sons, inspired by his father's example, followed him into this special area of education. Later, as an ordained Presbyterian clergyman, George exercised an invaluable ministry as Superintendent of the Kinghan Mission in Belfast. The award to him of an honorary Doctorate of Divinity in 1998 by the Union Theological College in Belfast was thoroughly deserved.

1

In the past many farmers were unwilling to allow their sons to forsake the land for careers in other spheres, being of the opinion that they should stay at home to gain the experience necessary to enable them to carry on the family tradition. William James Atkinson, my maternal grandfather, was one such. While the eldest of his sons, Bob, left the family farm at an early age for the world of business in Belfast, his three brothers, Joe, Sam and David (always known as 'Davy') were obliged to become farmers. The village-schoolmaster, recognizing my uncle Joe's considerable academic potential, did his utmost to persuade my grandfather to allow the boy to further his education, but to no avail. Uncle Sam was an omnivorous reader with a keen interest in solving the puzzles which appeared in various newspapers and journals. Over the years he won countless prizes including such valuable items as canteens of cutlery. I seem to have inherited his love of cross-words.

Before her marriage, my maternal grand-mother had frequently appeared as a soprano soloist at church concerts in the north-east Armagh area and her husband was a competent flautist (or 'flute-player', as James Galway might have described him.) Apart from Davy, the members of their family were good singers with Sam having been singled out on one occasion for praise by Captain C J Brennan, the Organist of Belfast Cathedral, for the lead which he gave to the tenors at a diocesan choral festival.

Joe was the principal cornet-player and Davy played the trombone for many years in Poyntzpass Silver Band. Previously Davy had been a member of Ballylisk Accordeon Band which had been trained from scratch by a modest, naturally-gifted, self-taught amateur musician called Billy Lavery who spared no effort to ensure that the band's performances were of a consistently high standard. He must have spent countless hours of his spare time, often working late into the night, making special arrangements of the pieces which the band played and his musical manuscript, with every note beautifully formed, was a joy to behold. 'Full many a flower is born to blush unseen.'

Although Ballylisk Accordeon Band is now defunct, Poyntzpass Silver Band, founded in1951, goes from strength to strength with an impressive record in competitions. An invaluable asset to the local community, the band, in addition to fulfilling its traditional marching role, is a popular attraction at concerts and enhances the music at various church services particularly during the pre-Christmas period. In addition to pieces composed specifically for brass band, the repertoire includes numerous arrangements of a very wide range of other music.

It is perhaps surprising that my mother, being the only girl in the family and her father's favourite, was not allowed to continue her education beyond the village school. The nearest grammar school, nine miles away in Portadown, was not accessible without a car and few farmers had one at that time. In her early teens she cycled weekly to Portadown for piano lessons. I know that it was always a matter of regret to my mother that she was denied the opportunity to develop her abilities further. In years to come, she and my father saw to it that their children were more fortunate. In her twenties my mother was accepted for training to be a nurse at the Royal Victoria Hospital in Belfast. However, my grandmother's accident and subsequent incapacity forced her to return home after about a year. Unfortunately, she was never in a position to resume her training.

My parents had met when my father was serving with the full-time police reserve (known as the 'A' Specials) at Tandragee in the early 1920s, a time of great unrest in the country at large. In fact, on one occasion when he was at home in Co. Monaghan on leave, my father was walking along a country road with some friends when an IRA sniper's bullet, no doubt meant for him as a policeman, killed one of his companions. Thereafter, when on leave, he stayed with a maiden aunt who lived on the northern side of the Border in Co. Fermanagh. In due course my father departed for Australia where he was to remain for ten years. He thoroughly enjoyed this period of his life, often reflecting nostalgically about it. Indeed, he might well have settled there and, had my mother been prepared to join him, would undoubtedly have done so. Evidently, while he was abroad my

Harry's father and mother with Stanley Heyburn (message-boy) outside the shop in Church Street, Bangor c1940

father had written to ask his brother, Charlie, to call on my mother and attempt to discover whether or not she expected him to come back after an absence of ten years for, at that time, they were not formally engaged. Having been informed that his return was anticipated, my father nobly forsook the attractions of the Antipodes and embarked on the long boat journey back to Ireland. My parents were married in November 1934.

The newly-weds settled in Bangor, Co. Down where they rented a shop and dwelling in a working-class area of the town. Most of the small terraced houses in Church Street had, on the ground floor, a drawing-room to the front with a living-room and tiny kitchen to the rear. At No.44 the shop replaced the drawing-room. Confined, therefore, to one small room with her growing family, my mother was to find life at times very difficult in the coming years. Upstairs, in addition to the bathroom, there were three bedrooms one of which had just about enough space for a bed and a small chest of drawers. The toilet was outside in the back yard.

It might be appropriate to include at this point, by way of a digression, some information about my siblings and their later lives.

I was born in October 1935, my brother David in December 1938, and my sisters Margaret and Norma in November 1940 and April 1945 respectively. My mother was quite a fluent pianist despite having had only a limited amount of tuition in her youth, while my father had been known to play the fiddle at country dances in Monaghan and later in Australia. It was not surprising, therefore, that they encouraged all of their children to develop the musical ability which they had inherited. David, Margaret and I were sent to piano lessons whereas Norma was the only one of us who learned to play the violin, progressing in due course to membership of the Belfast Youth Orchestra. David also took up the clarinet which he studied with John Johnston, a member of the BBC Northern Ireland Orchestra and an outstanding teacher. A reel-to-reel tape-recording of Mozart's *Clarinet Trio (K498)* made by David, a viola-playing friend, and me in the 1950s gives some indication of David's considerable potential.

All four of us went to Trinity Public Elementary School in Bangor and Regent House Grammar School in Newtownards. David later read Modern Languages (French and German) at Queen's University, Belfast. Tragically, terminal illness brought an all-too-early end to a life that was full of promise. (See Chapter 3.)

On leaving school Margaret entered the Civil Service. In 1967 she married Fred Clark in St Anne's Cathedral, Belfast where they were both members of the choir. Fred and Margaret lived for two periods in England, the first, in the early 1970s, at Leighton Buzzard in Bedfordshire and the second (1983-86) near Hereford. They share a love of church music and have sung in various choirs over the years. Both would regard their participation in a performance of Mendelssohn's *Elijah* in Hereford Cathedral given by the amalgamated church choirs of the area with orchestral accompaniment as one of the high points of their musical experience. Margaret and Fred with their two children, Jonathan and Christine, returned to Northern Ireland in 1986 with Margaret resuming her career in the Department of the Environment the following year. She retired in 2005. An avid reader of a wide range of literature, Margaret, like me, enjoys grappling with cryptic crosswords.

Norma always had a clear sense of vocation. From her childhood she wanted to make a difference and thought that the best way to do that would be to become a nurse. After training at the Royal Victoria Hospital (RVH) in Belfast (1964-67), followed by midwifery training at the Simpson Memorial Maternity Pavilion in Edinburgh (1968-69), she undertook a course in Tropical Nursing in London, hoping to serve abroad as a missionary. Unfortunately, the onset of ME was to enforce a change of plan. On her return to Belfast in 1970 she was engaged initially in general and cardiac intensive care at the RVH, before moving to the Accident and Emergency Department in 1971 where she worked for the next four and a half years, three and a half of them as a sister. At that time, with the province rocked by the continuing onslaught of the 'Troubles', she and her colleagues were under intense emotional and physical pressure as they strove to deal with the results of terrorist outrages virtually every day. Among the most horrific of these was the bombing of the crowded Abercorn Restaurant in Belfast in 1971. Often the nurses had to receive casualties with their body parts in plastic bags. At the end of 1975 Norma left the RVH to commence teacher training and spent the rest of her career in nurse education - fifteen years in the Belfast Northern College of Nursing and eleven subsequently in the University of Ulster (UU) where she was involved in the preparation of teachers of nursing, midwifery and health visiting as well as other disciplines. While at the UU she was awarded a PhD for a thesis entitled 'The Role of the Arts in the Teaching of Caring'. With her flair for language, she has often written poetry some of which has been set to music. During her time on the staff of the RVH, and later the College of Nursing, she found herself often using this talent in a lighter vein in order to compose and deliver 'odes' as tributes to colleagues at retirement and other celebrations. From time to time she was even known to appear on video as the Queen, Margaret Thatcher and various other celebrities!

Previous tenants of No.44 Church Street, Bangor had remained for comparatively short periods, none of them having been able to make a success of the shop. With his enormous capacity for hard work and with my mother's support, my father was to prove more than equal to the

Three generations – Harry with his father and grandfather c1937

challenge which faced him. Despite the unfavourable economic climate of the 1930s he established a grocery business which flourished by dint of his heroic efforts. Given the cramped conditions in which we lived, storage space was at a premium in our house and my father built three sheds in our yard and garden. He grew vegetables and later had a green-house constructed which provided him with a fine crop of tomatoes and lettuces each summer. My mother's soda and wheaten farls, baked on a gas hot-plate in our tiny kitchen or 'scullery', were also very popular with our customers. Unfortunately, this activity had a detrimental effect on my mother's health and in due course she was taken to hospital suffering from pneumonia. The doctor strongly advised her to dispense with her hot-plate and to reserve her energies for the upbringing of her four children. My father now had to set off on his message-bicycle early each morning to a home-bakery across the town, returning with the day's supply of soda, wheaten and potato farls for the shop.

When World War II broke out in 1939 I was four years old. I can vividly remember the air-raid shelters which were built in our streets and the large metal tank, erected outside our shop, which was filled with water for the use of the Fire Service should the need arise. My father joined the Home Guard and was regularly on duty throughout the night. When the air-raid sirens sounded, the rest of the household took refuge under the stairs or under our stout mahogany dining-table, listening anxiously for the ominous drone of approaching enemy aircraft.

During the war years certain school buildings were commandeered by the military authorities and fitted out to serve as hospitals or convalescent centres, school classes being accommodated in any available premises in the town. Consequently, three of my years as a pupil at Trinity Public Elementary School were spent in mission halls and the headquarters of a local troop of Rover Scouts. Faced with a considerable range of abilities and without what members of their profession would today regard as basic resources, our teachers contrived to deliver the curriculum. The so-called 'Three Rs' (i.e. Reading, Writing and Arithmetic) were the focus with the Creative Arts receiving scant attention. One teacher, Mr Lindsay from Newtownards, who was held in awe by all of the boys since he was said to have been a boxer, showed us how to make flowers from hazel-nut shells and endeavoured to introduce us to musical literacy through tonic sol-fa. Unfortunately, there was no continuity from year to year and the torch which he had lit was allowed to go out.

Throughout my childhood, school holidays were spent at my uncles' farm at Ballyshiel in Co. Armagh. In fact, for a short time during the war I attended the school in the neighbouring village, Clare. Although I missed my friends in Bangor, there were aspects of life in the country which were very appealing. Most of the effects of rationing were unknown here for there was always a plentiful supply of eggs, butter, bacon, etc. I recall with some relish the appetising cooked breakfast with which each day began. Uncle Sam made delicious bread from 'Indian' wheaten meal and this, fried until it was golden brown, was irresistible. There was little cholesterol-consciousness in those days!

I was glad to help on the farm, collecting eggs, feeding the cattle and poultry, and rounding up the cows for milking. The search for eggs, laid 'away' by some hens under hedges and in various places around the farm-yard, rather than in the hen-houses, was always exciting. The highlight of the year was undoubtedly the harvesting of the crops at the end of the summer. Through a long-standing, reciprocal arrangement the farmers helped one another with this vitally important task and it was good for my morale to be regarded as part of the busy team, tying sheaves of hay, corn and wheat, arranging them in stooks, and building ricks. I always looked forward eagerly to riding on top of trailer-loads of hay and straw as they were brought home to the farm-yard for storage.

The mid-Ulster dialect spoken in that part of Co. Armagh held a great fascination for me and some interpretation was necessary at first. It was delightful to make the acquaintance of words such as *for(e)nenst* (by, near), *higyard* (probably from the Irish *agard*, a hay- or corn-yard) and the almost onomatopoeic *sheugh* (from the Irish *seoch*, a ditch). Probable western-English influence can be traced in the open pronunciation of certain vowel-sounds: *ow* for *o* before *ld* or *ll* (*cold* = *cowl*, *hold=howl*, *roll= rowl*). Another feature is the use of interdental *t* before *r*: *drum* = *dthrum*. Perhaps the most distinctive characteristic of this dialect is the glide which has developed after *k* and *g* before *a*, *e* or *i*. This tendency is particularly marked before *a*: *cap* = *kyap*; *cant* = *kyant*. On my return to school in Newtownards after the long summer vacation my class-mates were quick to spot traces of the mid-Ulster dialect in my speech and they teased me mercilessly. I think that they looked on me as something of a country bumpkin.

The sanctity of Sunday was scrupulously observed in the country districts in those days; only absolutely essential tasks such as milking were undertaken. I accompanied Uncle Davy on foot to the small parish church, to which the family had always belonged, near the village of Clare about two miles away, shortening the journey in summertime by crossing the intervening fields and streams. At the church, the men-folk always allowed the ladies to go inside while they remained outside for a chat which at times seemed to follow an established script. For example, at New Year the opening gambit was always, 'How did ye get the Christmas over?' The inevitable reply was, 'Och, quietly, quietly.' When someone died, he or she was said to have 'got away' and if the deceased had been very ill the comment was that it had been 'happy for him/her.' Someone with a poetic gift might have made something of this quaint, rural social-interaction.

The Rector, Mr Johnston, a kindly gentleman with a southern-Irish county background, looked after the parish of Loughgilly in addition to Clare where the one Sunday service was at 3.30p.m. A short time before the service began he would come out of the church to greet the farmers who had arranged themselves in a line to shake hands and to be engaged briefly in conversation. Then, with a glance at his fob watch, he led the men inside to begin the service. One Sunday afternoon he preached on a text which has remained with me ever since because it seems to encapsulate the very essence of Christian living. It is Micah chapter 6, verse 8, 'And what does the Lord require of thee? To do justly and to love mercy and to walk humbly with thy God.'

The wonderful language of the Authorised Version of the Bible, and of the Book of Psalms in particular, appealed to me strongly from an early age. I noted that certain people of my Uncle Joe's generation, and older, had absorbed it to such an extent that occasional direct quotations from it would appear quite naturally in their conversation. In those pre-revision days, the *Book of Common Prayer* was to be found everywhere, uniting all levels of churchmanship. Some of its imagery had, of course, a special relevance for farmers, e.g. 'We have erred and strayed from Thy ways like lost sheep.' Although the music at the little church at Clare may have been lacking in polish, with dear Gladys McMahon doing her best to conjure support for the singing of the congregation from a very wheezy old harmonium, there was, nevertheless, a genuinely devotional atmosphere during its simple services.

Forty-odd miles away, Bangor Abbey, which I regard as my spiritual home, stood at the end of Church Street. Built on the site of a famous sixth-century monastery, the Abbey together with the care of its parishioners had been the responsibility of the clergy of Bangor Parish

Church (St Comgall's) until 1941 when it regained its independence with the appointment of the Revd James Hamilton as its Rector. Our entire family was involved in the life of the parish. My father was a member of the Select Vestry and a sidesman, my mother was for a number of years superintendent of the junior Sunday School and my brother, two sisters and I in the course of time joined her in the church choir. Each of us was a member of at least one of the other organisations which in those days, with comparatively high numbers on their rolls, were a significant aspect of the Parish's social ministry.

My mother was also for many years the Organist at the private chapel on the Dufferin and Ava estate at Clandeboye on the outskirts of Bangor with a service at mid-day on Sunday. A hoisted family standard would indicate that the Dowager Marchioness was in residence and she was likely to be accompanied at Matins by the members of her current house-party who might include eminent English politicians and other VIPs. Predictably, at the last moment before the service began, a footman would enter the chapel carrying on a silver salver the list of the hymns which

Her Ladyship had selected from *Hymns Ancient & Modern*! My poor mother had to set aside those which she had carefully chosen in accordance with the lectionary from the *Irish Church Hymnal* (*ICH*) and hastily find the new ones, with familiar tunes in the *ICH*. The Marchioness in her selection paid little heed to liturgical requirements or the seasons of the year for that matter. Even when there was snow on the ground she would include her particular favourite, 'Summer Suns are glowing.'

Among previous Organists of Bangor Abbey had been Dr Edred Chaundy who later served at Armagh Cathedral and Dr E Norman Hay, who, writing under the pseudonym 'Rathcol', was for many years the famously caustic music critic of the *Belfast Telegraph*. A particularly

Harry and his brother, David – choristers at Bangor Abbey c1946 *(Pidduck Photography, Bangor)*

demanding choir-master, Dr Hay would sometimes threaten to keep his singers locked in the church with him on rehearsal night until he was satisfied with their performance!

Mr Joseph Douglas was the Organist when I joined the choir at about the age of seven. He was a very competent amateur musician who used the rather limited tonal resources of the Evans & Barr organ very effectively. For his voluntaries he drew heavily on the Romantic repertoire then in vogue with music by William Wolstenholme *et al.* being frequently heard. Mr Douglas directed the mid-week full choir rehearsal from the organ console, the adults being allowed to sit in the choir stalls, with rugs wrapped round them on winter nights, while we boys were obliged to stand throughout on the cold stone floor, a state of affairs which we greatly resented. Composers represented in our bound volumes of anthems and canticle settings included Handel (excerpts from *Messiah*), Brahms ('How lovely are Thy Dwellings' from *The German Requiem*), Mendelssohn (*Hear my prayer*), S S Wesley, Sullivan, Goss, Ouseley and Attwood as well as such lesser figures as J Varley Roberts, whose setting of *Seek ye the Lord* allowed our leading tenor, Mr Bob Marshall, to come into his own. Other favourites (of Mr Douglas, at any rate!) were *O for a closer Walk with God* by Myles B Foster, *The radiant Morn hath passed away* by the Revd H H Woodward and *The Day is past and over* by J Christopher Marks, Organist of St Fin Barre's Cathedral, Cork 1860 - 1903. It says much for the competence of the choir of Bangor Abbey that Mr Douglas could decide in the course of a service which anthem or setting of the canticles was to be sung when he saw how many members were present. During the first lesson he would circulate a piece of paper with a number on it. This referred to the particular item(s) in our anthologies which he had selected.

The choir was augmented at Harvest Thanksgiving, Christmas and Easter by other adult singers, some of whom may have been former members, and on these occasions we might also have visiting soloists. Among the latter was Miss Mary Johnston, a well-known soprano, whose singing of 'With Verdure clad' from Haydn's *Creation* greatly impressed us all. Equally unforgettable, but for quite different reasons, was a visiting bass soloist who will have to be nameless! On one occasion I was puzzled to note that this gentleman was already in his place in the choir stalls when we entered them. When it came to the point in the service at which he was to deliver his solo, I was again puzzled that the whole choir stood although we had nothing to sing.

At lunch my mother was unusually quiet and was clearly very upset about something. When I raised questions about the visiting bass soloist at Matins, she was forthright in her condemnation of what had happened.

It appeared that he invariably sang best when he had fortified himself with some strong drink, as he had done that morning, and that the entire choir had been asked to stand during his solo to disguise the fact that he was being supported on either side by two of the choirmen! This rather bizarre incident was the talk of the Parish for many a day afterwards.

Among the twenty-plus boys in the Abbey choir were a number who possessed promising voices and who had genuine musical potential. It was regrettable, therefore, that we were given no training in voice-production and sight-reading. We were left largely to fend for ourselves, picking up the music as best we could and relying entirely on our ears. The truth was that, since the choir was essentially one of mixed adult voices including a confident group of sopranos, the boys were regarded as little more than a rather decorative appendage.

When they were kneeling for the prayers the boys were likely to be literally making their mark on the inner sides of the varnished panels of the choir stalls. Over the years the initials or, more frequently, the names of generations of choristers had been etched by busy finger-nails. While this time-consuming process could take months to complete, very good progress could be made during those services which included the Litany. In my early days in the choir, I felt moved to add my name to this primitive record and set about the task with gusto. For some unaccountable reason I confused the letters 'b' and 'd', consequently misspelling my own surname! I have often regretted that I did not attempt to salvage the panel in question when the old choir-stalls were replaced in the late 1950s in the course of a major refurbishment of the Abbey marking the 1400th anniversary of its foundation.

In those days Bangor Abbey Sunday School met at three o'clock on Sunday afternoons. A number of the choir-boys including myself, all aged about eleven or twelve, were in the same class and we were secretly in love with Greta Wallace, the very attractive young lady who was our teacher. We vied with one another for the privilege of sitting beside her, often arriving absurdly early in an effort to make sure of one of the two prized seats. No other class was so attentive to its teacher. Greta was happy to indulge her adoring audience by spending the minimum of time on the invariably dull set lesson in order to read us a passage from some work of fiction which was more to our liking.

At the age of about eight I had been sent for piano lessons to Mr Frank Parsons, the Organist at First Bangor Presbyterian Church. Since Mr Parsons was reputed to be a kindly gentleman, my mother considered that, as a teacher for her precious young son, he would be preferable to Dr Ernest Emery, the highly gifted but rather volatile Organist at Bangor Parish Church. Mr Parsons, though delightfully avuncular, was not, unfortunately, a good piano teacher and my recollection is that he could have been much more demanding. He seemed to be prepared to settle for adequacy rather than motivate his pupils to achieve higher standards. Technique received scant attention and most of the music which he selected was not sufficiently challenging. He seemed unwilling to enter me for examinations which he said, 'were only for lazy people.' However, my mother prevailed.

My parents were determined that their children should have the benefit of the grammar school education which they had both been denied. They opted for Regent House School in Newtownards which was co-educational, rather than Bangor Grammar School, and each morning, from the age of eight, I joined the lively band of boys and girls who travelled by bus to the neighbouring town.

With about 400 pupils on its roll, Regent House was at that time a comparatively small school by modern standards. Mr Rogers, the headmaster, then approaching retirement, presided benignly over what was essentially a very happy establishment. One of my abiding memories is of the gargantuan football matches which took place each day at lunchtime in the playground in front of the school with, it seemed, most of the school's male population taking part! All this was to change, however, with the advent of Mr Rogers's successor, Lieutenant-Colonel James McDonald. With his army background, Mr McDonald was a stickler for discipline and, although he was not popular with the pupils, he was respected, not least because he had been an international cricketer whose spin bowling was said to have troubled an Australian touring team.

As far as those of us in the junior classes were concerned, Music meant a period of forty minutes, once a week in the assembly hall, singing such unison songs as 'Aiken Drum' under the direction of Mr Ernest Browne, a charismatic Maths teacher who conducted the Ards Choral and Orchestral Society. We thoroughly enjoyed these entertaining sessions with Mr Browne (or 'Chisel-chin' as he was affectionately known) who was something of a 'character' but we did not learn anything about music. There seemed to be a complete absence of basic resources. The recorder was unknown! Out of the goodness of his heart, Mr Auterson who taught English, shared his great love and considerable knowledge of music with any pupils who cared to join him occasionally after school hours to listen to some of his 78 rpm gramophone records.

Of the succession of visiting part-time Music teachers who came to the school to take the upper-school classes, by far the most successful was Robert Simpson who later joined the staff at Stranmillis Training College in Belfast. With his winning personality and engaging sense of humour Bob was able to draw fine singing from the young ladies and gentlemen in the fifth and sixth forms. On Friday afternoons when we second-formers had a double-period of Algebra in a room adjoining the assembly hall in which he was taking his rehearsal, I always tried to finish as quickly as possible the exercises set by our teacher in order that I could listen to the stirring three-part harmony (SA&B) arrangements of songs from the *Cantemus* collection like 'From high Olympus' which filtered through to me from next-door.

Like most of my peers I sat and passed the first 11-plus examination in Northern Ireland in 1947. Having had little by way of formal preparation for this examination at Regent House, we simply relied on our own intelligence to see us through. There was certainly none of the intensive private coaching which was to become a widespread practice in later years and I was not aware of any panic. I was delighted that my father would no longer have to pay the school fees which he could ill afford.

The next academic objective was the Junior Certificate Examination (JCE) which was taken when we were about 14 years old. Most of those who were candidates would agree that, as a state examination based on a prescribed syllabus, it served as a significant and useful staging-post on the road to the Senior Certificate Examination which was then the culmination of one's grammar school education. It is very regrettable that it was eventually withdrawn.

With many of us sitting the JCE in ten subjects, we were expected to apply ourselves to our studies and to undertake a substantial amount of homework each evening. The Science syllabus called for, among other things, a thorough knowledge of a number of experiments. Our teacher, Mr Clements, commanded the school's battalion of the Army Cadet Force and his impressive weekly drilling of his troops in the playground always attracted a sizeable crowd of passers-by. He was a man to be feared and his teaching/revision method was simple. Having drawn the basic diagram for a particular experiment on what was then called the 'blackboard', he would proceed to go through the sequence of stages in the process. If, when he had finished, we assured him that 'all was clear', the members of the class had to come to the black-board in turn and go through the details of the experiment, from memory of course. Mr Clements was not at all pleased if anyone omitted something or confused the order of the stages. Having listened nervously to about thirty outlines of every experiment, it is little wonder that, by the time the examination arrived, we were thoroughly conversant with them all. It is, perhaps, not surprising that the marks in Science were consistently high.

Mr J A Auterson, or 'Jake', as he was known, another one of the 'characters' on the school's teaching staff, seemed to take some pride in wearing a gown which was in shreds! He encouraged us all to read as widely as possible and to make a point of listening, as he did, to Walter Allen's informative weekly radio programme on English literature. For five shillings (i.e. 25p) I purchased *The Reader's Guide*, published by Penguin, which contained a planned syllabus for those who wished to broaden their knowledge of particular subjects. The serialized dramatisation of Hardy's novels on the old BBC Home Service on Sunday evenings appealed to me so much that I read his entire output in a matter of weeks.

'Jake' helped us to appreciate what constituted good writing and expected us to express ourselves clearly and cogently in the essay which we were required to write for him each weekend. The return of this work with his corrections was awaited with a mixture of eagerness and anxiety for 'Jake' was wont to make his comments publicly. As exercise-books were sent skimming across the room in the direction of their owners he might utter a word or two of commendation or censure. Occasionally, when I had been moved to indulge my liking for a high-flown phrase, he would snap, 'Enough of this Jonsonese!' I cannot help wondering what 'Jake' would have made of the abuse of the English language which is so common today among broadcasters, journalists and others who ought to know better.

For enthusiasm and dedication the palm belonged to Miss May Holmes who was our French teacher. The basket attached to the handle-bars of her bicycle seemed to be always full of exercise books and during break and lunch-time she could usually be found in a classroom with a pupil going over his or her homework. As in the case of English, the weekend essay called for a major effort on our part and Miss Holmes marked this with great care. Each Tuesday she appeared with lists of all the mistakes made by the members of the class. These were discussed and their corrections noted by everyone. We were then required to write out in our 'fair copy' books the amended version of our essays and Miss Holmes completed the process by inspecting this work to ensure that it was error-free. Thirion's book of French irregular verbs was our bible and Miss Holmes expected quick reponses when she tested our knowledge of these. Hesitation could result in detention after school! Something of a human dynamo, Miss Holmes was known as 'The Buzzer'. Such was the thoroughness of her teaching that when I sat the A-level examination there was only one word on the papers with which I was unfamiliar. This was 'gisaient', the third person plural of the imperfect tense of the verb 'gésir' meaning 'to lie (horizontal)'. I am not likely to forget it!

As the 'A' stream, our class consisted of bright, well-motivated children who appeared to thrive on the competitive atmosphere which prevailed. My friend, Philip Barker, and I would have regarded it as decidedly *infra dig* if we had been beaten by one of the girls. Our strategy was to reserve our best French accent for the examinations, having lulled the girls into a false sense of security by our rather casual approach to the reading and speaking of the language at other times.

The Barker family had moved to Bangor from Birmingham on the appointment of Philip's father to the post of Chief Engineer at the Post Office in Northern Ireland. Philip and his brother, Alan, were sent to continue their education at Regent House with Philip joining my form. With a great deal in common, we became very good friends. Philip was a highly intelligent boy who had an exceptionally disciplined approach to all that he undertook. Being both very competitive, we probably brought the best out of one another although it has to be admitted that we did once come to blows.

Our piano teacher, Mr Parsons, entered us for a piano-duet class at Bangor Musical Festival at which the adjudicator was Dr Harold Darke, the well-known organist and composer. The other competitors in the class were girls. Awarding us the first prize Dr Darke said that he was very pleased to see two boys playing together, a rare enough sight even at that time. It was gratifying to have scored another victory over the girls!

After a brilliant career at school and at Queen's University where he completed the four-year degree course in three years, Philip Barker went on to London University for a further year to gain the professional diploma at Imperial College. He then joined IBM, rapidly progressing to a post in senior management. Sadly, we lost contact after he was transferred to Germany and we never met again. In later years I learned that Philip had died at the age of forty-four after a very serious illness.

My piano lessons with Mr Parsons were continuing and I was steadily working my way through the Associated Board examinations. When I asked him if I might learn to play the organ he was dismissive, saying that my legs were too short. He might have offered to introduce me to music for the manuals only, of which there is an abundance, but he made no such suggestion. I was *very* disappointed.

However, my gloom was dispelled with the appointment of Mr R Huston Graham as Organist of Bangor Abbey in 1950. An architect by profession, Huston opened up to at least one teenage boy a new, exciting musical world. While he was an efficient choirmaster, his organ-playing was simply a revelation. Before and after the services we were treated to fine performances of works from the standard repertoire selected with an unerring sense of occasion. Sometimes when Huston felt that he should perhaps make a concession to the less-discriminating members of the congregation, he would allow himself to indulge in a little 'ear-tickling', as he described it, by playing something like Easthope Martin's rather saccharine *Evensong*. I was delighted when he readily agreed to give me lessons and under his kindly tutelage I was soon coming to terms with Percy C Buck's *First Year at the Organ*, a volume long-since displaced in the affection of teachers by more modern courses. Although it lacked information on such matters as period performance practice, its exercises were models of their kind and provided the student with a sound basic technique. On Sunday afternoons, when I knew that Huston was at home, I would go into the church with my friend Philip Barker in tow. Having taken a few volumes of music from Huston's cupboard in the choir-vestry, I would endeavour to play as much as I could on the organ while Philip was admirably tolerant.

It was not long before I was able to accompany an entire service with hymns, a chanted psalm, and canticles. I was also very happy to assist Huston by writing out about twenty copies of the weekly service sheet for the members of the choir. I should imagine that he was amused to note, as he must surely have done, that his protégé was not only using green ink, as he himself did, but that his handwriting was being painstakingly copied! The long-term result of this devotion is that my signature has remained very similar to his, with the surname's characteristically large initial letter G. I had found a hero.

Some friends advised me that my piano-playing would benefit from a change of teacher and suggested that I should enrol with Bertram Jones, a Welshman with a well-established reputation, whose pupils had included some of the province's leading pianists. Accompanied by my faithful friend, Philip Barker, I called on Mr Parsons to inform him of my decision to discontinue my lessons. Mr Parsons chatted enthusiastically about the music of the coronation service of Queen Elizabeth II which had taken place earlier that afternoon (2 June 1953) and did not enquire about the reason for our visit. My courage having utterly deserted me, we eventually withdrew leaving Mr Parsons, no doubt, wondering why we had called. Afterwards I took the coward's way out of the situation by sending him a letter.

Bertram Jones was a remarkable man who, in order to keep himself physically fit, avoided using public transport as far as possible. Each day he walked from his home in the Stranmillis area of Belfast to the city centre where his studio, situated on the top floor of commercial premises, was reached by climbing several steep flights of stairs. With his brief-case and rolled umbrella, he was a familiar sight striding purposefully along the street, his back as straight as the proverbial ramrod. When he shook hands, his grip was vice-like! There was little else in his one-roomed studio apart from two pianos, an upright and a grand. The pupil began his/her lesson with a sequence of finger-exercises, of Mr Jones's own devising, on the rather dilapidated upright and then moved to the grand

Bertram L Jones (aged 91) MA (h.c.), Queen's University, Belfast, July 1988 *(Photo: Vincent Smith)*

piano for scales, pieces and sight-reading. Mr Jones expected his pupils to come thoroughly prepared and rumour had it that over the years, more than one, who had evidently failed to do the requisite amount of practice, had been sent packing! I found the lessons stimulating even if the comments and directions which he scribbled in my notebook were virtually illegible. There was very much more to playing the piano and making music than I had hitherto realised.

After Huston Graham had been giving me organ lessons for two or three years he said that he felt that he should pass me on to Dr E H Emery, the eminent Organist at Bangor Parish Church (St Comgall's) with whom he himself sought occasional consultation, particularly about the playing of Bach. Ernest Emery's DMus degree was from Edinburgh University where it had been awarded for distinguished performance during the professorship of the renowned, Donald Francis Tovey. Dr Emery told me that the extent of Tovey's knowledge of music was such that he could readily play on the piano, from memory, quite extensive excerpts from any work which one cared to mention.

The focus of Ernest Emery's life was the fine Hunter three-manual instrument at his disposal at St Comgall's and he was a masterly player. No one had ever heard him play a wrong note! As the foremost organist in Northern Ireland, Dr Emery gave frequent recitals and contributed regularly to the series by leading British players broadcast on the network by the BBC on Sunday mornings. A cricket-loving Yorkshireman, he had been in his youth an articled pupil at Manchester Cathedral and was subsequently Organist at Garston Parish Church. It is said that the Revd R C H Elliott (later Dean of Belfast and Bishop of Connor), met Ernest Emery when

Ernest H Emery at the organ of Bangor Parish Church c 1959 *(W T Kirk, Photographer, Bangor)*

they were on military service together in France during the First World War. After the War the two men were reunited when Ernest Emery was appointed Organist at St Comgall's where Mr Elliott was then a curate. Given his outstanding ability as an organist, Dr Emery might have been expected to obtain a cathedral post in the course of time. However, it has to be admitted that he was inadequate as a choir-master. Neither would his lack of a really good general education nor his highly temperamental nature have served to advance his cause.

As indicated earlier, Dr Emery's playing was the epitome of accuracy. His accompaniment of the services was highly colourful with the texts of the psalms in particular, inspiring him to great heights. The awe-struck choir and congregation would be submerged beneath something approaching full organ, with pedal trills conjuring up thunder-claps or the lions roaring after their prey! A notable feature of his rather idiosyncratic style of accompaniment was the way in which he brought the choir in at the beginnings of hymns, psalms and canticles. Having played over the tune or chant he would sound the bass note of the opening chord on the pedals as an anticipatory up-beat and his singers, after years of practice, would respond promptly. With regard to the registration of Bach, 'the Doctor' was not averse to the odd romantic touch such as highlighting a particular entry of the 'subject' or 'answer' in a fugue by playing it on a powerful solo reed.

Life was now very full as approaching 'O' and 'A' level examinations meant an increasing load of set homework and private study. I also endeavoured to keep up regular piano and organ practice as well as attending the weekly meetings of the Scout troop attached to Bangor Abbey. I helped my father in our shop after school and on Saturdays when business was always especially brisk. In addition to serving customers, I would deliver orders on a message-bicycle to houses in the surrounding area. Like all who knew him, I had the greatest respect for my father and wished to help him as much as I could. Although I was keenly interested in sport, playing both rugby and cricket, I was rarely available to represent the school because matches usually took place on Saturday mornings.

Nevertheless, I was able to assist as a stage-hand with the mounting of the annual drama festival at Regent House. In March 1953, during my final year at the school, I appeared before the foot-lights in the sixth-form's entry for the competition, playing the part of the High King of Ireland in Gerald McNamara's hilarious comedy, *Thompson in Tir-na-n-Og*. The eponymous hero, an Orangeman who had been accidentally killed at the Sham Fight at Scarva, finds himself in the land of Gaelic-speaking mythological figures. The play reveals the extent of their ignorance and incomprehension of each other's tradition, a constant theme in Irish

Form VI Latin Class at Regent House School 1953; from left, Harry, Thomas Waugh, Mollie McDonald, Mary Angus, Joyce McClelland, Shirley Bristow, Rosemary Fromson and Margaret Orr

history. Thompson was played superbly by the late Thomas Waugh, a Billy Bunter-like figure, who proved to be an ideal casting. Our performance benefited greatly from the considerable experience of the theatre which Mr Stewart, our History teacher, brought to its production and it was not surprising that we won the competition. Afterwards I was flattered to be invited by Mr Stewart to participate in one of Bangor Drama Club's forthcoming productions but, with rehearsals taking place on Sundays, which were strictly observed in our household, I had to decline.

My mother was determined that her eldest child should become a clergyman and admitted that, when I was born, she had dedicated me to God's service. Now this appeared to my teenage mind to be most unfair since I had not been allowed any say in the matter. As head-chorister I had sung occasional solos, and when I read lessons from time to time my mother ensured that their delivery was well-nigh perfect. I was to discover that both the members of the congregation and the clergy saw me as a potential ordinand. Our curate presented me with a New Testament in Greek. When rectors were asked to send possible candidates for the ministry from their parishes to a one-day conference for senior school-boys, I was coerced into attending, taking my younger brother with me for company. Only when my mother at long last saw that her persistence was in vain did she concede that perhaps my vocation might be to serve God and His Church through music.

Dr Emery encouraged me to seek a post as an organist but my applications were usually turned down, without interview, on the grounds that at seventeen, I was too young to undertake such a responsibility. Although I should have preferred a post in a Church of Ireland parish, I was happy and somewhat relieved to be asked by the Kirk Session of Shore Street Presbyterian Church in Donaghadee to take a choir rehearsal and to play the organ for two Sunday services. Mr Luke Semple, the kindly Clerk of Session, had said to me beforehand that if they liked me and I liked them the job would be mine. In all probability I had been the only applicant and I was duly appointed.

At that time any student at Regent House wishing to take Music at either 'O' or 'A' level of the Senior Certificate of Education had to seek private tuition, the subject not being one of those offered at the school. In fact Music was regarded as having little or no academic credibility. When Mr Griffith, the Vice-Principal who taught us Geography, found one day that he had a few minutes to spare at the end of a lesson, he decided to ask each member of the class in turn what career he or she would ultimately like to pursue. Those who hoped to be lawyers, medical practitioners, teachers, architects etc. had his approval. When I said that I wanted to be a musician both he and the rest of the class burst out laughing. I was acutely embarrassed. 'Don't be silly, Grindle,' he replied, 'Music is only a hobby!'

Undaunted, I went to see Professor Ivor Keys at Queen's University in Belfast. He explained that without 'A' level Music, I should have to sit the matriculation examination in the subject to gain entry to his department. Mr Griffith, having realised that my intentions were serious, arranged for me to join the one 'A' level Music candidate at the school when she took the aural tests and to have a chat with Mr T S Turner, H M Inspector, afterwards. Mr Turner was most encouraging and told me that, since I had done very well in the aural tests, without preparation, it was a pity that I had not been entered for 'A' level Music.

When the Senior Certificate 'A' level results were published, I was delighted to discover that I had come first overall in French in Northern Ireland and that I would receive a special prize presented by the French Government. No one at Regent House was more pleased to hear this news than Miss Holmes, our indefatigable French teacher, to whom I owed a deep debt of gratitude for her constant guidance and support. The euphoria at the school was heightened by the headmaster's granting of a day's holiday to staff and pupils.

It was about this time that I met Dr Chaundy. Born in Oxford in 1871, Edred Martin Chaundy was the son of a lay-clerk in the choir of Christ Church Cathedral who supplemented his meagre income by organizing concerts in the neighbouring villages, the admission charge being one penny. As a small boy, Edred was called upon to act as accompanist on these occasions and this experience enabled him to develop his extraordinary musical ability. He told me that the programmes at his father's concerts were rather *ad hoc* affairs for their constitution relied heavily on the available local talent. The artists might include such figures as the blacksmith.

Singers in particular were wont to arrive without copies of the music to be performed. As he waited in the wings with one of the soloists, the small accompanist would listen intently while a few bars of the next song were hummed

Edred M Chaundy c1908

into his ear. Fortunately he was blessed with absolute pitch and instantly identified the key. On the platform he would improvise a suitable prelude only to discover sometimes that the singer was in quite a different key. The young Chaundy soon became so adept at making the necessary adjustments to his accompaniment that few in the audience were probably either aware that anything was amiss or conscious of the astonishing skill being demonstrated in saving the situation.

In due course Edred Chaundy went up to Oxford University to read for degrees in Arts and Music. His father having only recently died, he was probably not in a fit state, either emotionally or mentally, to sit his MusB finals. Parry and Stainer were the examiners and he always modestly attributed his success to Stainer's humanity in very trying circumstances. He was destined to achieve even greater academic distinction with the attainment of the degree of Doctor of Music in 1908.

Most of his later life was spent in Northern Ireland. He held Organist posts in Enniskillen, Belfast (St Mark's, Dundela and St George's), and Bangor Abbey prior to his appointment in 1920 to Armagh Cathedral. An exophthalmic eye complaint, which was ultimately to force him to retire in 1935, so impaired his vision that he was unable to read musical notation of normal size at more than a few inches' distance. Consequently he was obliged to play all service accompaniments from memory and to rely on his prodigious gifts as an extemporiser for the provision of voluntaries.

The late Mr Frank Parsons recalled a visit by the Ulster Society of Organists and Choirmasters (USOC) to Armagh Cathedral towards the end of Dr Chaundy's time there. Having accompanied the choir expertly during Evensong, Dr Chaundy launched into a recital of organ music which delighted the listeners who had heard none of it before. They learned later that the entire programme had been improvised!

Dr Chaundy spent his last years in Bangor where he lived with his second wife, Beulah, a former children's photographer, in a tiny house in Ashley Gardens. Callers were always welcome particularly when they were prepared to make music. One might find oneself desperately trying to keep pace with his knobbly but nonetheless nimble fingers in piano duets or accompanying him when he played one of his stringed instruments, for he was very much a musical all-rounder. *Allegro* movements were invariably taken *molto vivace* with Dr Chaundy cheerfully exhorting one to greater sight-reading efforts.

He was very interested in horticulture and introduced me to the plants *Anthemis* and *Azelea Palestrina* which, he declared, should have a place in the garden of every church musician. He maintained his clarity of thought and his happy, positive outlook right to the end. I consider it a privilege to have known him.

CHAPTER TWO

1953-61 | UNIVERSITY, SCHOOL-TEACHING AND FIRST ORGANIST POSTS

In the early 1950s most of the students going to university from Regent House went to Queen's with a few accepting places at Trinity College, Dublin. We could not avail ourselves of the options which might have been on offer at one of the larger Belfast grammar schools. One could only dream about such places as Oxford and Cambridge. Without a second foreign language, I was obliged to study Medieval French at Queen's and as subsidiary subjects I naturally chose Music, having passed the matriculation examination, and Latin.

In 1953, when I entered the University, the Head of the Modern French Department was Professor Bisson who seemed to inhabit a world of his own. One day in my final year I called to ask him for a testimonial; he looked at me blankly and said that 'freshers' were to remain outside! The testimonial when it eventually materialised was both brief and vague. I showed it to Dr Godin who held the post of Reader in the Department and he informed me that the Professor gave this same testimonial to everyone. Dr Godin provided me with one which was of some value.

The other eccentric on the staff of the French department at that time was Mr Japolski who was, I think, of Polish extraction and whose nickname was inevitably, 'Jalopy'! His behaviour could be decidedly odd. For example, we might enter his room for a lecture to find him laughing uproariously and we would be obliged to sit and wait patiently until he had settled down. Sometimes he was to be seen, with a mischievous grin on his face, stealing up behind a colleague in the street and tapping him playfully on the shoulder as a child might do. However, Mr Japolski came into his own when he played the piano and his occasional lunch-time recitals in the Whitla Hall were always well worth hearing, his performances of the music of Debussy being especially fine.

It was generally agreed that Dr Henri Godin, as the outstanding academic in the department, should have held the chair and it was a shame that he had to wait until comparatively late in his career to realise

23

what must have been his long-term ambition. 'Dr G.', as he was known among the students, was an example to us all and we regarded him with something verging on veneration. He told me that when he came to Northern Ireland in 1936 he had instantly fallen in love with the province and its people. Always perfectly groomed, he was the archetypal French gentleman. Except for the word 'foreign', which he pronounced 'foring', his English was flawless. He delighted in finding French influence in local surnames, e.g. 'Sinnamon', and in local dialect. His recounting of a brief conversation with a Belfast bus conductor, who had said that the weather was so cold that 'it'd cut the neb aff ye' (i.e. 'it would cut your nose off') brought the house down!

The members of our class were invigorated by the weekly challenge which Dr G. issued when he set a passage of highly idiomatic English to be translated into equally idiomatic French. As a master of this art he brought his considerable ingenuity and vast knowledge of literature to bear on the various problems raised by the text and never failed to impress us with his solutions. Once when I felt that I needed to increase my vocabulary I asked Dr G., who was the custodian of the departmental library, for an appropriate book. With a twinkle in his eye and the comment, 'That should do the trick!', he handed me a copy of *A rebours* by Huysmans. So many of the words in this were new to me that even after a few pages I had increased my vocabulary considerably.

Dr G. took a keen interest in his students and kept scrapbooks of press-cuttings, etc. about their post-university careers. In his earlier years at Queen's he had made something of a name for himself as a jazz-musician; he was an authority on art and a highly proficient photographer. He also had a passion for water-wheels. The passing years did nothing to diminish his thirst for knowledge and when I visited him shortly before his death he touchingly expressed his concern that there was 'still so much to learn'.

I understand that in those days it was rare, and it may well be still, for a university to have a separate department of Medieval French. The lecturer in charge of the subject at Queen's was Dr Margaret Pelan who hailed from Lisburn in Co. Antrim. She jealously guarded her domain. Dr Pelan insisted on lecturing in French but, unfortunately, her accent was such that it made note-taking extremely difficult. (I used to think that she had something in common with the Prioress in Chaucer's *Canterbury Tales* to whom 'the French of Paris was unknowe'.) The wide-ranging course included the study of morphology, phonology, semantics and palaeography in addition to a representative selection from the literature of the period. Despite the attraction of such a broadly-based syllabus, I cannot say that I was inspired by the teaching in this department. Medieval French badly needed a Dr G!

With the young and energetic Philip Cranmer now at the helm, the Music Department was quite a different proposition. Derryvolgie House, a large Victorian villa on the Malone Road about a mile from the University, housed both Education and Music at that time. Professor Cranmer clearly enjoyed his interaction with the students and we felt that we all belonged to a very happy family. His colleagues were the ebullient Denis Arnold, an Italian Renaissance specialist, who was later to succeed to the Chair of Music at Oxford University and Evan John, a pianist and organist who also played the French horn, violin and viola. Denis Arnold recommended that we read *Lucky Jim* in which Kingsley Amis paints a very unflattering picture of one 'Evan Johns'. (It is said that Evan John's subsequent court action against the author resulted in the payment of derisory costs. This story, however, may well be apocryphal.)

Philip Cranmer and Denis Arnold were the members of staff who made things happen in the Music Department even if performance standards were sometimes not what they might have been. Philip was a first-class pianist and a quite outstanding accompanist. I have an indelible memory of one of the annual Hamilton Harty Memorial recitals in which he partnered the well-known tenor, David Galliver, his superb technique allowing him to make light of an extremely demanding programme. The University Choir or 'Big Choir', as it was known, was open to all comers and there was no audition. The result of this was that, on the night of a performance, the chorus might be augmented by a number of young men who were not necessarily singers but who were determined to gain access to the post-concert party! It was inevitable that such a motley chorus would live dangerously and it became traditional to give two performances, one in each half of the programme, of such works as Constant Lambert's *Rio Grande* and Beethoven's *Choral Fantasia*, in the hope that the second might be an improvement on the first! The University Singers, a chamber choir formed later by the Professor with entry by invitation/audition, achieved much higher standards in a very varied repertoire. My future wife, Heather, was a founder member.

The other choir was Denis Arnold's Renaissance Group, a small *ad hoc* vocal ensemble consisting almost exclusively of music students, which regularly presented programmes of Italian and English madrigals interspersed with appropriate keyboard music played by Mr Arnold on his virginal. Now and again we would be called together in the late afternoon to sight-read a number of items for performance later that evening as illustrations to one of his extra-mural lectures in some out-lying part of the province. Despite being grossly under-rehearsed our contributions were always enthusiastically received by these small and, doubtless, undiscriminating audiences.

The concerts organised by the Music Society provided a platform which was shared by staff and students. It was an invaluable experience to play and sing before what was at once a critical but sympathetic body of one's peers and tutors. Among the interesting projects suggested by Professor Cranmer was the playing of Bach's *48 Preludes and Fugues* in the course of an academic year with every member of the Department undertaking to perform at least one prelude and fugue at each concert appearance. Incidentally, Philip Cranmer chose to celebrate his eightieth birthday on 1 April 1998 by playing Bach's *'48'* in the church hall at Clayton, the Sussex village where he and his late wife, Ruth, had lived so happily in their retirement.

The year 1953 also saw the beginning of my career as a church musician. Most young people continue to undertake this work on the basis of a course of organ lessons and without adequate coaching in the vitally important choir-training aspect of it. Apart from purely musical and technical matters, there is also the question of people-management. Obliged to learn largely by doing, one inevitably makes mistakes. However, the members of the choir of Shore Street Presbyterian Church in Donaghadee were very tolerant of their young Organist as he learned his trade. A number of fund-raising events enabled us to purchase a set of copies of *The Church Anthem Book*, edited by Walford Davies and Henry Ley, and the opportunity to learn new music was welcomed.

Everything sung by the choir had to be available in both staff notation and tonic sol-fa because some of the tenors and basses could read only the latter. When the two forms of notation were printed separately and in different formats, as they sometimes were, time could be lost in rehearsal when it was necessary to locate a particular place in the score. It was necessary to be very patient! Should the ladies, many of whom were members of the Ards Choral Society, dare to suggest that life would be much easier if everyone were to sing from staff notation, the men were quick to remind them that those members of the choir who were fluent readers of tonic sol-fa were much more accurate than the others. This retort was enough to silence the ladies who knew that the claim could not be denied.

The Harvest Festival was the major event of the year. With each congregation in the town being allocated a different Sunday, it was possible to attend all the special services that were held in Donaghadee and a great many people chose to participate in this annual church 'crawl.' It was only to be expected that these circumstances would give rise to a certain amount of competition between the churches especially with regard to the music and the floral decorations. On one occasion at least, Mr Joseph Russell, who was in charge of the decorating of Shore Street

Church, excelled himself and doubtless his counterparts elsewhere when his spectacular creation took the form of life-size representations of a tractor and a horse each drawing a plough which together covered most of one of the side walls of the building. A photograph of Mr Russell's masterpiece appeared in the local newspaper.

One of my lasting memories of the two years which I spent at Shore Street is of the preaching of the minister, the Revd Tom Patterson. From Co. Donegal where his Scottish forebears had no doubt settled at the time of the Plantation, Mr Patterson, a deeply spiritual man, often shared some of his visionary experiences with us in the course of his wonderful sermons.

Although the regular diet of hymns, metrical psalms and paraphrases was leavened by the inclusion of an anthem and/or introit at each service, I looked forward to the day when I might find a post in a parish church where there would be greater scope for music within the context of the incomparable Anglican liturgy. I must also admit that I had not found Shore Street's Hammond electronic organ a particularly satisfying instrument to play. In 1955 an opportunity arose at Willowfield Parish Church on the Woodstock Road in East Belfast where a successor was being sought for Mr Aubrey Hickman, a highly accomplished musician, who played the viola in the professional Olin String Quartet and who was also a lecturer in Music at Stranmillis College. This time there was competition for the post, with an interview and an audition and I was very pleased to be appointed with effect from January 1956.

Now I had rather innocently assumed that the dignity of the worship which I had known at Bangor Abbey, with its robed choir and a rector whose conduct of the services reflected his great sensitivity to the requirements of the liturgy, was to be found elsewhere in the Church of Ireland. Therefore the informal atmosphere both before and during services at Willowfield, with its decidedly 'low church' ethos, came as something of a shock. (It will be noted that, unusually, the church was not named after one of the Saints.) The members of the unrobed choir did not process but took their places in the choir stalls in ones and twos during the five or ten minutes prior to service time. The refusal of the Rector, the Revd John Frazer, to wear a cassock was no doubt a statement of his position on churchmanship. His long surplice reached to his large boots. Regarded with some amusement by most of his fellow clergy, Mr Frazer had an eye for the ladies and was not above telling the odd risqué story. Before wedding services he was wont to move among the assembling guests entertaining them with wisecracks which were greeted with frequent outbursts of laughter. It gave me no pleasure to provide organ music as a background to this unseemly merriment and it was little wonder that brides-to-be increasingly invited one of the curates to officiate at their weddings although the Rector still expected to be paid a fee. I had great admiration for the parishioners who, though clearly embarrassed by their Rector's behaviour, showed true Christian forbearance towards him while being unswervingly loyal to their Church.

No devotee of church music, Mr Frazer even contrived to thwart my efforts to improve standards. Since the chanting of the psalms, for many one of the most beautiful aspects of Anglican worship, is an art which calls for intensive and regular practice, I would allocate to it a considerable proportion of time at the weekly choir rehearsal. On the following Sunday, and usually without prior notice, Mr Frazer would occasionally announce a psalm other than that which had been previously appointed and we had prepared, adding that this psalm would be said rather than sung. The exasperation of both the choir and myself can be imagined!

Like a number of the more proficient church choirs in Belfast in the 1950s, that at Willowfield Parish Church was capable of giving a good account of itself in annual performances of excerpts from Handel's *Messiah* at Christmas and/or Easter as well as in a range of other music. This well-balanced body of about thirty singers had a blend of experience and youth in all parts with the contraltos being the most consistently competent. Albert Allen who, as a boy, had been a chorister at Armagh Cathedral, inspired confidence in his fellow basses while the outstanding soloist was James Rowan, the possessor of a superb tenor voice. James had been auditioned and been offered a contract by the Carl Rosa Opera Company during one of its visits to Northern Ireland but he had ultimately decided somewhat reluctantly not to accept.

Members of the Choir of Willowfield Parish Church , Belfast c1960 with Harry seated in centre of front row

I was glad to have at my disposal at Willowfield a two-manual pipe-organ. This sounded quite impressive in the Church's resonant acoustic and I thoroughly enjoyed practising in the empty building. Bach's *Six Trio Sonatas*, the organist's *Gradus ad Parnassum,* are at once technically challenging and sublime music. Dr Emery suggested that I should play the first of these (in E flat) when I made my début at the annual composite recital given by invited members of the USOC in St Anne's Cathedral on 3 November 1956. Faced with the large audience which this event always attracted I was naturally very nervous but, with Dr Emery's reassuring presence as my page-turner and with his whispered words of encouragement between movements, the performance (I was told!) went well.

In July of that year I had attended a summer course in French language and literature at Strasbourg University. As this was the first time that I had been out of Ireland the experience was for me, at any rate, something of an adventure. It was exciting to find oneself in the midst of an assembly of several hundred students from various countries in a beautiful European city. My room-mate, Henning Lundt Nielsen from Denmark, was perhaps rather more interested in some of the young ladies than in furthering his French studies which meant that he was not infrequently absent from classes. On the plus side he was a fine clarinettist and a recital which he and I gave in the great hall of the university was very warmly received by an audience which, judging by its size, must have included most of the students and staff.

Albert Schweitzer, one of the most famous alumni of Strasbourg University, had established an annual recital of the music of Johann Sebastian Bach in St Thomas's Church (in Strasbourg) to mark the great composer's birthday on 28 July, 1750. The organ recitalist in 1956 was Edouard Nies-Berger who had collaborated with Schweitzer on the completion of a new edition of Bach's organ works (published by Schirmer, New York) on which the latter had previously worked with Charles-Marie Widor. On the morning of the recital I visited St Thomas's where I met Mr Nies-Berger and Albert Schweitzer's elderly sister who was with him. That evening the church was filled for a memorable recital of a representative selection of Bach's organ music with chorale preludes being prefaced by the singing of the relevant chorales by a choir under the direction of a young relative of the eminent French conductor, Charles Munch.

Illness in the early part of 1957 seriously affected my studies for my final honours degree examinations at Queen's in June of that year. Consequently I did not achieve as high a classification as was expected. I subsequently learned that two of my class-mates had successfully sought a deferral of their entry for the examinations until a later date but, unfortunately, I had not been aware that this concession could be granted in certain circumstances.

Having also studied Music for two years at Queen's, I could have stayed on for a further two in order to take a BMus degree had I been able to raise the necessary funding. This being out of the question, I was obliged to seek a teaching post in a local school. It so happened that the Principal of Park Parade Secondary School, Mr Tommy Holland, a tenor in the choir at Willowfield Parish Church, was looking for someone to assist with both French and Music. He gave me to understand that if I were to accept this position I should be well placed to succeed the current Head of Music, Peter Hinckley, who had indicated that he would like to pursue his career abroad.

Once at Park Parade, I could see that Peter would be a very difficult act to follow. His musical gifts and personal charisma were such that he was an exceptional teacher. A graduate of the Royal College of Music (RCM) and a brass specialist, he had persuaded the school governors to purchase a set of instruments to allow him to form a brass band and this, combined with the large choir of girls, always sounded very impressive at concerts in the sumptuous arrangements which Peter made specially for them. His appointment to an important advisory post in Canada robbed the school of an irreplaceable member of staff.

Because it was not obligatory for graduates to have an education certificate in order to gain entry to the teaching profession in the 1950s, I had never stood in front of a class prior to my arrival at Park Parade School. Now while the acquisition of a PGCE does not necessarily guarantee the holder's success in the classroom, the course followed includes periods of supervised teaching practice with assessment of performance. As a probationary teacher, I had to submit schemes of work and lesson notes regularly to the principal for his approval and subject inspectors were liable to visit the school at any time to see how I was faring.

The French inspector did not think too much of my efforts to teach the language to girls in one of the lower forms. He suggested that, rather than strive to inculcate the elements of grammar and simple vocabulary (which he regarded as an 'academic' approach), I should ask the girls to keep scrap-books and write short paragraphs (in English!) about French fashion. I'm afraid that I was not convinced of the value of this type of exercise. As for the boys in the upper forms, they were simply not interested in Music, with the result that class-management could sometimes be extremely difficult.

By the middle of the first term, I was exhausted at the end of many a school day and would go home to bed while my senior colleagues, who seemed to control their classes with the utmost ease, headed for the golf-course. Encouraged by my friend and mentor at Queen's, Dr Godin, I had embarked on research into Music in the work of the French Existentialist poets. However, life for me at Park Parade was proving so stressful that we both soon realised that this absorbing project would have to be shelved. The migraine headaches which were to plague me over the ensuing years undoubtedly date from this time. Indeed, my general health suffered to such an extent that my doctor insisted that I take some time off to recover.

Early in 1958 I applied for a post as a teacher of French at my old school, Regent House. I also went to have a preliminary chat with Mr McDonald, the Headmaster, who admitted that he was really looking for a lady to coach hockey. The fact that I was a hockey player myself seemed to count for nothing. Mr Holland readily granted me permission to have an afternoon off to attend the formal interview and was convinced that, as a former Regent House pupil, I would be appointed. Having narrowly missed the bus to Newtownards, I telephoned Mr McDonald to explain my predicament, to offer my apologies and to ask if I might be interviewed later in the afternoon. He informed me that his favoured candidate for the post was now a man in his final year at Queen's who had a 'blue' for rugby. It would not be necessary for me to make the journey.

When Park Parade reopened after the summer vacation I spotted in the staff-room a tall, athletic young man who was a member of the congregation at Willowfield Parish Church. He told me that he had been appointed as a teacher of French at Regent House, that he had failed his degree examinations and that, pending the 're-sits', he had accepted a temporary post at Park Parade. In fact he never took up this post but decided to join the Royal Air Force in the interests of the further development of his career as a rugby player. As a result my younger sister Norma, then in the fifth form at Regent House, had to make do with a series of inadequate supply teachers who were of little help to her and her peers as they prepared for their 'O' level examinations at the end of the year.

My experience at Park Parade had made it clear to me that I was not cut out to be a secondary schoolteacher and, with my morale at a very low ebb, I decided to resign. I did not ask Mr Holland for a testimonial because I knew that he would have been unable to make many positive comments about my work. My salary as Organist at Willowfield Parish Church together with fees for weddings etc. provided me with a small income which I augmented by teaching piano privately (at 2 guineas, i.e. £2.10, for 10 half-hour lessons) and by giving students individual tuition in French.

In 1959 I was invited to become the conductor of the Victoria Male-Voice Choir. Founded in 1917 this choir, having in its halcyon days won a number of awards at competitive musical festivals both in Northern Ireland and in England, had fallen on leaner times in recent years and was in need of an increase in membership as well as reinvigoration. I was to discover that the men who sang in male-voice choirs were rarely members of mixed-voice choirs because they preferred socialising and making music with other men. Since few of them could read music with any degree of fluency an inordinate amount of rehearsal time was taken up with what is known as 'note-bashing'. Nevertheless, once they had learned their parts and could sing with confidence, they made a stirring sound even if the inevitable preponderance of bass voices made it difficult to achieve a satisfactory balance. Tenors have always been in short supply.

The men looked forward to the concerts which we gave around the province. During the interval most of them made for the nearest hostelry, some invariably failing to return by the agreed time. I am not likely to forget those occasions when I was obliged to go on to the platform to begin the second half of a programme without the full complement of singers, the late-comers sheepishly reappearing in the ranks in the course of the opening items. I should like to think that the Victoria Male-Voice Choir made some progress during the two years that I was its conductor and although Kenneth Roberton, the adjudicator at Bangor Musical Festival, did not place it among the prize-winners, he commended the choir for its disciplined singing, its suitably robust rendering of an arrangement of *The Lincolnshire Poacher* receiving special mention together with enthusiastic applause from the audience.

When I heard that Mrs Henrietta Moran had come to live in Bangor I paid her a visit to seek her advice and help. Singing under her maiden name, Henrietta Byrne, she was considered to be one of the finest soprano soloists that Ulster had ever produced. A Music graduate of Trinity College, Dublin and an accomplished pianist, organist and choir-trainer, Henrietta made a very significant contribution to the musical life of the province as a concert artist and broadcaster as well as in the field of education. I was warmly welcomed into the busy Moran household and was soon regarded as one of the family by Henrietta, her husband Edwin (the Postmaster in Newtownards) and their two children, Isabel and Stephen. Isabel was later to study singing at the Royal Academy of Music (RAM) with Dame Eva Turner and have a distinguished career as a contralto soloist in New Zealand.

Henrietta suggested two objectives, firstly, that I should endeavour to add further musical qualifications to the LTCL piano teacher's diploma which I had passed in December 1957 and, secondly, that I should try to widen the scope of my musical activities in order to increase both my experience and income. On the academic side she recommended that a degree in Music should be the ultimate goal. To this end she set about giving me a thorough grounding in harmony and counterpoint, both strict and free. She also introduced me to Dr Havelock Nelson, the staff accompanist at the BBC in Belfast and a leading figure on the Northern Ireland musical scene to whom countless aspiring young musicians have been indebted for assistance as they have striven to establish themselves in the profession.

Through his numerous contacts Havelock was able to open many doors. I soon found myself acting as an accompanist and adjudicator at competitive musical festivals, playing the organ and piano in productions by the Grand Opera Society of Northern Ireland in addition to assisting him with both the rehearsals and actual performances of his Studio Opera Group. In fact, when Havelock was abroad undertaking one of his adjudicating engagements in 1959 he left me in charge of preparations for the next production.

I had also met Dr H K Andrews who had offered to give me some help (by correspondence) with fugue and other contrapuntal procedures. Dr Andrews was born in Comber, Co. Down and educated at Bedford School, the RCM, Trinity College, Dublin, and New College, Oxford, gaining doctorates of music at both Universities. He later taught at the RCM and lectured at Oxford where he was Director of Music at New College Chapel. His analytical studies of the compositional techniques of Palestrina and Byrd are authoritative as is his *Oxford Harmony, vol. ii.* Correspondence is, however, a rather unsatisfactory substitute for personal contact and, although I once travelled to Oxford to have a lesson with Dr Andrews, I did not derive as much benefit from his tuition as I had perhaps expected.

In addition I had a few lessons from Dr A J (Archie) Potter, one of the most gifted figures on the Dublin musical scene. Born in Belfast in 1918, Potter was a chorister at All Saints' Church, Margaret Street, London. Later he studied at Clifton College, Bristol under Dr Douglas Fox and at the RCM where he was a pupil of Vaughan Williams. He was awarded the MusD degree at Trinity College, Dublin in 1953. It is said that during the final examinations one of the invigilators, seeing Potter slumped across his desk, hurried to his side assuming that he had taken ill. He was, in fact, asleep having completed the three-hour paper in a third of the allotted time. Elected to a professorship in composition at the Royal Irish Academy of Music (RIAM) in 1955, Potter was also a noted music journalist and broadcaster. Earlier in his career he had been for a time a vicar choral at St Patrick's Cathedral, Dublin.

In 1960 I entered the choir of Willowfield Parish Church for two classes at the Belfast Musical Festival. As the most important event of its kind in Northern Ireland it attracted large numbers of entries in those days. On the nights of the choral competitions the main hall of the Assembly Buildings was usually packed with the competing choirs and their groups of supporters. In the prevailing highly-charged atmosphere some choirs might excel themselves while the performances of others might fall short of expectation. The Willowfield choir-members did not let either themselves or their conductor down and, although they were unplaced in one of the classes, they were runners-up in the other, the adjudicator, Dr Eric Thiman being particularly impressed by their expressive singing of Psalm 42 to what he informed us was his favourite chant (by Walford Davies). We were all greatly encouraged by this result. Dr Thiman's comments had been very constructive and it was evident that we had given a good account of ourselves.

Each year at the Belfast Musical Festival a special award was made to the young conductor who, in the opinion of the adjudicator, had shown the greatest promise in the course of the competitions. Named after a well-known Ulster musician (of English extraction), the John Vine Memorial Bursary enabled the recipient to attend a course in choral conducting at the Downe House Summer School of Music in Berkshire. I was thrilled to be declared the winner of this award in 1960.

Such courses as those at Downe House are of great benefit not only from an educational point of view but also because of the opportunities which they afford for interaction with both members of staff and one's fellow students. In addition to attending the various classes during the day, all were expected to come together in the evening to rehearse (for performance at the end of the week) Verdi's *Requiem* under the direction of David Willcocks, the famous Director of Music at King's College, Cambridge with Professor Philip Cranmer accompanying on the piano. It was fascinating to observe this great choir-trainer at work with a large, unbalanced body of singers of very mixed vocal ability.

That summer I also attended orchestral conducting courses at Canford School in Dorset (under George Hurst who was then the conductor-in-chief of the BBC Northern Orchestra), and at Bromley in Kent. Of these the latter was the more interesting and I considered myself very fortunate to be one of the eighteen selected participants. It was based at the spacious home of the Misses White both of whom were members of the Bromley Symphony Orchestra of which the distinguished conductor Sir Adrian Boult was the patron. A small string orchestra had been assembled with a pianist filling in the wind parts. Sir Adrian, a recognised authority on the subject, proved to be an excellent tutor generously sharing with us the fruits of his vast experience. His philosophy, neatly expressed in the opening sentence of his helpful *Handbook on the Technique of Conducting*

Sir Adrian Boult (centre, front row) with those attending his orchestral conducting course at Bromley, Kent, August 1960; from left, back row: John Hind (former Director of Music at Campbell College, Belfast), Eric Fletcher and Harry

was that 'the object of technique in all art is the achievement of the desired end with the greatest simplicity and economy of means'. He himself had been profoundly influenced by Arthur Nikisch, the renowned Austro-Hungarian conductor, particularly with regard to rehearsal methods. Sir Adrian strongly disapproved of anything smacking of showmanship which, while it might have a measure of audience appeal, served only to distract the musicians who required the conductor's gestures to be concentrated in the point of his stick in their line of vision just above their stands. He personally used a very long, white baton with rubber bands wound round its cork handle to help him to maintain easy control of its movement. Unnecessary use of the upper arms was discouraged. One day when a student was not responding to his admonishment, Sir Adrian took a long piece of rope and bound the hapless fellow in such a way that he could move only his lower arms!

The members of the chamber orchestra, whose patience must have been severely tried at times, were most co-operative. The rehearsal schedule allowed each of the participating conductors a fair share of time on the rostrum and we all agreed that we had learnt a great deal not only from our own mistakes but from observing the mistakes which others made. An additional benefit was that we were given complimentary tickets for the Henry Wood Promenade Concerts taking place in the evenings at the

Royal Albert Hall. Naturally the technique of each Prom conductor came in for detailed critical assessment by the members of our party both after the concert and during the following day!

Some of my friends at the Bromley course had urged me to give serious consideration to coming to London to continue my studies, and when I returned home after what had been a hectic but hugely enjoyable period of musical activity I discussed the matter with my parents as well as with Henrietta Moran. All were agreed that I was now probably in a position to derive the utmost benefit from such a move. London appeared to be beckoning and they felt that if I were meant to go there a way would open up for me.

A further episode occurred in 1960 which appeared to emphasise the advisability of this decision. Dr Emery, who had served as Organist at Bangor Parish Church for the previous forty years, was about to retire and a successor was being sought. Because of the high esteem in which he was held, he was asked to act as advisor to the Select Vestry in its quest for a suitably qualified musician. The post was advertised widely in both the local and national press. Assuming that I would not be considered for what was after all one of the most important parish church Organist positions in Northern Ireland, I did not apply.

One Saturday afternoon as I was on the point of setting off to play hockey, I received a phone call from Archdeacon George Quin, the Rector of Bangor Parish Church, who said that both he and Dr Emery would like me to come along later that afternoon to meet them and to play the organ for them. Somewhat puzzled by this request and, in addition, rather tired after a tough game in the course of which I had received a few nasty blows on my hands, I turned up at the church where I played some of the pieces which I was currently studying with Dr Emery. He also asked me to undertake a number of keyboard tests. Still puzzled, I then withdrew with them to the vestry where they discussed the post with me. Although they did not say as much, it is probable that, unable to find a suitable candidate among the many applicants, they had decided to give consideration to someone who was already well known to both of them. While they thought that I was capable of meeting the musical demands of the post, they hesitated to offer it to me perhaps because at this stage I lacked sufficient experience and suitable qualifications. 'If only you had gone away, Harry', the Archdeacon said more than once in the course of the interview. Dr Emery may also have been unwilling to appoint someone as his successor who would have come from so 'low' a church as Willowfield. I should simply *have* to go away.

The Grindle Family c1960. From left: Harry, David, and parents standing with Norma and Margaret in front

CHAPTER THREE

1961-62 | FURTHER STUDY AND SCHOOL-TEACHING IN LONDON

I was interviewed for two school posts in London and was offered both of them. The one which seemed immediately more attractive was in the small choir-school at Westminster Abbey but on further consideration I decided against accepting it. In addition to my teaching and boarding duties I should have been responsible for the supervision of the choristers' leisure activities including travelling with them to sports fixtures in various places. It was evident that I should have been left with little time for my personal studies.

The Revd Donald Atkinson, the enthusiastic young headmaster of Friern Barnet Grammar School (FBGS) in the North Finchley area, was warmly welcoming and promised that he would find me the quiet 'digs' which I was seeking. He also pledged me his full support when I joined the staff of his school in September 1961 to teach French and Music and to take over from him the direction of the school choir. He was to be as good as his word on both counts.

In the meantime I gladly accepted an invitation from Alan Angus, Head of Music at Campbell College in Belfast, to assist him during the Easter term. An independent boys' school run on English lines, 'Campbell', in its magnificent woodland setting on the outskirts of the city, had an excellent academic and sporting record. Teachers were shown due respect and life was very civilized, with morning coffee and afternoon tea taken in the very comfortable staff common-room and dinner served in hall. The arts in general had a high profile. There were a number of very talented musicians among the boys including the sons of the professors of Music at both Queen's University, Belfast and Dublin University (Trinity College). In the upper school there were some fine pianists, one of them of concerto standard.

From the outset I knew that I was going to enjoy my time at 'Campbell.' Alan gave me a varied timetable which included a mixture of class-teaching and individual piano lessons. He also allowed me to take rehearsals and conduct the performances of the incidental orchestral music which had been specially composed for the production of Shakespeare's 'King Lear' scheduled for the end of term. I was sorry to leave the school at Easter.

While I had been eagerly looking forward to the next phase of my life, a dark cloud was gathering on the horizon. My brother, David, who was in his third year at Queen's studying French and German, had early in 1961 injured one of his knees in a hockey match. Our local GP, not suspecting that any serious damage had been done, merely applied a bandage. David continued to attend lectures travelling to and from Belfast every day. Soon, his knee having swollen to the size of a football and with David now quite unable to walk, he was confined to bed. Further investigation revealed that cancer had developed. Although as a family we did not have a great deal of money to spare, every avenue was explored in an effort to arrest the progress of the disease. A very expensive dietary régime which initially promised much failed like everything else to have the desired effect.

At such times one is made keenly aware of life's priorities. With David's health deteriorating over the summer months, my instinct was to inform the headmaster at FBGS of the gravity of the situation and ask if, in the circumstances, I might be allowed to postpone my arrival at the school. On the other hand since, for David's sake, we were determined to remain as positive as possible, a decision was taken that there should be no change in my plans.

It was, therefore, with a heavy heart that I began teaching at FBGS in September 1961. I flew back to Northern Ireland each week-end to visit David in Musgrave Park Hospital in Belfast and was shocked to note the accelerating decline in his condition. My distraught mother rarely left his bedside. David's passing in October, at the age of twenty-one, spared him any further suffering, knowledge which afforded us some consolation in our grief. We learned afterwards from one of his closest friends that, although David had gone along with us in looking forward to a bright future when he would have recovered, he had known for some time that he was terminally ill. Visitors and fellow-patients had wondered at the courageous way in which an increasingly frail young man had borne his suffering. It must have been obvious to everyone that it was David's unshakeable Christian faith that sustained him. Indeed, while he was still able to communicate with others, he did not hesitate to testify to that faith and to the transforming effect which it had had on his own life. He was a shining example to us all.

I was deeply grateful to my colleagues at FBGS for their sympathy and support during what had been a very distressing time. However, once back at school again, I was caught up in a busy round of activities.

FBGS was a small Church of England independent school for boys which was managed by a board of trustees with the rector of St John's Parish Church, Friern Barnet, acting as warden. In 1961 there were about 145 pupils on the roll. Because there was then no sixth form at FBGS, the boys had to go on to another school to study for their 'A' levels. The eager, well-mannered little boys in the first form were a delight to teach and I always looked forward to the periods which I spent with them. At the end of each class, as they left the room, many of them would come forward and express their gratitude for the lesson. I had never met such courtesy before. One day when I was introducing a recording of some violin music played by Yehudi Menuhin, a boy put up his hand: 'Please, sir, he lives round the corner from me in Hampstead!'

I think that I could claim to have had a good rapport with all of the age-groups. Of course, an interest in sport on the part of a teacher is always a recommendation as far as boys are concerned and when they discovered that I played cricket, they organised a challenge match between teams led by David Smart, who taught Geography, and myself. The poster advertising this match suggested that it would have something of an international flavour. Although I am fairly certain that David does not have a single drop of Scottish blood in his veins, the name of everyone on his side was given the prefix 'Mac' while the names of the 'Irish' eleven all began with 'O'. While I cannot recall the result, I do remember that the match was eagerly anticipated and that on the day there was much hilarity.

Despite the restrictions imposed by lack of space and limited resources, FBGS was a pleasant place in which to work. Discipline was maintained easily throughout the school (draconian measures were never necessary) with the prefects carrying out their duties efficiently under the leadership of Philip Hartree, an exemplary Head-boy.

The teaching staff of seven included the Headmaster who taught History. The three older teachers, all approaching retirement, were Miss Stella Davies (Art), Fred Newmarch (Maths), and William Gross (General Subjects). Fred Newmarch, formerly a commissioned officer in the Royal Army Service Corps, was always referred to as 'The Colonel.' Mr Gross, a chain-smoker and very eccentric, slept in a deck-chair at night!

My two very able younger colleagues were David Smart and Keith Ramsay (English). David was also in charge of games. Having been stationed during his military service at Ballykinler in Co. Down, he delighted in addressing me occasionally in an exaggerated version of the Ulster accent with its flat vowels and distinctive inflections. In my capacity as assistant games master, I was usually happy to help David as much as possible. Nevertheless, the running of the preliminary heats for the various events during the weeks prior to the annual sports day sometimes threatened to result in my being late for a lesson with one of my teachers or to curtail severely the organ practice which I had booked in one of the local churches. With David looking after the track events in another part of the park, I would put my charges through their paces in the field events in record time in order to gain my freedom. I even encouraged the boys participating in both track and field events to come to me first. Knowing full well what I was about, David would take up his megaphone and make it clear to me and to the entire neighbourhood that, 'track events take precedence over field events.' He still continues to remind me of this regulation.

Keith Ramsey's annual dramatic production in the Easter term was always one of the highlights of the school year. A very gifted director, Keith drew from the boys acting of an exceptionally high quality in plays by Shakespeare and Shaw. Auditions were keenly contested and the enthusiasm engendered was such that those who had been unsuccessful in their quest for a part were quite happy to work behind the scenes. Involvement in some way was the thing.

Both David and Keith sang in the school choir which rehearsed during lunch-hour three times a week. With the Headmaster singing tenor (while keeping an eye on attendance!) members had to have a good reason for absence. At morning prayers each day in St John's Parish Church across the road from the school, the choir led the singing of the hymns with Colonel Newmarch accompanying us on the organ. This instrument, said to have been built by 'Father' Henry Willis, the greatest of the nineteenth-century British organ-builders, made a splendid sound in the resonant acoustic of the lofty church. Although I was permitted to practise on the organ at St John's, I rarely did so because the heavy old tracker action made the playing of faster music well-nigh impossible when the manuals were coupled.

Eric Fletcher, whom I had met at Sir Adrian Boult's conducting course in Bromley, had kindly offered to help me with my preparations for the ARCO diploma examinations. A former Cambridge organ scholar and Assistant Organist at Peterborough Cathedral, Eric was a very fine musician. (He had been the organist on the early Argo recording of Easter Matins made by the King's College Choir under the direction of Boris Ord.) Eric gave me lessons at St Paul's, Portman Square where he was at that time Director of Music and, in return, I acted as his assistant when required at services, accompanying the choir while he conducted. Occasionally I would stay overnight at his spacious ground-floor apartment in Holland Park. The property was owned by the daughter of Eric Milner-White, the former Dean of King's College, Cambridge who had composed the original bidding prayer and drawn up the order of service for the famous Festival of the Nine Lessons which has been adopted throughout the English-speaking world. I noted with interest that the bed-linen bore the famous family name.

Having successfully sat the ARCO examinations in January 1962, I was present at the distribution of diplomas at the end of the month. The well-known architect and Surveyor of the Fabric of Westminster Abbey, Mr Stephen Dykes Bower, brother of the Organist of St Paul's Cathedral, and himself an organist, gave a talk on 'The Placing and Appearance of the Organ'. Dr Herbert Howells's speech of thanks to the speaker, a man of many parts, was carefully considered and its delivery was characteristically measured. The opening was arresting: 'I remember one day, in the morning, a certain man giving a lecture on the chamber works of Brahms, and the same day, in the afternoon, the same man explaining why milk in bulk is blue'.

I had hoped that Eric Fletcher would be able to continue to act as my mentor. However, with his heavy work-load (he was also Director of Music at St Dunstan's College, SE 6), it was impossible for him to find the time to see me as regularly as was necessary. I should have to seek help elsewhere.

The previous Headmaster of FBGS, the Revd Philip Thomas, had gone to teach Religious Studies at Queenswood, a large independent school for girls at Hatfield in Hertfordshire where his wife, Marjorie, was in charge of the Music Department. Marjorie, an accomplished organist, who was at that time one of the few women to hold the Fellowship of the Royal College of Organists (FRCO), was to prove to be an invaluable advisor and friend. She had inherited her musical gifts from her parents, both professional singers, who had appeared as soloists in performances under the direction of Sir Edward Elgar. Her only son Alan, a former head-chorister at Magdalen College, Oxford, studied viola at the RAM before taking up a post in the orchestra of the Royal Opera House, Covent Garden. Outgoing and the very soul of kindness, Marjorie Thomas took me under her wing, generously giving me the run of her house which was situated not far from FBGS.

For organ lessons she recommended Douglas Hawkridge, the Organist at St Columba's Church of Scotland, Pont Street and a member of the teaching staff at the RAM. Being a member of the panel of examiners for the RCO diplomas, he was thoroughly conversant with the requirements and with the instrument used for the practical part of the examinations - a very important consideration. Under his expert guidance, I entered for and passed the ARCM diploma in Organ Performance in July 1962. Marjorie suggested that I seek help from Dr Eric Thiman with the written part (i.e. harmony and counterpoint) of the FRCO diploma which we had identified as my next objective.

Eric Thiman's career is confirmation of the truth of the dictum that hard work as well as talent is necessary for ultimate success. The death of his father at an early age made the eleven-year-old Thiman realise the need for self-reliance. On leaving school he became a booking-clerk at London Bridge station but, finding that this was a 'dead-end' job, he resolved to follow his true métier and become a musician. Composition was a positive obsession. Apart from some early part-time study at Trinity College of Music and the Guildhall School of Music, Thiman was self-taught. He obtained the FRCO diploma in 1921 (winning the Turpin Prize) and six years later, after some coaching from Dr Harold Darke, the DMus degree at London University. At the age of twenty-seven he was the youngest successful candidate ever. Later he was appointed to a professorship of both harmony and composition at the RAM and from 1952 was an examiner to the Faculty of Music at London University. He also served for a time as Dean of the Faculty. Exceptionally, Eric Thiman was not an Anglican but a life-long member of the Congregational Church in which his father had been an ordained minister. From 1957 he held the post of Organist and Director of Music at London's City Temple, the 'cathedral' of Congregationalism.

Thiman was a prolific composer, his output including numerous works in most genres. He is undoubtedly best known for his vocal music, both sacred and secular, which has long enjoyed a widespread popularity. Always eminently practical and melodically attractive, its essential appeal is to amateur singers. There are those who would dismiss Thiman as a purveyor of mere *Gebrauchsmusik* ('functional music') and while it is true that his style has its limitations as well as a certain predictability, a text will sometimes move him to produce something of quite exceptional quality. *Draw nigh and take the Body of the Lord*, a setting of words from the seventh century Bangor Antiphonary commissioned in 1960 by the choir of my home parish, Bangor Abbey, Co. Down, is one such piece.

Countless students will have had good cause to be grateful to Eric Thiman for his excellent text-books on harmony, counterpoint, musical form and fugue which are admirably succinct distillations of a fund of knowledge of all four subjects. Those who, like me, were fortunate enough to receive personal tuition from him would, I am sure, agree that he was an inspiring teacher. He had an incredible facility on paper, writing a fugue, complete with episodes in triple counterpoint, as one might dash off a letter. He was also an exceptionally gifted improviser. On one occasion, after he had examined and commented on a passacaglia which I had written, he said, 'You might have done this' and, having played over the bass theme on the piano, he proceeded to add a series of increasingly complex variations incorporating virtually every conceivable contrapuntal device - at once a *tour de force* and a spur to greater efforts on my part.

I found at 13 Wycliffe Avenue, the home of the Freestones, the most peaceful and comfortable of havens. Mrs Ellen Freestone was the school secretary at FBGS and her husband, Frank, worked in local government. Their only son, Paul, whom they had adopted, was a lively twelve-year-old with a very keen interest in sport. Paul attended FBGS and sang treble in the school choir. Although he did not take undue advantage of our relationship as members of the same household, I had to remind him from time to time of the deference which a teacher at such a school was entitled to expect from a pupil.

In an effort to save on bus fares, I bought a second-hand bicycle on which to travel to and from FBGS. During the severe winter of 1962 when there were heavy snow-falls with sub-zero temperatures in the early morning, having sometimes gradually lost the feeling in my fingers and hands en route to school, I would have to bathe them in hot water to restore the circulation.

There were few spare moments during most days what with a busy round of classes to teach, rehearsals to take, homework to mark, lessons to prepare and personal study as well as organ practice to be done. I allowed myself one evening in the week off to attend a badminton club at a local church. On the other evenings the Freestones kindly allowed me to take over their drawing-room and piano for an hour or two to practise keyboard tests.

On Sundays I went with the family to the morning service at a nearby Baptist church where the hearty congregational singing was given a strong lead by the lively Welsh Organist. I usually attended Evensong at Hampstead Parish Church which in those days had a choir of men and boys of cathedral standard under the direction of Martindale Sidwell. Mr Sidwell contrived to divide himself between this church and St Clement Danes in the Strand, by employing capable assistants at both churches. He would appear in person at one in the morning and at the other in the evening! Regarded as one of the outstanding choral conductors of his day, he was also a professor of organ at the RAM. Many of the country's leading church musicians of the next generation have readily acknowledged the extent of the influence on them of his teaching and of his relentless pursuit of excellence.

On the odd Sunday evening I went with Frank and Ellen to the small chapel at Kensit Memorial College which was situated in extensive grounds on one side of Wycliffe Avenue. Many of the houses on the other side of the avenue were owned by the trustees of this institution where missionaries called the Wycliffe Preachers were trained for the Protestant Truth Society. Tenants, among them the Freestones, were expected to attend services in the College Chapel at least occasionally, joining the sparse, elderly congregation in what was sadly a rather dull act of worship. If the regular 'organist' were absent, I would volunteer to accompany on the harmonium the Moody and Sankey hymns which were the standard fare. At my first appearance exception was taken to my playing of 'Amens' at the ends of hymns (as printed!) and I was careful not to repeat this transgression subsequently.

Those responsible for the conduct of the services were invariably rather severe and conveyed little of the joy of the Christian Gospel. However, humour could intrude as it did one evening when a solemn elder was bringing future events at the College to the attention of the congregation. Due to an unfortunate slip of the tongue, the showing of one of the 'Fact and Faith' films was announced as a showing of a 'Fact and Filth' film. Frank Freestone, who was present, told me that he for one could scarcely contain himself!

Sunday afternoons might find me assisting with a Crusader Bible-class for grammar schoolboys at Christ's College at Finchley. I enjoyed playing the fine piano with its sonorous bass in the school assembly hall and afterwards chatting to some of the very bright lads who were present. Most of them had never before met anyone from Northern Ireland.

From time to time I would travel into central London to attend Evensong at either St Paul's Cathedral or Westminster Abbey or, as a special treat, take the train to Cambridge to visit the chapels of King's and St John's Colleges to listen to their celebrated choirs under the direction of David Willcocks and George Guest, then at the height of their powers. It was possible, because of the times of the services on a week-day, to attend Evensong at both chapels and it was interesting to compare the sounds of these two outstanding choirs. The singing of the psalms was particularly fascinating with the characteristically fastidious approach of Willcocks making the greater impact and giving much food for thought. There is no doubt that in the early 1960s the King's and St John's choirs were in a class of their own, the continuous supply of alert choristers and young choral scholars with fine, blending voices enabling two consummate choir-trainers to achieve performances of the very highest quality.

In this context I must mention the music at All Saints', Margaret Street in central London where the Organist and Choirmaster at that time was Michael Fleming. The magnificence of High Victorian Gothic architecture and worship in the Anglo-Catholic tradition (with, in those days, the ladies of the congregation on one side of the central aisle and the gentlemen on the other) combined to make a deep impression even on someone of an evangelical persuasion like myself. While the singing of the choir was superb, its exceptionally well-drilled movements had a unanimity which I have never seen equalled elsewhere. Alas, the church's choir-school closed in 1968. Since then a mixed-voice choir, with sopranos having replaced the trebles, has maintained the exacting musical standards for which All Saints', Margaret Street has always been justly famous.

London, of course, is a veritable hive of musical activity with hundreds of concerts and recitals competing for an audience every day. The father of one of the boys at FBGS was the manager of the BBC Concert Orchestra and he frequently sent me complimentary tickets. With the high admission prices to London events well beyond my limited means, I was truly thankful for this bounty. The tickets gave me access sometimes to the best seats in the house and I might even find myself enjoying the unaccustomed luxury of a private box whenever the concert programme was one that was lacking in popular appeal. I was sometimes in the invited audience at the BBC studios at Maida Vale on a Sunday afternoon for the concert by the BBC Symphony Orchestra regularly broadcast 'live' at 3.00p.m.

It is also possible in London to come across a first-rate concert in what appears to be an unlikely place. One day while out walking in the Finchley area, I saw a poster outside a small, rather nondescript Congregational church advertising a concert there the following Saturday evening by the Finchley Choral Society (President: Mrs Margaret Thatcher, MP). The programme (Parry: *Blest Pair of Sirens*; Dag Wiren: *Serenade for strings, Op.11* and Mozart: *Requiem, K.626*) looked attractive, so out of curiosity, I went. The well-trained choir was accompanied by a small string ensemble of, as I learned afterwards, professional players drawn from one or more of the top London orchestras with the wind parts being supplied by the organist. The conductor was Alan Barlow. The deftly-played Dag Wiren *Serenade* was for me a very exciting discovery, although its final *alla marcia* movement, in which the composer parodies the German 'goose-step', was already familiar as the signature-tune of the BBC television programme *Monitor*. Altogether this concert was one of the most enjoyable that I have ever attended.

At FBGS we set two objectives for the choir during 1961-62. The first of these was quite an ambitious carol service which would include a certain amount of unfamiliar music and the second, by way of a climax to the school year, a concert in mid-July at the end of the summer term. With my arrival at the school having been delayed due to my brother's death and with the consequent reduction in the rehearsal time available, we all had to work extremely hard. The boys were very responsive. For the carol service in St John's we were allowed to borrow the robes belonging to

The Choir of Friern Barnet Grammar School, London, December 1961

the church choir in order that we could look the part and an appreciative congregation of over three hundred parents and friends came along to support us.

It was the Headmaster, I think, who discovered that the well-known guitarist, John Williams, was a former pupil of the school. Then aged twenty and on the threshold of what was to be an illustrious international career, he kindly agreed to be our special guest artist at the summer concert. His superb playing of music by Bach, Fernando Sor, Granados and Villa-Lobos delighted the large audience and inspired the other artists to give of their very best. The programme which had opened with the singing of all three verses of the National Anthem also included contributions from the school choir, vocal solos by the Headmaster and two of the trebles, one of them being Paul Freestone, and piano duets played by Marjorie Thomas and me.

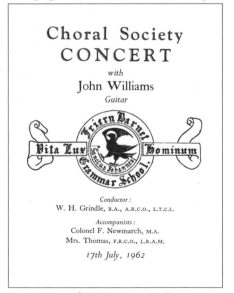

Choral Society
CONCERT
with
John Williams
Guitar

Conductor :
W. H. Grindle, B.A., A.R.C.O., L.T.C.L.

Accompanists :
Colonel F. Newmarch, M.A.
Mrs. Thomas, F.R.C.O., L.R.A.M.

17th July, 1962

Programme of FBGS Summer Concert, July 1962

Incidentally, one of the trebles in the school choir was destined to have a notable career on the pop music scene. This was Simon Nichol who in 1967, at the age of seventeen, was a founding member of *Fairport Convention* which took its name from Simon's home ('Fairport') where the band rehearsed. Although I cannot claim any credit for Simon's success, one of my later piano pupils (perhaps *despite* my teaching!) has made a considerable name for himself ('Duke Special') on both sides of the Atlantic as a pop musician.

In August 1962 I joined the support staff at the Summer School of Music at Dartington Hall in Devon. This was directed by Sir William Glock who, as Controller of Music at the BBC, was able to attract the leading artists of the day to give performances and master-classes. It was inspiring to watch these great musicians at work in rehearsal and on the concert platform. At meal-times one might find oneself in the company of members of the world-famous Amadeus String Quartet or solo artists of the calibre of Julian Bream, the renowned guitarist. For me it was especially interesting to sing, when my duties permitted, in the Course Choir which, in the concert at the end of each week, gave a performance of a major choral work under the direction of such conductors as Imogen Holst, George Malcolm, Paul Steinitz and Bernard Keefe. I remember that I was particularly struck by the originality of Stravinsky's harmony in the *Symphony of Psalms* and moved by the wonderful sequence of transcendental alleluias with which the work ends.

One day in the early summer of 1962 I had received an urgent telephone call from Archdeacon Quin. The post of Organist at Bangor Parish Church was vacant and he wanted me to apply for it. How the vacancy arose I do not know. I had been thoroughly enjoying life in London and had not thought of returning to Northern Ireland after only one year, if at all. God's ways, however, are not our ways. If I were to be appointed to Bangor Parish Church, I should be able to live at home with my still-grieving parents and lend them some support.

I duly applied for the post and attended for interview and an audition with the church choir. The Select Vestry had asked Captain C J Brennan, the Organist at St Anne's Cathedral, Belfast to act as advisor to the sub-committee set up to make a selection from the short-listed candidates. I was appointed and returned to London to inform the Headmaster at FBGS. He expressed his bitter disappointment at the news but genuinely wished me well. Being a very sympathetic person he realised what my return home would mean to my parents. Because I had to serve my notice, I should not be able to take up the post at Bangor Parish Church until mid-October 1962. I was giving up a great deal to make this move but it seemed to be inevitable.

There were to be other staff changes at FBGS. David Smart went on to teach successively at the King's School, Worcester, Marlborough College, and Dulwich College where he remained until his retirement from the profession. The Headmaster was appointed to the post of Principal at a state comprehensive in the Midlands. Keith Ramsay had left FBGS in 1961 for Frensham Heights, a progressive boarding-school associated with Bedales. He later entered third-level education, lecturing in Drama at Hull University prior to his appointment as Head of the Drama Department at the Bishop Grosseteste College of Education, now a university, in Lincoln.

In his book, *The Lincoln Mystery Plays: A Personal Odyssey* (2008), Keith gives an enthralling account of his revival of these fifteenth century dramatic presentations of episodes from the Bible and of his productions of them with a travelling troupe of actors, not only in Britain but also in Europe and the USA over a period of some thirty years. The conferment on Keith of a DLitt. degree by his university in 2008 was an appropriate recognition of what was a major cultural achievement.

FBGS was run by its Board of Trustees until 1994 but, with pupil numbers falling and the school's finances consequently in a precarious state, its future looked very bleak. Negotiations with John Catt Educational Ltd, the owner of Woodside Park Preparatory School, led to the amalgamation of the two schools. Now a co-educational establishment known as 'The North London International School', this prepares students for the International Baccalaureate Diploma examination.

CHAPTER FOUR

1962-64 | BANGOR PARISH CHURCH

The post of Organist at Bangor Parish Church had a number of very attractive aspects. In the first place there was the rather exceptional provision of accommodation. For a mere peppercorn rent, which had been reduced in 1956 to one shilling (i.e. 5pence) per annum, one had the use of a spacious three-storey, terrace house conveniently situated on Hamilton Road at a short distance from the church. Because I intended to live with my parents and would therefore not require the house, the Select Vestry increased my annual salary from £300 to £450. The Organist's house was initially converted to serve as a curatage and later sold.

The church had what was generally considered to be one of the finest organs in Ireland. Built in 1919/20 by Messrs A Hunter & Son of Clapham, London, this organ replaced one made in 1885 by the Belgian firm, Annessens et Fils of Grammont. It is probable that Ernest Emery, who had recently been appointed Organist of the church, drew up the specification of the new instrument and had the oversight of its installation. He told me that Mr Hunter, the head of the firm, himself came to Bangor and stayed for a fortnight at his own expense to ensure that the tonal finishing met his rigorous standards. Such was his pride in this organ, that Dr Emery guarded it jealously.

Harry at the organ of Bangor Parish Church, 1963 *(W T Kirk, Photographer, Bangor)*

50

Woe betide anyone who dared to gain access to it without his permission! If he discovered during a service that the tuning of one or two of the pipes was unsatisfactory, he would go into the chamber during the sermon to make the necessary adjustments. With most of the lights in the church switched off while that in the chamber was on, the movements of his spidery shadow were clearly visible by those seated in the nave. On such occasions, the preacher was in danger of losing the attention of at least some of the congregation! During the first weeks of his retirement prior to his departure from Bangor, he visited the church each day simply to gaze fondly at the fine instrument which he had been delighted to play for the previous forty years.

The church choir, which in 1962 had a membership of between fifty and sixty boys, ladies and men, included a number of promising young singers. Among these was the eighteen-year-old Norma Burrowes whose 'star' quality was obvious to everyone. After graduating in Music at Queen's University, Belfast, Norma studied singing at the RAM in London, making her professional debut in 1972. Through frequent appearances at some of the world's great opera houses she soon established herself as one of the outstanding sopranos of her day. Best known for her performances of Handel, Purcell, Haydn and Mozart, Norma also excelled in light opera, particularly Gilbert and Sullivan. She toured extensively as a concert singer and made several acclaimed recordings of a varied repertoire. On her retirement from the operatic stage in 1982 she settled in Toronto where she teaches singing at York University. The degree of Doctor of Music *(h.c.)* was conferred on Norma Burrowes by her *alma mater* in 1979.

I knew that I could count on the support of the Rector, Archdeacon George Quin, a wonderful Christian pastor, whose life was lived in the service of others. In those halcyon days he was assisted by three curates. It was a privilege to be a member of this happy family with the Rector as its father-figure and his equally warm-hearted wife, Nora, a medical practitioner, always concerned about our welfare.

Finally, a large proportion of the congregation at Bangor Parish Church had a real appreciation of music and the importance of its role in the liturgy. I was sure that my efforts to extend the repertoire and the range of musical events to include occasional recitals would be welcomed and encouraged. In this latter connection my ultimate aim was to raise the considerable sum necessary to provide a lasting memorial to Ernest Emery whose name, more than any other, will always be associated with the Church's music.

At our preliminary meeting to discuss the way ahead the Rector began by telling me that my first assignment would be to 'get rid of the 10 o'clock choir!' On Sunday morning there were at that time two services of Morning Prayer, one at 10.00a.m. and the other at 11.30a.m. with the church choir singing at the latter. (The earlier service was known as 'The Golfers' Service' because many of those attending it made for Bangor Golf Course immediately afterwards!) During the previous year eight members had either left the choir of their own volition or had been asked to leave by my predecessor. These dissidents together with a few of their friends formed a small *ad hoc* choir to lead the singing at the 10 o'clock service. Visitors who had come to this service expecting to hear music of a high standard had expressed to the Rector their disappointment with the performance of what they had assumed was the church choir. Archdeacon Quin had decided that something must be done immediately and that the newly-appointed Organist should be his agent!

I had no difficulty in dealing with the men of 'the 10 o'clock choir' most of whom I already knew well. They had expected that I would be making changes and raised no objection to the choir's disbandment. However, as far as the ladies were concerned it was quite a different matter! It was arranged that they would meet me at the home of one of them. I was greeted with great warmth and treated to a delicious afternoon tea. They told me how delighted they were that I had come to Bangor Parish Church and how much they were looking forward to the future of its music. I suddenly realised that they had, in fact, been expecting me to invite them to return to the church choir. There was nothing for it but to bite the bullet.

The Choir of Bangor Parish Church, 1962 (Photo: Gordon Hamilton, Bangor)

Once the real object of my mission was known, cordiality instantly gave way to bitter disappointment tinged with anger and, conscious that I had outstayed my welcome, I beat a hasty retreat!

When I reported back to the Rector he said that on the following Sunday I should have to explain to the congregation at the 10 o'clock service the absence of the usual choir and what provision I was going to make for its replacement. As required, I duly announced that in future, the singing at the 10 o'clock service would be led by a section of the church choir. Fortunately the members of the church choir willingly gave me their backing and a rota system was devised to enable the new arrangement to operate satisfactorily.

Having solved my first problem I could look forward to the carol service on the Sunday before Christmas with a repeat on Christmas Eve. The Select Vestry kindly agreed that it would be appropriate to use the collection at the second of these services to establish 'The Dr E. H. Emery Memorial Fund' with the object of erecting a stained-glass window in the Church. Since the members of the choir shared my determination to achieve as high a standard as possible no one complained when I called for a number of extra rehearsals. In fact these were without exception very well attended. Lacking an assistant, I myself had to act as both conductor and organist. I am certain that the preparation of the six unaccompanied items in particular was a salutary experience for the choir. In a matter of weeks there was a marked improvement in the overall quality of the choir's performance with a consequent increase in confidence. The carol services attracted large congregations with some of those who had attended the first one returning on Christmas Eve for a second helping. We were greatly encouraged by the many expressions of appreciation which we received, one of them being from the members of the Select Vestry. The choir's morale had been given a major boost.

I was never able to discover what sort of audition prospective choir members were previously expected to undergo. Indeed, in some cases at least there may have been no audition at all. Consequently there were a few singers who should not have been admitted to the choir. One of these, a 'bass', had great difficulty in holding his part despite the fact that he was flanked by experienced and musically secure colleagues. This gentleman was wont to 'lose the plot' suddenly, especially in the hymns and psalms, and to begin singing the melody at his pitch. I persuaded two or three of the more elderly sopranos (not without some difficulty) to sing contralto. Only *in extremis* would I ask someone to leave a church choir and then not without first seeking the permission of the incumbent. In some instances such a course of action can result in a congregation losing an entire family.

In the choir at Bangor Parish Church there was a soprano who would faint from time to time in the course of a service, invariably when something was being sung. Because we could not very well continue to the end of a longish item while the unfortunate lady lay on the floor, we would have to stop, in mid-phrase, to allow her to be carried into the vestry for attention. When one of these incidents had brought a premature end to what was promising to be a particularly good performance of a new anthem, I sought an interview with the Rector. I expressed to him in the strongest possible terms my own sense of frustration and that of the other members of the choir. He was very sympathetic and understood the absurdity of the situation. I had patiently tolerated her consistently flat singing but the havoc caused by her fainting was the last straw! With the Rector's permission, I asked her to leave the choir. Shortly afterwards the mother of the lady in question came to see me to plead her daughter's case. She told me how much pleasure her daughter derived from singing in the choir and that if I were to hold a rehearsal on every night of the week she would always be present. As regards the flat singing, she wondered whether the rest of the choir might perhaps have compensated for it by singing sharp! Certain lines *have* to be drawn, however, and that was the end of the matter.

With the Dr Emery Memorial Fund successfully launched at Christmas 1962, the choir committee and I drew up a schedule of events in an effort to attract further financial support in the coming months. Dr Emery himself had established a tradition of recitals on Sunday evenings during the summer months each year. In these he was sometimes joined by his friend Dr Ernest Stoneley, a fine violinist who was Head of the Music Department at the Methodist College, Belfast, and by one of his favourite sopranos, Miss Joan Page, whose voice, he said, was ' like a boy's'. We thought that it would be appropriate to revive this tradition and I arranged to give recitals on each of the Sundays in July with a vocal and an instrumental soloist on each occasion. These would begin at 8.30p.m. to allow those attending evening services at other churches in the town to attend.

In the 1960s a popular fund-raising event at churches was the 'Guest Tea'. Although this usually took place in the evening, what was served to the invited guests amounted to afternoon tea and this was followed by a varied musical programme with a collection being taken up for a particular cause. It was decided that such an event, scheduled for April, should be our major fund-raising effort in 1963. With the Boys' Brigade, Boy Scouts, Mothers' Union, Bowling Club, Young Wives' Group, Girl Guides and Badminton Club each willingly accepting responsibility for a table, a capacity attendance was guaranteed. Not only was a sum of well over £170.00 raised but the enthusiatic co-operation of so many organisations had resulted in one of the most successful parish events that anyone could remember.

Collaboration with other choirs can have both musical and social benefits. The choirs of Bangor and Willowfield Parish Churches visited Carrowdore Parish Church, Co. Down in June 1963 to sing Evensong at the invitation of its Rector, the Revd John Bell who had been a curate at Willowfield during my time there. It was a pleasure to share the direction of the music with John Lyttle, my successor as Organist at Willowfield, who continues to serve the church faithfully in this capacity some forty-seven years later. I also gave a short organ recital. Early the following month the fine choir of St James's Parish Church, Belfast came to join us in a further Choral Evensong with Leslie McCarrison, the Organist of St James's, and I dividing the conducting and accompanying duties between us. Each of the choirs sang three anthems and combined in one, the large body of over eighty singers together with the organ making a splendid sound. (The final service in St James's on 29 June, 2008 prior to the Church's closure was a sad occasion and particularly so for my friend, Billy Adair, who had striven over the past twenty-two years to maintain its musical tradition with the loyal support of a small but very competent group of singers.)

In order to give the younger adult members of Bangor Parish Church choir the opportunity to sing a wider and more challenging repertoire, I formed the St Comgall's Singers. This chamber choir made its debut at a concert in the church on 15 December 1963. The centrepiece of a programme which included seasonal choral music by Vaughan Williams, Warlock, Walton and Joubert *inter alia* was a performance of a *Christmas Cantata* by Alessandro Scarlatti for solo soprano, string quartet and continuo. As well as chorale preludes by Bach and Brahms, the organ music included an attractive set of variations on *King Jesus hath a Garden* by the Belgian composer, Flor Peeters, with whom I was to study a few years later.

I also sought to increase the number of boys in the church choir and to take a more structured approach to their training which had in recent years been somewhat neglected. Because of the commitment expected from the boys and their parents, I had asked the Select Vestry to give serious consideration to making a small regular monthly payment to each of the boys, the amount of this being dependent on attendance and application. Hitherto the boys had received a mere half-crown (i.e. 12½ pence) each year at Christmas. While I was disappointed that this proposal did not meet with the Select Vestry's approval, I was grateful for the provision of a new piano for use at rehearsals in the choir's robing-room.

I am sure that other choir-masters would agree that working with boys can be a most rewarding experience and that their absence to-day from most parish church choirs accounts to a considerable extent for the continuing shortage of tenors and basses. Their behaviour can sometimes be a source of amusement. At a boys' rehearsal one day at Bangor Parish Church I had been emphasising the importance of posture and its effect on breathing and voice-production. I said that one was unlikely ever to see a chorister depicted on a Christmas card with his face buried in his music. Indeed I went so far as to issue a challenge. Should any boy be able to produce such a picture, I would give him half-a-crown. Months later when I had quite forgotten about the challenge, a boy handed me an envelope after a rehearsal. Assuming it was a message from his mother, I put it aside intending to look at it later. However, the boy said that I owed him half-a-crown. I promptly opened the envelope to discover that it contained a Christmas card on the front of which were three choristers. Whereas the posture of two of them was exemplary, the face of their companion was hidden by his carol-book. I had to pay up!

Since coming back to Bangor I had been accepting private pupils for both piano and organ and, at the invitation of Alan Angus, I had been delighted to rejoin the staff of the Music Department at Campbell College in a part-time capacity to teach piano. In early 1963, having been successful in the examinations for the FRCO diploma, I decided to make the choir-training diploma of the RCO my next goal. In preparation for the examinations for this I had some singing lessons from Mrs Carys Denton, at the time one of Belfast's leading singing teachers. I also enrolled for a special intensive course organised by the RSCM at Addington Palace near Croydon specifically for intending candidates for this diploma. To facilitate those coming from a distance this course was scheduled to take place over a number of days immediately before the examinations. Virtually all of the candidates, among whom were a number of Oxford and Cambridge organ scholars and at least one future English cathedral organist, duly assembled at the RSCM for what proved to be a most valuable course. Both the practical and written aspects of the syllabus were thoroughly covered. The candidates in turn were required to rehearse the resident choir of music students in each of the set pieces of music before a staff panel including the Director of the RSCM, Dr Gerald Knight, formerly Organist at Canterbury Cathedral. The present Assistant Organist at Belfast Cathedral, Ian Barber, from Holywood, Co. Down, then a student at both the RSCM and RCM, who was a member of the choir, told me that he and his peers eagerly looked forward to this event each year. In collusion with the resident choirmaster, they took great delight in devising a series of well-disguised 'inaccuracies' in order to test the aural perception of the unsuspecting candidates. This ensured that, as far as the candidates were concerned, the experience was both a taxing and a salutary one!

For the practical examination at the RCO a small group of professional singers was provided who, by the time my turn arrived, were singing slightly flat due, no doubt, to tiredness. When the results were published I was gratified to learn that I had not only passed but had won the John Brook Memorial Prize, awarded each year to the candidate who gains the highest mark in the practical and *viva voce* part of the examination. Among the congratulatory messages which I received was one from The Incorporated Society of Organists of which organisation Mr John Brook had been the first secretary.

It has always been traditional at the RCO distributions of diplomas for a distinguished organist to play a short programme of pieces selected from those set for the next examination session. On 26 January 1963 we listened spellbound to an extraordinary musician. Dr Douglas Fox, for whom a brilliant career had been forecast, had lost his right arm in World War I. Showing astonishing courage and resolution he came to terms with a handicap which would have overwhelmed most keyboard-players. Careful rearrangement of the music allowed him to encompass within the very wide stretch of his left hand most, if not quite all, of the notes usually played by the right hand. This was done so cleverly that it was often difficult to tell what had been omitted from the original version. His performance of the pieces by Bach, Schumann, Parry, Vaughan Williams and Hindemith, some of which would have severely tested the technique of players possessing all four limbs, was a veritable *tour de force*. The audience had been at the same time thrilled and humbled.

For the previous few years it had been the custom for the Ulster and Leinster Societies of Organists and Choirmasters to hold an annual joint meeting at venues alternately north and south of the Border. In 1963 it was the turn of the Ulster Society to act as hosts and Bangor was the chosen rendezvous on Saturday 25 May. At Bangor Abbey the visitors heard an interesting selection of choral music sung by the church choir under the direction of Rob Anderson. Earlier they had been to Bangor Parish Church where I had played a programme of organ music by modern French and English composers.

In the course of November 1963 I gave a recital on the organ of All Saints' Parish Church, Clooney, Londonderry following the rebuilding and enlargement of the instrument by the Irish Organ Company; at the Belfast Festival at Queen's University, I took part with Evan John, the University Organist, in a joint recital on the organ of the Sir William Whitla Hall; at the annual recital by members of the USOC at Belfast

The Clergy of Bangor Parish Church, 1963: the Rector, Archdeacon George Quin, with his curates (from left), Robin Eames, George Martin and Robin Ellis

Cathedral I played César Franck's *Chorale No 2 in B minor* and, to keep the momentum of our fund-raising campaign for the Emery Memorial Fund going, I gave a recital at Bangor Parish Church. In addition to the busy round of seasonal services in December at the church, I played the organ for the annual Christmas concert given by the Bangor Harmonic Society when the programme included a varied selection of carols in addition to music from Handel's *Messiah*.

A new curate had joined our clerical team in September 1963. Although it had seemed at one time that his future might lie in the field of academic law, the Revd Dr Robin Eames had chosen to answer God's call to take holy orders. He still regards his time at Bangor Parish Church as one of the happiest periods of his life. Robin added a men's club to the already long list of flourishing parish organisations and he rejoiced particularly in the Church's musical tradition. I found in him an ardent supporter and we were soon firm friends. With the Rector's agreement the choir sang Evensong on one Sunday afternoon in the month at an earlier time than the congregational service of Evening Prayer, Robin acting as cantor. I know that he derived great satisfaction from his participation in the music of the liturgy and he was assiduous in his preparation. For someone so young Robin possessed a remarkable maturity which was combined with something of the gravitas which so became him when he was translated to the highest office in the Church of Ireland. His courteousness and personal charm enabled him to relate with the utmost ease to all sorts and conditions of men and women. 'He had a great way with him,' as one parishioner put it and his sense of humour was delightfully mischievous.

Archdeacon Quin occasionally turned up on Sunday morning without a sermon when it was his turn to preach, the previous days having been taken up perhaps with his various diocesan duties and some of the nights with ministering to the seriously ill and dying. As they made their way along the west end of the church behind the choir during the processional hymn, the 'Arch', as he was affectionately known, would ask Robin to preach in his stead. With little time in which to select an appropriate text and marshall his thoughts, it is little wonder that Robin sometimes seemed to be preoccupied as he took his part in the service! He acknowledges his gratitude to George Quin for regularly putting him on the spot in this way because it enabled him to develop the invaluable skill of thinking on his feet. I very well remember Archbishop Robin's funeral tribute to George Quin's wife, Nora, at the service in Bangor Abbey many years later. Delivered without notes of any kind, it painted a complete picture of a very gracious lady who had been a mother to all of her husband's curates. The person seated next to me remarked afterwards that, while no one would have guessed, this eloquent address had probably been put together in Robin's mind as he drove to the Church. Given the increasing demands on his time, particularly during the 20 years when he was Primate of the Church of Ireland, he had to depend heavily on this invaluable accomplishment.

A Thursday afternoon might find a group consisting of two of the curates, Robin Eames and Robin Ellis, both churchwardens, the Rector and me at Carnalea Municipal Golf Course. Apart from Archdeacon Quin who played off a low handicap, none of us could claim to possess any golfing skill whatsoever. Although he must have been exasperated by our inability to hit the ball any appreciable distance in the right direction, 'the Arch' showed true Christian forbearance as he patiently exhorted us to better efforts. Now and again when a misdirected shot by one of his companions had narrowly failed to decapitate a player on a neighbouring fairway, he would intervene to avert what might have been a very angry confrontation. One day we were on the first tee watching a member of our party preparing to launch his round. A fraction of a second after he had played his drive with all the force he could muster in order to impress the rest of us, there was the sound of shattering glass to our right as the ball, hit with a prodigious slice, went through a locker-room window! On another occasion when Robin Eames and I were playing a round at Carnalea we were on the tee at one of the short holes on the 'back' nine. As a result of Robin's heavily-sliced iron shot the ball came down from a considerable height on the roof of an adjacent bungalow where it seemed to bounce around for several seconds before falling to the ground. Robin took refuge behind a hedge leaving me to face the furious resident who had come out to remonstrate with the offender. On our next visit to Carnalea we noticed that a huge screen made of heavy-duty wire-mesh had been set up between the tee and the bungalow in question!

An important date in the social life at Bangor Parish Church was the Archdeacon's Cup golf competition held annually at Bangor Golf Club of which George Quin was a member. While it was originally intended to be an exclusively parish event, its eventual wider promotion resulted in an increasing number of entries from all parts of the province. Competitors ranged from those who played off scratch, to 'duffers' like myself and all able-bodied men in the congregation were expected to participate. An attractive range of prizes was always on offer with good play at all levels of the game being suitably rewarded. This rather special day was invariably rounded off with everyone sitting down to a traditional 'Ulster Fry' in the clubhouse.

Although there was still a considerable sum of money to be raised to cover the cost of the stained-glass window which was to be the memorial to Dr Emery, it was decided to arrange to have the window installed in time for dedication by the Bishop of Down and Dromore, the Rt Revd Dr F J Mitchell, on Easter Sunday 1964, a suitably festal occasion for such an important event in the history of the parish. Appropriately sited beside the organ, the window depicts St Cecilia, the Patron Saint of Music and Musicians, playing a portative organ. The design also incorporates the opening bars of Charles V Stanford's setting in B flat of the *Te Deum*, a particular favourite of Dr Emery's, together with the text: 'We praise Thee, O God: we acknowledge Thee to be the Lord'. In addition to this setting the music at the service of dedication included what is arguably Edward Bairstow's finest anthem, *Blessed City, Heavenly Salem* in which the soloist was Norma Burrowes. Dr Emery's only son, Trevor and his wife came from their home in Surrey to join the very large congregation.

The boys of the choir and I were frequently asked to provide the music at weddings both at Bangor Parish Church and elsewhere. Occasionally the presence of a group of the adult members might be requested instead. One day I was visited by a leading florist from Newtownards who said that he wanted the wedding of one of his daughters in a Presbyterian church in the town in April 1964 to be particularly special and that he would spare no expense to ensure that it was. Clearly bent on impressing the numerous guests, he asked me to bring as large a body of singers as I could muster. He handed me a substantial wad of notes to cover fees, saying that if more money were required I had but to ask. With the wedding being on a week-day, some of the adults were naturally unavailable because of business commitments but boys from the fine choir at Campbell College, among them a few excellent altos, were very happy to join us to sing a selection of anthems and to earn some extra pocket-money into the bargain. The wedding attracted widespread public and press attention with some coverage on the evening television news programmes. This unusual interest in a family wedding was no doubt due to the florist's avowed intent to break the world record for the greatest number of blooms used in the decoration of a church! I have yet to discover whether or not he realised his ambition.

Although I had been at Bangor Parish Church only since mid-October 1962, I had been so busy that it seemed to have been a much longer period. It was exhilarating to be a member of the staff of such a lively parish in which the further development of the church's music was both encouraged and appreciated. In particular one's efforts to raise standards of performance while making regular additions to the repertoire met with general approval to which some members of the congregation occasionally gave gratifying written expression. Equally there were a few people who did not hesitate to make their feelings known when they found the work of certain modern composers not to their liking. One Sunday morning after we had given Benjamin Britten's invigorating setting of the *Jubilate* (published in 1961) what was probably its first 'airing' in Northern Ireland, I was accosted by an angry gentleman who was evidently appalled. 'I have never heard anything like it in my life!' he bellowed. I am quite sure that he had not!

With my piano teaching at Campbell College, an increasing number of private pupils and frequent engagements of one kind or another, in addition to my work at Bangor Parish Church where in May 1964 my salary was increased to £41.00 per month, I was fully occupied. I could not have been happier! Bangor was a very pleasant place in which to live and I might well have been content to remain there had not another even more important church music post in Belfast been advertised in the press. In January 1964 Captain Charles J Brennan gave notice of his intention to resign as Organist and Director of the Choir at St Anne's Cathedral with effect from the end of June after sixty years' service.

C J Brennan was born in Gosport, Hampshire in 1876. He held

Organist posts at Clifton, Bedfordshire, Strabane, Co. Tyrone, and Elmwood Presbyterian Church, Belfast prior to his appointment as the first Organist of the new Belfast Cathedral in 1904. Due to his having been a commissioned officer in the Royal Irish Fusiliers in World War I, he was thereafter always known as 'Captain' Brennan. Small, rotund and dapper in appearance he had a commanding, Churchillian presence and was highly regarded as a choral conductor. Mr Brennan directed the Ulster Male Voice Choir as well as two Belfast operatic societies and his services were sought-after as a conductor at the periodic diocesan festivals of church choirs which were once musical and social events of some importance. He was a noted vocal specialist with a large teaching practice and the author of a useful text-book, *Words in Singing* (London,1905). From 1908 Charles Brennan also held the post of City Organist, his popular recitals on the fine Hill organ in the Ulster Hall filling the auditorium on Saturday nights before the advent of the cinema.

It appears that when Captain Brennan was seventy years old, in the hope that he might be prompted to make way at the Cathedral for a younger man, a lavish dinner was held in his honour in the Grand Central Hotel. A number of speakers were eloquent in their praise of Captain Brennan and his fine record of musical achievement. In the course of his reply, he declared that he was delighted to know what widespread satisfaction his work had given over the previous forty-two years. That being the case, everyone would be pleased to hear that he intended to continue to serve the Cathedral as its Organist. This he did, despite the loss of sight in one eye and increasing deafness, for a further eighteen years.

'The Conditions and Particulars of Appointment' document, a copy of which was sent to those seeking information about the post of Organist and Master of the Choristers (as it was now styled) at Belfast Cathedral, stated that candidates aged between twenty-five and thirty-five would be preferred and that consideration would be given to making the appointment pensionable. (In fact, no arrangements were made for a pension for the Organist until 1972!) The salary offered for what was clearly considered to be part-time employment was £500.00 per annum and there was no provision for accommodation. Those in leading positions in other professions at that time would have expressed their surprise at what they considered to be an inadequate financial return for the occupant of such a responsible post. Since a cathedral appointment has always been regarded by professional church musicians as the ultimate goal, many have been prepared in the past to accept insufficient payment in order to enjoy the prestige and musical satisfaction which it brings. Today leading church musicians expect much more realistic salaries and conditions of employment and it is not unknown for the director of music at a so-called 'parish church cathedral', such as St Anne's, Belfast, to be classed as a 'full-time' member of staff and to be paid accordingly. In due course I was to realise how comparatively well off I had been at Bangor Parish Church!

Now, given the tradition of appointing men from 'across the water' to important positions in the arts in Northern Ireland, I was at first hesitant to apply for the post at Belfast Cathedral. Nevertheless, encouraged by close friends and having given the matter prayerful throught, I took the plunge. There were forty applicants. I was shortlisted with three Englishmen, one of whom was resident in Northern Ireland.

On my way to the cathedral for the interview and audition, I met a fellow-member of the USOC who, not knowing where I was going, proceeded to give me his version of the list of applicants for the Cathedral post together with the names of those short-listed. I was amused to discover that he evidently did not rate me worthy of consideration!

The interview panel included the secretary of the Cathedral Choir whose wife was one of the middle-aged sopranos. His question was an obvious one, 'I suppose that, were you to be appointed, you would wish to make this an all-male choir?' To which I replied that I hoped that the appointee, whoever he might be, would take the choir as it was and help it to achieve its full potential.

I remember Terence Lovett, the conductor of the BBC Northern Ireland Orchestra, once saying to me that he never could understand why we chose to have Englishmen coming across to Ulster to boss us about. (He put it much more graphically!) There were those who did not approve of my appointment to Belfast Cathedral and who were of the opinion that the post should have gone to an Englishman. However, I was overwhelmed by the enthusiastic reaction of the vast majority to the news. These good people wished me well, many of them expressing their delight that a native of the province had succeeded to this important position.

Of the scores of letters which I received, three were particularly moving. The first was from Mrs Lena Smart, an elderly neighbour in Church Street, Bangor, who had known me since childhood and who had continued to take a kindly interest in my progress over the years. The second, obviously written with great difficulty, was from The Revd Joseph Lindsay, then Rector of Warrenpoint, who had been a curate at Bangor Abbey when I was a chorister there. As a boy he had sung in the choir of St Patrick's Cathedral, Dublin and his fine tenor voice was a very welcome addition to the Abbey Choir. While he was with us, Joe suffered a severe stroke which left him paralysed down one side. Although in time he courageously resumed his clerical duties it was only with increasing difficulty that he was able to carry these out. His death at an early age was widely mourned. The third letter, from my friend Robin Eames, was such a sincere expression of appreciation that I shall always treasure it with the others.

At Bangor Parish Church, Archdeacon Quin was, as usual, the very soul of kindness. He told me that he had recently had a phone call from the Dean of Belfast, the Very Revd Cuthbert Peacocke who wished to know how the Archdeacon found me as a colleague. 'Unfortunately, I was unable to say anything against you,' he said ruefully.

In the months remaining before I was to take up duty at the Cathedral, I wanted to make sure that the outstanding amount on the Dr Emery Memorial Window was raised. I organised another series of weekly Sunday evening recitals beginning on the last Sunday in June and continuing to the end of August. While I was on holiday, recitals were given by Huston Graham, Ian Barber, Jack Young and Donald Davison. On 30 August, my last Sunday at Bangor Parish Church, the accomplished Ulster soprano, Mavis Beattie, joined me in a programme which included music by Bach, Haydn, César Franck and Jean Langlais. Because all those who had participated in the recital series did so without payment, we were able not only to reach our target but found ourselves with a surplus. This was used to purchase two trophies, one each in memory of Dr and Mrs Emery, for Bangor Musical Festival with which both had had a close association. By the time I left Bangor Parish Church I had passed the first two parts of the MusB degree at Trinity College, Dublin. However, such was the nature of the challenges which lay ahead that it would be a number of years before I should be in a position to commence study for the final examinations.

A visit to London in July 1964 with Jack Young, the Hon. Sub-Organist at Belfast Cathedral, for the RCO's centenary celebrations made for a very pleasant interlude. In the course of five days we heard recitals by some of the leading organists of the day with Gerre Hancock, representing the American Guild of Organists, making the greatest impression. Playing from memory, as we were afterwards informed, he displayed consummate technique and control in a wide-ranging programme which began with Bach's magnificent *Fantasia and Fugue in G minor (BWV 542)* and ended with Liszt's typically flamboyant *Prelude and Fugue on B-A-C-H*. At St Paul's Cathedral and Westminster Abbey we heard some fine choral singing. Before and after Evensong at the latter, the brilliant Simon Preston treated us to masterly performances of Bach's *Prelude and Fugue in E minor (' The Wedge') (BWV 548),* Franck's *Choral in B minor* and the *Introduction and Fugue* from Reubke's monumental *Sonata on Psalm 94.* At a Henry Wood Promenade Concert in the Royal Albert Hall the BBC Symphony Orchestra, under Sir Malcolm Sargent, gave a rousing of Elgar's *Second Symphony*. On the social side there were the President's reception at the RCO, an official reception by the Corporation of London at Guildhall, a garden party at Addington Palace (the headquarters of the RSCM) where we were addressed by the Director, Dr Gerald Knight, and, as a finale, a splendid centenary dinner at the Connaught Rooms.

Blessed with beautiful summer weather, this exceptionally well-organized event was an unqualified success. The memory of it stayed with me for a long time afterwards and served to inspire me as I embarked on what was to prove to be perhaps the most demanding phase of my career.

CHAPTER FIVE

1964-65 | Belfast Cathedral

I t is regrettable that for Belfast to gain an Anglican cathedral it was found necessary to sacrifice a fine example of eighteenth-century church architecture. Built in 1776 at his own expense by the Earl of Shaftesbury, St Anne's Parish Church was in the Classical style, having a western portico and a tower in four stages with a cupola. The church remained in use while the great Hiberno-Romanesque cathedral, designed by Sir Thomas Drew, was constructed around it and was demolished in 1903 on completion of the cathedral's nave. The erection of the impressive west front was achieved by 1927 with the quire, apse and ambulatory, begun in 1955, being consecrated in 1959. In 1965 a public appeal was launched for £200,000 to complete the cathedral by building north and south transepts together with a central crossing. Samuel Bennett Crooks, who was to be an outstanding dean, held office from 1970 to 1985, a critical period in the cathedral's history. Blessed with vision, courage, and a dynamic personality, Dean Crooks proved to be the right man in the right place at the right time. With the province's infamous 'Troubles' well under way and given the consequent bleak economic outlook, he could see that this major building project was in urgent need of reappraisal. Work was temporarily suspended while this was carried out. By mid-1971 a modified plan which would allow for the addition of the south transept and the crossing had been approved with Easter 1973 as the target date. A further £200,000 was sought in 1972. The south transept was consecrated in 1974 and the north transept seven years later. The elaborate, original plans had included an impressive tower which the foundations, on unstable, reclaimed land, could not, in fact, have supported. This being the case, a spire, in the form of a slender needle-like structure forty metres high and made of stainless steel and titanium, was added in 2007 as the finishing touch to a building which had taken over a hundred years to complete.

Harry at the organ of Belfast Cathedral in 1965

The Cathedral Church of St Anne, Belfast is unique in having no diocese of its own. Although the Cathedral stands in the Diocese of Connor, much of the city is in the Diocese of Down. Hence, in Belfast Cathedral are to be found two stalls, one for the bishop of Connor, whose diocesan cathedral is in Lisburn and the other for the bishop of Down and Dromore, who has two diocesan cathedrals. Such an eccentric arrangement seems to be peculiar to the Irish system of ecclesiastical organisation.

The first organ to stand in Belfast Cathedral was that built in 1781 by Johann Snetzler for St Anne's Parish Church. Isaac Nichol, the Organist of the church from 1874 until its demolition in 1903, has passed on to us this description of the instrument as he found it: 'The great organ (8 stops) was much as Snetzler left it - of exquisite beauty, fulness [sic] and richness of tone. The full organ blended to absolute perfection, forming one grand 8ft tone . . . wood pipes most exquisitely made.' There were five stops on the swell manual and one 16ft pedal stop. In 1875 a major overhaul was carried out by William Hill & Son of London who extended the compass downwards to CC as well as altering the tuning to equal temperament and making some additions to the specification. These brought the number of speaking stops up to seventeen. The Snetzler organ was re-erected by Evans & Barr of Belfast in the new cathedral on a gallery at the east end of the north aisle. When the decision was eventually taken to replace this lovely old instrument with the much larger one which was considered necessary in such a vast space, the Snetzler organ was sold for £250 to the Revd Joseph Stewart who presented it to the Church of Ireland Young Men's Society. It was set up in the Society's Clarence Place Hall in August 1907 but was sold for scrap in the 1950s.

Today, when every effort is made to preserve high-quality craftsmanship, one wonders why there was no attempt to salvage at least some of the pipe-work from the Snetzler organ and to incorporate it in the new one. With Andrew Carnegie having promised £800 towards the cost of a new instrument, the contract was awarded to Messrs Harrison & Harrison of Durham. Completed in 1907 and opened by Walter Alcock, this, the first entirely new cathedral organ to be built by the highly-esteemed Harrison firm, was erected temporarily at the east end of the south aisle. The intention was to move it to a loft in the transept when this was built and at that point to add a fourth manual. This was not achieved until 1975. (For a detailed account of the history of the organ at Belfast Cathedral see: *The Cathedral of St Anne, Belfast and its Organs* by David Drinkell [Organist 1988-2002] in *The Organ* Vol.69, Number 272, Spring 1990.)

Although a choir school had been thought desirable, and provision had accordingly been made in the plans for its inclusion in the completed building complex, there has never been one at Belfast Cathedral. It is difficult to understand why a choir school could not have been built in a city which is at the centre of an area having the greatest density of Church of Ireland membership in the entire country, and which at the turn of the nineteenth century had the support of many men of substance and influence. Doubtless, not for the first time in the history of the Irish cathedrals, available funds were diverted to other uses.

Belfast Cathedral, being of the parish church type, has never had regular week-day services, in any event without a choir school it would have been difficult, if not impossible, to maintain them. Sunday Matins or

Eucharist (11.00a.m.) and Evensong (3.30p.m.) have always been choral with, for many years, a further service of Evening Prayer of a parochial nature at 7.00p.m. (This was discontinued in 1984 in the interests of economy.) The Cathedral Choir has sung the two choral services, while a separate so-called 'evening' choir of adults trained by the Assistant Organist replaced it at the 7.00p.m. parochial service. Up to 1964 the Assistant Organist's duties also included taking the boys' rehearsal on a Tuesday (5.00-6.00p.m.), acting as organ accompanist at the Christmas carol services and for the performance of an appropriate choral work at Passiontide, as well as deputising for the Cathedral Organist when he was on holiday. In Captain Brennan's time, the Assistant Organist might also be called upon at the carol services to play an obligato on the set of tubular bells which stood near the organ console. Also to be found in the organ loft was a pair of timpani and a wooden music-stand complete with light attachment. For many years a timpanist had been in attendance regularly at services to reinforce, at Captain Brennan's discretion, accompaniments to anthems, canticles and hymns, a set of marked volumes being provided specifically for the timpanist's use. So far I have not come across any reference to this novel practice being followed anywhere else.

One would have expected Belfast's new cathedral to have a choir of men and boys as is the custom at most Anglican cathedrals, and indeed visitors have often expressed their surprise at the presence of ladies in the choir stalls of St Anne's. From conversations I had with Captain Brennan it is clear that their inclusion was due to his personal preference. He admitted to a dislike of the male-alto voice. The choir which he established was therefore made up of about 20 boys, 10 sopranos, 6 contraltos, 6 tenors and 10 basses i.e. almost twice as many singers as in most other cathedral choirs. Mr Harry Wood, a son of the composer, Charles Wood, and a member of the choir of St Peter's Parish Church on the Antrim Road in the city, was at Evensong one Sunday at the Cathedral. Somewhat taken aback by the length of the choir procession, he remarked to a friend afterwards, 'As I stood there, the half of Belfast went by!'

In 1917 there were ten paid adult 'solo' singers in the Cathedral Choir whose inadequate salaries the Dean recommended should be increased. It appears that efforts were then being made by other churches to induce some of these singers to transfer their services by offering larger salaries. A revised scale of annual payments ranging from £12 to £20 was agreed. By 1968 the number of paid singers had been reduced to seven, each of whom received £60 per annum, while the choir librarian's salary had been increased to £50.

The choir which Captain Brennan had established in 1904 and which he had maintained over the ensuing six decades was in effect a choral society

Captain C J Brennan at the organ of Belfast Cathedral on the day of his retirement, June 1964 *(Cathedral Archive)*

rather than a cathedral choir in the accepted sense. No doubt when both Captain Brennan and his adult singers were much younger this body of over fifty voices was capable of producing fine effects. Endowed with a commanding presence and a very ready wit he would certainly have been a purposeful and lively director of operations. In his latter years in particular when he had long passed the normal age for retirement, and when many of the ladies and gentlemen of the choir were no longer in their vocal prime, standards of performance declined. The ten basses were allowed to dominate, the marked vibrato of some of the more mature sopranos made blend with the boys' voices impossible and intonation was a perpetual problem.

I have learnt in recent years that, according to chorister lore, the 'new Organist got rid of the ladies from the choir and made bonfires of the old music!' What actually happened was rather less sensational and there were, in fact, no bonfires. Although both the choristers and the younger adult members of the Cathedral Choir welcomed their new Director and the fresh approach which they hoped and, indeed, expected that he would bring, the older ladies and gentlemen, with a few exceptions, were less favourably disposed towards him. There was a resistance to change on the part of a number of these singers, some of whom were given to informing me frequently that 'Captain Brennan always did this or that' or 'never did this or that.' In the case of music with which the choir was familiar, no matter how I might try at the mid-week rehearsal to shape the performance as I saw it, at the services on the following Sunday it sometimes seemed to me that *I* was being conducted by the choir which, despite all my efforts, had reverted, perhaps not altogether unconsciously, to its former way of doing things. One had a better chance with unfamiliar music although I was criticised for daring to introduce a new item on my very first Sunday, not that Vaughan Williams's *O taste and see* should hold any terrors for the members of a cathedral choir who should be able to sight-read it with ease.

Most of those who found the new régime not to their liking resigned from the choir over a period of time during which they were increasingly uncooperative. (I even received an anonymous telephone call!) There was only one case of my finding it necessary to ask someone to leave the choir at this juncture. This was a soprano whose hearing-aid vibrated when she was flanked by other singers. Therefore she had to be placed at the end of the choir-stall next to the desk occupied by the clerical Vicar Choral. He found the stridency of her voice unbearable, as I did much further away at the organ, and thoroughly approved of my decision.

Among the basses was an elderly gentleman who had in his earlier years been one of the province's leading oratorio and concert soloists, his magnificent, sonorous voice thrilling audiences far and wide. Now, partially deaf, he had difficulty in hearing directions at rehearsals and seemed to be incapable of singing in tune. A widower who lived alone with his cat, his membership of the Cathedral Choir meant everything to him and it would have been heartless of me to have deprived him of it. In fact he was one of the few senior members of the choir who had been whole-heartedly supportive of the new régime which, he enthusiastically admitted, had given him a new lease of life. Although at times my ingenuity

Belfast Cathedral Choir outing to Newcastle, Co. Down in mid-1960s. From left: Huston Graham, Harry, Jim and Betty Drennan and the Revd John Nolan *(Cathedral Archive)*

and patience were severely taxed, I considered that it was my duty, as a Christian, to enable a charming older man to continue to experience for a few more years the joy which he obviously derived from his singing.

As far as the choristers were concerned, I decided that I myself would take their Tuesday rehearsal, in addition to that on a Saturday morning, and extended its duration from an hour to an hour and a half, with the agreement of the boys' parents, to enable us to cover more ground. This important rehearsal had previously been the responsibility of the Assistant Organist, Huston Graham, my former organ teacher, with whom I was delighted to be reunited. Huston was glad to be relieved of this duty because, as an increasingly busy professional architect whose work took him to all parts of the province and beyond, he did not always find it possible to be at the Cathedral by four-thirty on a Tuesday afternoon.

The Cathedral Board agreed to allocate a sum of 5 shillings (i.e. 25pence) per month per boy to be used at my discretion to improve discipline and as a 'positive incentive for good work.' One member of the Cathedral Board expressed concern that such regular payments to the choristers might make them professional singers. Hitherto they had each received small quarterly amounts, which varied according to a boy's place in the pecking order, plus 10 shillings - 50p - at Christmas. I devised a system by which marks were awarded for correctly answering questions, reading musical intervals and phrases, etc. with inattention, talking and such misdemeanours resulting in the deduction of marks.

The Head-Chorister kept a record of each boy's score. At the end of the month a boy could receive more or less than 5 shillings depending on his attendance record and performance, with any money left in the 'kitty' (as a cumulative result of deductions or 'fines', as they were known) going to the boy with the highest number of marks to his credit. Boys, of course, thrive on competition and indiscipline was soon a thing of the past as the energies of the wayward underwent sublimation. I was permitted to buy a set of chant-books for the choristers who had previously been without them. Apart from their normal use in conjunction with the psalter, these volumes were an invaluable resource in the teaching of music- reading.

It had been the tradition to appoint head-choristers solely on the basis of seniority. To ensure that the holders of these two key positions would be worthy of them, possessing the requisite musical and leadership qualities, I convinced the Vicar Choral of the advisability of making merit the sole criterion on which future appointments should be made. Consequently the two boys selected in September 1964, Gordon Wilson and Stewart Haslett, proved to be ideal choral prefects, their musical prowess and responsible discharge of their duties winning them the respect of their peers.

Choristers' rehearsals usually took place in the cathedral hall, a rather dilapidated building situated in a yard at the east end of the Cathedral itself, lacking the desks and other appropriate furniture which would be taken for granted at any other cathedral. (My friend, Donald Leggatt, the Northern Ireland Representative of the RSCM and Director of Music at Campbell College, always delighted in referring to this building rather grandly as 'The Song School'.) We all looked forward to having better accommodation at some time in the not-too-distant future. The old, clapped-out, upright piano was promptly replaced by a small, second-hand grand, purchased for £105, which greatly facilitated the conduct of the choristers' rehearsals.

As far as I know, my predecessor had had no difficulty in recruiting boys. The Cathedral Choir in his day seemed to attract a steady stream of good-quality candidates for audition. By the 1960s, however, the complexion of things had changed. With music rapidly developing in the schools (orchestras as well as choirs were now the norm) and with the establishment of schools of music in the city, musical boys were faced with a variety of outlets for their talents, and, of course, a boy's school had prior claim on his time and attention. The once-steady stream of auditionees became a trickle and then dried up altogether. It was clear that if the treble section of the choir - indeed the choir itself - were to survive, it would be necessary for me to pay regular visits to local primary and preparatory schools, where entry for a competitor could be obtained, in order to make the boys aware of the existence of the Cathedral (many had never heard of it) and of the advantages of being a chorister. Armed with illustrated brochures about the choir and the training offered, I began a visiting campaign which I carried on throughout my eleven years at Belfast Cathedral.

In the past, boys had left the Cathedral Choir as a matter of course when their voices began to change. It was generally believed that it was advisable for the singing voice to be rested for a period of perhaps two or three years while the changes of pitch and quality took place and that to continue singing during this time was to risk doing irreparable damage to the delicate vocal chords. In this way over the years scores, if not hundreds of potential altos, tenors and basses must have been lost to the Cathedral Choir in particular and perhaps, in some cases, to church music. Experts are agreed that if the use of the changing voice is carefully monitored to ensure that strain is avoided and that if it is allowed to develop naturally, it is possible for a boy to sing through this period of vocal and emotional insecurity as his musical experience is further extended and enriched. The Young Men's Choir, which I formed and which sang at 10.00a.m. Matins on the first Sunday of the month, allowed past-choristers to continue their close association with the Cathedral pending the return which a number of them would later make to the Cathedral Choir as adult singers.

Another matter requiring urgent attention was the reorganisation of the choir's music library. At each adult singer's place in the choir stalls there was a locker which contained, in addition to a chant-book, psalter, hymnal and a copy of *The Church Anthem Book* (edited by Walford Davies and Henry Ley), several bound collections of anthems and services which were probably compiled in the early years of the century. Much of this music was no longer in general use in cathedrals. Items from the Tudor and early Stuart periods were usually in the old untransposed editions which were now out of date e.g. Gibbons's *'Short' Service* appeared in the F major version published by Novello. Every locker also contained a copy of each of the other items which had been added to the repertoire in more recent years.

With the help of the librarian I rescued these loose copies, many of them crumpled and torn, and, having sorted and repaired them, stored them until they were next required. As for the volumes of services and anthems, I took these home to Bangor in batches on the train. I had no car. In the evenings during the summer months of 1964 my mother my two sisters and I set to work with razor-blades to take these volumes apart. Copies of music which I intended to retain in the repertoire were carefully preserved, while the remainder were not set on fire (contrary to popular belief) but, being Cathedral property, were kept in a safe place in the crypt. The separation of the copies in the volumes belonging to the choristers was not such an arduous task because these volumes were falling apart already!

On my first Sunday at the Cathedral I had noted that one of the choristers was without his Eton collar and bow while the general appearance of a few others also left something to be desired. The Dean and the Vicar Choral agreed that it would be necessary to find a lady who would be willing to iron surplices each week as well as supervising the robing of the choristers. We were very fortunate that Miss Anne Johnston consented to undertake these duties for she was to prove to be an indispensable member of the Cathedral Staff. A dress-maker by profession, Anne Johnston was happy to assume further responsibilities as 'Mistress of the Robes', a role in which she took great pride, rendering sterling service over many years. In addition to repairing and altering robes as the need arose, Anne made collars and cuffs for the ladies of the choir as well as a complete set of new surplices for the boys and men. She also made a protective cloth cover for every hymn-book, psalter and chant-book.

Those numerous choristers who knew Anne Johnston and her sister, Maureen, who was always on hand to offer assistance, remember them both with great affection and gratitude. Their generosity, like that of favourite maiden aunts, seemed to know no bounds. Almost every Saturday evening they entertained the choristers at their home on the Springfield Road. There would be a show of slides taken on holidays or on choir outings, the opportunity to sample recordings, mostly of church music, from the vast Johnston collection and, of course, a 'scrumptious' meal. Anne and Maureen took a keen interest in the boys' welfare, rejoicing with them in their personal triumphs and commiserating with them in their disappointments. Together with the Vicar-Choral, the Revd John Nolan (himself a former chorister), who held a Bible-class for the boys each Sunday morning, they exercised a very important pastoral ministry in the young lives committed to their charge.

As far as the Cathedral's music was concerned, the emphasis was now largely on new repertoire. In early October 1964 Harvest Festival Matins included Vaughan Williams's *Te Deum in G,* composed for the enthronement of the Archbishop of Canterbury in 1928, and Britten's lively setting of the *Jubilate* with, at Evensong, anthems by the sixteenth century composer, Robert Whyte (*O praise God in His Holiness*), Schubert (*The Lord is my Shepherd*) and Gustav Holst (*Lord, Who hast made us for Thine own*). Although there were no objections to Britten's *Jubilate,* as at Bangor Parish Church, a few people expressed to me their disapproval of the beautiful sets of Tudor responses which I was introducing and which they found too ornate. One lady, as I recall, had an aversion to the division into four syllables of the word 'temptation' (i.e. temp-ta-ti-on) to be found, for example, in Robert Stone's lovely setting of the Lord's Prayer. I am glad to say that such outspoken dissenters constituted a rather small minority.

With the approach of Christmas the pace of life quickened as preparation for the carol services, in addition to Matins/Eucharist and Evensong on Sunday, increased markedly the intensity of rehearsals. At this time of year it has always been the custom for the choristers to visit hospitals and residential homes to sing carols to the patients. Sometimes an invitation might be received for the whole choir to provide seasonal music at a social event such as the annual Christmas lunch of The Rotary Club of Belfast in December 1964. Having sung a varied selection of choral arrangements, the choir gave a lead to the assembled company in a group of well-known carols, with Huston Graham and I playing, as an instrumental interlude, *A Fantasia on Christmas Carols* for piano duet by the Belfast composer, Dorothy Parke.

I had been asked to give the sixth in a series of gramophone record recitals at the Belfast Central Library earlier that month. These recitals had been organised in an attempt to bring the library's new record-lending service to wider public attention. I enjoyed making my selection and then introducing works by Monteverdi, Gibbons, Corelli, J S Bach, Wolf, Hely-Hutchinson and carol arrangements by Malcolm Sargent. It was interesting to juxtapose a performance on the organ by Simon Preston of Bach's Advent chorale prelude on *Wachet auf!* ('Sleepers, wake!') with that by the Swingle Singers. Victor Hely-Hutchinson's charming *Carol Symphony* is probably still not as well known as it deserves to be. I was pleased to hear later from the City Librarian, Mr Ivor Crawley, that the recital had gone down well with the audience and that there had been numerous enquiries about the recordings subsequently.

Christmas carols would seem to have an irresistible appeal for the public at large. Even those who would rarely, if ever, be seen in church during the rest of the year, come in their hundreds to join with regular worshippers at the Christmas services, in particular the Festival of the Nine Lessons. At Belfast Cathedral this has always been held on the afternoon of the Sunday before Christmas with a repeat on Christmas Eve when it can be a case of 'standing room only.'

It had long been the tradition for the BBC to broadcast the first of these carol services live on the Northern Ireland wavelength. At Christmas 1964 advice given to me years before by my friend Tim Turner, the Schools Music Inspector and Organist of Holywood Parish Church, enabled me to deal effectively with a tricky situation. On the Wednesday evening prior to the broadcast, BBC staff were present at the choir rehearsal for a run-through of the carol service which was to begin with an introit sung at the west end of the Cathedral from where the choir would make its way to the choir stalls in the course of the processional hymn. The members of the choir took up their positions at the west door in three rows, one behind the other with the choristers in front. After the singing of the introit (at the rehearsal) the head-engineer rushed into the building and insisted on rearranging the singers in the interests of achieving what he assured me would be an altogether better result as regards the transmitted sound. I despaired as I beheld my choral ranks now in such disarray that it would have been well-nigh impossible to derive an orderly procession from it. Tim Turner had told me that at the run-through before a live broadcast he always deferred to the wishes of the producer/engineer whereas during the actual broadcast he did as he personally saw fit. Following Tim's example I made no fuss and tried to reassure the members of the choir who were perplexed by this countermand of my instructions. On the morning of the broadcast I told the choir to line up in the afternoon before the service in the normal way. The engineer, out of sight in his control room and preoccupied with the transmission, would be none the wiser.

Such proved to be the case. When the broadcast was over he appeared to be very pleased, 'My rearrangement of the singers for the introit made a huge difference to the overall sound. I was delighted with the result!' I was happy to allow the engineer to have all the credit he claimed.

I had been asked by the BBC to record a short programme of Christmas organ music to be transmitted after the carol service. This, the first of a number of broadcast recitals which I was privileged to give over the years, included music by Bach, Brahms, Karg-Elert, Edward Bairstow and Ivan Langstroth, a contemporary American composer. Amongst appreciative correspondence were letters from listeners not only in Northern Ireland but also in England where there were some people who tuned in to the carol service from Belfast Cathedral every year. One of these, George Booth, a retired gentleman had, as a young employee of Peter Conacher Organs, Huddersfield, worked on the instruments in St Columb's Cathedral, Londonderry and St Macartin's (Church of Ireland) Cathedral, Enniskillen. He said that, as usual, he was also looking forward to hearing the service from King's College, Cambridge as well as that from St Patrick's Cathedral, Dublin which followed it on Christmas Eve (on Radio Éireann).

It had been the custom at Belfast Cathedral to mark Passiontide with a performance of an appropriate substantial choral work such as Brahms's *German Requiem* or an abridged version of Bach's *St Matthew Passion* accompanied by the organ. I had decided that Fauré's beautiful and justly-popular *Requiem* would be an admirable choice for 1965 with the addition of a few shorter pieces such as Allegri's *Miserere*. In buoyant mood I went to London, hired the requisite fifty-odd copies of the score from United Music Publishers and brought them back to Belfast on the plane in order to avoid any possible delay in their arrival by post.

The members of the choir, most of whom had not sung Fauré's *Requiem* before, took to it instantly and, with rehearsals going very well, the performance on Maundy Thursday was eagerly anticipated. It should perhaps be recorded that during my predecessor's time settings of Latin texts were avoided except in cases where an English translation was available. Although the *Requiem* was not being sung in the context of a service but rather as part of a concert programme, there were evidently some people who had objections. Consequently, after 'a lengthy discussion' at a meeting of the Cathedral Board at the end of February 1965, it was decided that Fauré's *Requiem* 'should be performed as planned unless the Dean, after examination of the translation, considered that it was open to question on theological grounds.' I was called to a meeting with the Dean, the Vicar Choral and the Canon Theologian at which the last-named, armed with a metaphorical blue-pencil, went through the work excising those sections of which he could not approve. So little of the work survived his examination that I was left with no alternative but to scrap the project. I had been rather naïve. In future I would try to make sure that I did not allow myself to be carried away by my personal enthusiasm.

By way of compensation for this disappointment, I received an invitation from Anthony Smith to take part in two performances, on successive evenings, of Bach's *St John Passion* in Enniskillen on 30 April and 1 May 1965. As Director of Music at Portora Royal School and Organist and Choirmaster of St Macartin's Cathedral, Tony Smith was a key figure on the musical scene in Co. Fermanagh. An exceedingly able and enterprising musician, he was something of a pioneer in that relatively remote part of the province. Tony was determined that his performance of the *St John Passion* with his Fivemiletown Choral Society would not be merely another routine 'concert' version with a passive audience but that it would be in keeping with Bach's original concept. To this end he invited choirs from fifteen primary and secondary schools together with three school orchestras to participate in the chorales, with the choral society alone being responsible for the choruses. It should be added that, because of the vast number of young singers involved, the massed school choirs were divided, half of them taking part in each performance. Numerous preliminary rehearsals under Tony's direction ensured that cohesion of these disparate forces was achieved. A strong team of soloists was headed by the distinguished English tenor, Ian Partridge, who was the Evangelist. Accompaniment was supplied by an ensemble drawn from the BBC Northern Ireland Orchestra, Dr Havelock Nelson and I providing keyboard continuo on piano and organ respectively. The event was a conspicuous success and a personal triumph for Tony Smith who had masterminded it.

Among the so-called 'special' services at Belfast Cathedral in the early part of 1965 was the memorial service for the great British Prime Minister, Sir Winston Churchill who had died on 24 January. With every available seat in the Cathedral occupied, this was both a dignified and moving state occasion.

Appearances at concerts in the city and beyond served to bring the Cathedral Choir to the attention of many people who might otherwise have been unlikely to hear it. In April 1965 the choristers were invited to take part in the 88th annual concert promoted by the Belfast Masonic Charities. A very impressive affair, this began with a fanfare which heralded the entry of the 'Grand Masonic Procession' in full regalia. The substantial 70-page concert brochure, giving information about the proceedings and the participants, cost 6d (i.e 2½p) 'at least'!

BELFAST CATHEDRAL

✻

VISIT OF ULSTER AND LEINSTER SOCIETIES OF ORGANISTS AND CHOIRMASTERS

SATURDAY, 29th MAY, 1965, at 3 p.m.

RECITAL

by

The Cathedral Choir

Organist and Master of the Choristers
W. H. GRINDLE, B.A., F.R.C.O.(CHM), A.R.C.M.

Assistant Organist
R. H. GRAHAM

Hon. Sub-Organist
J. A. YOUNG

Programme of recital by the choir of Belfast Cathedral in May 1965

Accompanied on the piano by Huston Graham, the boys sang two songs in each half of the programme. In rehearsal it was evident that their favourite piece was Phyllis Tate's exuberant and highly imaginative arrangement of *Old MacDonald had Farm*. At the concert their totally committed performance of this delighted the audience.

In addition to some locally well-known vocal soloists, the artists also included the band of the Devonshire and Dorset Regiment, stationed at that time in Northern Ireland. Later, brass players and percussionists from this fine band would from time to time combine with the Cathedral Choir when such pieces as Vaughan Williams's familiar setting of *The Old Hundredth* were being sung at services.

The audience at the Masonic concert also heard a young Belfast cellist then in his final year as a student at the RAM and with a very distinguished career ahead of him. This was David Strange who was to be principal cellist of the Royal Philharmonic Orchestra 1973-85 and of the orchestra of the Royal Opera House, Covent Garden 1985-90. Now in 2009 the holder of a chair at the University of London, he is in charge of the String Department at the RAM as well as being Director of Studies for the European Union Youth Orchestra and a visiting professor in Melbourne and Salamanca.

The climax of my first year at the Cathedral was undoubtedly a recital which the choir and organists gave on Saturday 29 May for the Ulster and Leinster Societies of Organists and Choirmasters. The full choir sang a selection of anthems including Byrd's *Ave Verum* and Stanford's *Beati quorum Via* (both in Latin!), *Greater love hath no Man* (Ireland) and *My Soul there is a Country* (Parry) as well as Howells's *Collegium Regale* setting of the Magnificat and Nunc Dimittis. For many, one of the highlights was the choristers' performance of Handel's technically challenging aria, *Let the bright Seraphim*. Their *esprit de corps* was palpable and I have to confess that I was very proud of them and their achievement. Organ interludes were provided by Jack Young (music by Bach, Philip Cranmer and Norman Hay), and by me (my own *Improvisation on the tune 'University'* and John Cook's exciting *Fanfare*), with Huston Graham, who had acted as accompanist throughout the programme, bringing the recital to an end with Bach's great *Fugue in A Minor (BWV 543)*.

After the trials and tribulations of the previous months it was particularly satisfying to reach this point in the development of the Cathedral Choir. While I had anticipated that the period of transition would not be easy, I had not expected that it would bring quite as much stress and strain as it did. Although we had lost a number of adult singers, some of whom chose to depart just prior to the important festival of Easter, promising young voices were coming forward to replace them and the overall sound of the choir was improving with the introduction of countertenors.

CHAPTER SIX

1965-67 | Belfast Cathedral,
The Cathedral Consort

D uring July and August, the school vacation period in Northern Ireland, rehearsals were usually suspended at the Cathedral. The Cathedral Choir was, nevertheless, still responsible for providing the music at the Sunday services during these months when, of course, the congregation included many visitors from various parts of the world. It was essential to draw up a rota in consultation with the members of the choir who were, after all, voluntary except for the seven paid singers (see Chapter 5) to ensure that a balanced ensemble was always present, the repertoire to be sung being chosen accordingly. The choir also agreed to arrive in time for a short rehearsal before each service during the summer. Once they were convinced of the value of this pre-service 'warm-up', something which had long been a common practice at most other cathedrals and major parish churches, the members of the choir readily accepted it as part of our normal routine from the beginning of September 1965.

In addition to private piano and organ teaching, various engagements provided a very welcome supplement to my cathedral income (now £550.00 per annum), a fair proportion of which went on meals and daily return journeys by train from Bangor. When the Royal Liverpool Philharmonic Orchestra paid a very rare visit to Belfast in early September 1965 I was asked to play the organ part in Elgar's *Enigma Variations* which concluded the second of two concerts given by this fine orchestra in the Ulster Hall. Having discovered that I was not a member of the Musicians' Union, the manager of the orchestra hastily arranged to take out temporary membership on my behalf in order to avoid the risk of a strike by his players were they to find out. As far as I can remember this issue was never raised when, from time to time, I joined the City of Belfast Orchestra and its successor, the Ulster Orchestra, as a keyboard continuo player.

One of the most ambitious musical projects undertaken in the course of the 1965 Queen's University Festival was the mounting of two performances

81

(the first in Northern Ireland) of Benjamin Britten's *War Requiem* which had had its première at Coventry Cathedral three years earlier. Given on successive evenings in November in the Sir William Whitla Hall at the University and at St Anne's Cathedral, these performances, under the direction of the indefatigable Havelock Nelson, brought together the Ulster Singers, the McCready Singers, the Cathedral Choristers, the Olin Chamber Orchestra (drawn from the ranks of the professional BBC Northern Ireland Orchestra) and the largely-amateur Studio Symphony Orchestra. Terence Lovett, the recently-appointed conductor of the BBC Orchestra was in charge of the chamber ensemble while I directed the choristers. The soloists were the Dublin soprano, Veronica Dunne, the well-known English tenor, Edgar Fleet, and Eric Hinds (baritone) from Belfast. The performance at the Cathedral, the work's natural 'home', was particularly successful, the spaciousness facilitating the disposition of the forces involved and the sound benefiting from the resonance of the acoustic. One could only salute the courage and enterprise of Dr Nelson who in the course of his long career introduced a succession of major works to Northern Ireland audiences. I am sure that, like the Cathedral Choristers and myself, the other participants were grateful to him for enabling us to experience this undoubted twentieth-century masterpiece.

The autumn of 1965 had seen the launch by the Dean of an appeal for £200,000 to fund the completion of the Cathedral with the addition of north and south transepts and central crossing. As part of its publicity campaign, the local firm which had been engaged to promote the appeal conducted a series of interviews with leading figures in the Cathedral community whose profiles appeared later at regular intervals in issues of the *Belfast Telegraph*. An interviewer visited me at home in Bangor where he noted my collection of records among which were some belonging to a series featuring the organs and organists of various English cathedrals. He asked me if I should like to make such a recording. I replied that I thought that the fine Harrison organ in Belfast Cathedral was worthy of being included in the series and that I hoped that it might be one day after its long-overdue reconstruction had been completed.

Before he departed, the interviewer promised to send me a copy of the text prior to its submission for publication. When the piece arrived, its opening sentence, which, he later told me, was calculated to arrest the reader's attention, came as something of a shock, 'If Harry Grindle has his way the organ of St Anne's Cathedral will be heard around the world.' Since I hope that I am not the pushy, self-assertive individual that this statement might suggest, I telephoned right away to ask that the piece be withdrawn. The interviewer, while being unwilling to comply with my request, promised to carry out some research, the results of which he would communicate to me as soon as possible. This entailed his asking twenty people who, he said, knew me well, to read the offending text, with each being required to say whether or not the impression which it gave radically changed his/her estimation of me as a person. The responses, he informed me were uniformly negative - whatever that was meant to indicate! Nevertheless, on my continued insistence, he reluctantly agreed to withdraw the article.

The Cathedral Choir's continued improvement drew favourable comment from colleagues, visitors, correspondents and music critics. From time to time letters were appearing in the press expressing appreciation of both the rapidly-expanding repertoire and the standard of its performance. The choristers were establishing a reputation of their own with further participation in performances of major choral works in Belfast in 1966, making the first of what were to become regular appearances as the *ripieno* choir in Bach's *St Matthew Passion* which was then presented annually by the Ulster Singers under Havelock Nelson. Professor Philip Cranmer also invited the choristers to take part in a performance of the much-less-familiar *Hymn of Jesus* by Gustav Holst at Queen's University.

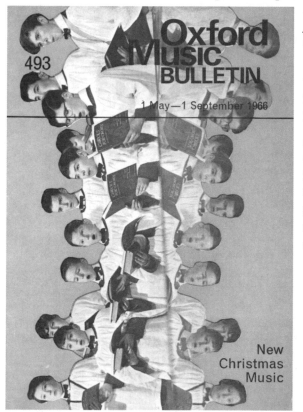

In December 1965 Mr G Victor Henry ARCO, the Managing Director of the Bank Buildings, a large department store in the centre of Belfast, invited the full Cathedral Choir to sing carols throughout the store to the crowds of late-night shoppers.

Cover picture of May-September,1966 issue of the *Oxford Music Bulletin*

The novelty of this appearance by the choir on commercial premises in the midst of the pre-Christmas rush naturally received a considerable amount of press coverage and there were photographs in most of the local newspapers. One of these showed a group of the choristers singing from copies of the first volume of *Carols for Choirs,* a popular anthology published by Oxford University Press (OUP), with the choristers' image clearly reflected on the surface of the glass counter behind which they were standing. Evidently this striking picture had appealed to someone in the publicity department at OUP because it adorned the front cover of the May-September 1966 edition of the *Oxford Music Bulletin* which carried information about newly-published Christmas music.

Jack Smith, a young bass in the Cathedral Choir, had for some time been trying to persuade me to give consideration to the idea of forming a smaller mixed-voice choral group to specialise in earlier repertoire. Like me, Jack was frustrated by the embargo in force at that time at the Cathedral on the singing of Latin texts in the course of services. Now, in my second year as Organist at St Anne's and with my *modus operandi* well established, I decided that I was in a position to take on another responsibility. Jack Smith's ideal would have been one voice to a part, but, as the director of this proposed new group, I opted for the larger number of singers that would give us some insurance against the emergency which would inevitably arise were someone to be unavoidably absent at the last moment.

The Cathedral Consort, consisting initially of sixteen singers, made its début in St Anne's on 11 June 1966 when the programme consisted of Byrd's *Mass for Four Voices*, a group of motets by Tallis, Byrd, Peter Philips and Pitoni, with organ music by Bach played by Brian Hunter, one of the countertenors. In his review of the concert in the *Belfast Newsletter* under the heading 'The Essence of all Music is Here,' Donald Cairns compared the small vocal ensemble to the string quartet particularly with regard to the high level of discipline and refinement of which each is capable. (This analogy would have pleased Jack Smith!) 'The Consort gave no sign of being a newcomer. Its work is stylish, sensitive, properly cool but never emasculated as the English tradition of cathedral singing sometimes seems to be . . . Byrd and Tallis and the rest were able to speak for themselves through an already highly-polished instrument . . .. How much they have to say and how elegantly they say it!'

After this successful launch the Consort gave a further concert in the Cathedral in September when Byrd's *Mass for Three Voices* was sung by two countertenors, two tenors and two basses, with the full Consort being heard in motets and anthems by Byrd, Gibbons and Purcell as well as Stanford's Three Motets Op.38 (*Justorum Animae*; *Coelos ascendit*

Hodie and *Beati quorum Via.)* From then on the Cathedral Consort never wanted for engagements. When the committee of the USOC decided to introduce a choral element into its annual members' recital in early October to lend some variety to the programme, the Consort was invited to make its third appearance at the Cathedral in a comparatively short period. On this occasion our contribution consisted of a repeat performance of Byrd's *Mass for Four Voices* together with the *Five Mystical Songs* by Vaughan Williams in which the soloist was Jack Smith. In the final song, *Antiphon* ('Let all the World in every Corner sing'), Dr Francis Jackson, then Organist of York Minster, kindly permitted us to use his very effective arrangement of the accompaniment for organ and piano, played respectively by John Boal and Huston Graham.

The members of the Cathedral Consort enjoyed exploring a broad range of music, both sacred and secular, although it is probably true to say that for most of them it was from singing Renaissance polyphony that they derived the greatest satisfaction. Among the members we were fortunate to have a number of fine solo singers who were heard from time to time and particularly when we were presenting varied programmes to some of the province's music societies.

It is salutary for someone who spends much of his or her time directing performances to play or sing occasionally under another conductor.

The Cathedral Consort in 1969. Back row, from left: Fred Clark, Dermot McConnell, Jack Smith, Ronnie Fleming, Jim Caves, Raymond Hastie and Brian Hunter. Front row, from left: Heather, Geraldine Roberts, June Houston, Harry, Freda Sloss, Ellen Rainey and Margaret Clark

Apart from what one may learn from the experience, it may even afford a little amusement.

In November 1966 I was taking part as continuo pianist with the Belfast Philharmonic Society and the Ulster Orchestra in a performance of Haydn's *The Seasons* conducted by Maurice Miles in the Ulster Hall. The soloists, all well-known on the British concert circuit, were Margaret Price, Kenneth Bowen and Gordon Clinton. At one point where Mr Clinton was due to deliver a passage of recitative, I noted that he was not standing. Maurice Miles, perhaps assuming that, for some reason or other, his bass soloist had decided to sing from a sitting position and not wishing to break the flow of the performance, brought the continuo cellist and me in. When there was no response from Gordon Clinton, who had not moved, Mr Miles indicated that we repeat the opening chord of the passage. After a brief pause and when it was evident that we were not going to hear from Gordon Clinton, Maurice Miles, by now clearly exasperated, conducted while the cellist and I played through the sequence of chords which constituted the accompaniment. Mr Clinton had evidently dozed off in the very warm hall while he awaited his next entry. Given the demands of the life of a leading concert soloist, with its round of rehearsals, performances and tiring travel, it is perhaps surprising that such an incident does not occur more frequently.

Although most of my own work was in Belfast and the surrounding area, sometimes it might take me outside the province. In February 1966 I visited Douglas in the Isle of Man to give a recital in Finch Hill Congregational Church with Eleanor Shimmin (contralto) and Alan Wilcox (bass), two popular local singers, to mark the reopening of the church. Two years earlier a fire had severely damaged the building and its contents, the organ having been reduced to such a state that it was beyond repair. The congregation of Christian Street (Primitive) Methodist Church in Peel, which had recently been closed, generously donated the redundant organ to the Congregationalists of Finch Hill. In the process of its installation in the Congregational Church this organ had undergone extensive rebuilding and enlargement by the Irish Organ Company of Belfast who at the recital also introduced their new *Cosgrove* organ, a compact and attractively-priced instrument designed to meet the needs of smaller churches. Later we were to have the use of a *Cosgrove* at Belfast Cathedral for part of the time that the Harrison organ was undergoing its major rebuild in Durham during the construction of the Cathedral's south transept (see also Chapter 7). While it was limited tonally, the *Cosgrove* proved to be an admirable organ on which to teach basic technique to beginners.

I had recently been giving consideration to the idea of having some lessons from one of the leading continental organists and I discussed the matter with my friend Leon Rittwegger who was then in charge of the music at Clonard Monastery in Belfast and who knew Flor Peeters, the renowned Belgian organist and composer, very well. With Leon's kind assistance a course of lessons was arranged for July 1966 with Professor Peeters, at that time Director of the Antwerp Conservatory and Organist at the Cathedral of St Rombout in Mechelen. As a composer, Peeters is especially noted for his organ music, his highly personal style being to some extent a synthesis of such elements as Gregorian chant, French Renaissance polyphony and Flemish folk-song from which he sometimes derived his thematic material. One of his best-known works, the *Toccata, Fugue and Hymn on Ave Maris Stella Op.28* is dedicated to his greatest friend, Charles Tournemire, whose improvisatory style would appear to have influenced its composition. In 1939 Tournemire bequeathed to Peeters the organ console that César Franck (his teacher and predecessor as Organist) had used at St Clotilde in Paris. This console which stood in the music room of his beautiful home, appropriately named *Adagio*, was one of Flor Peeters's most precious possessions and he was wont to refer to it when discussing the music of Franck.

Peeters was very proud of the fact that he had succeeded in completing a project similar to that undertaken by Bach in the *Orgelbüchlein* but which Bach had unfortunately left unfinished. This was to compose a series of chorale preludes covering the entire Church year. Much in demand as an organ consultant, he took great pride in the instrument which he had designed for his own personal use as well as for teaching in his music room.

I was, of course, already familiar with his three-volume treatise, *Ars Organi*, a summary of his teaching methods which places him firmly in the tradition of his great predecessor, Marcel Dupré. His advice about the performance of the French Romantic repertoire was of particular interest and it was inspiring to hear his playing of passages from his own pieces. While in Belgium I also had the opportunity to attend a series of outstanding recitals given in Antwerp Cathedral by Flor Peeters and other eminent European organists. Unlike similar events in Britain these recitals attracted capacity audiences. I returned to Belfast at the end of July after what had been a thoroughly stimulating experience and one from which I had learnt a great deal. Specifically, Flor Peeters had made some interesting suggestions about registration (i.e. use of stops). These I had carefully noted for implementation in my further exploration of the resources of the cathedral organ.

It is no exaggeration to say that, but for the vision and determination of Jack Young, Belfast Cathedral would not have the fine, four-manual instrument which now stands in its south transept. Jack was second to none in his devotion to the Cathedral, a devotion to which he gave written expression in characteristically flowery terms in his monograph, *Unfinished Pilgrimage*. His legal advice was invaluable to the Cathedral Board of which he was a long-standing member. A keen amateur musician with a two-manual organ in the drawing-room of his home, Jack longed for the day when the completed Cathedral would house in its north transept, as was then proposed, the rebuilt and enlarged organ of which he dreamt. Being Honorary Secretary of the Friends of Belfast Cathedral (FBC) he was in a position to exert considerable influence and he did not hesitate to do so in the interests of the Cathedral's music.

At Jack Young's suggestion the FBC undertook responsibility for the funding of the organ project and it gave him great personal satisfaction to report regularly on the steady growth of the amount invested for this purpose. The occasional legacy was always especially welcome! Faced with the daunting task of raising £200,000 to pay for the next phase in the building of the Cathedral itself, the members of the appeal committee, under the chairmanship of the Dean, must have been tempted to break the tenth commandment! Jack Young saw to it that his burgeoning organ fund remained intact.

The postponement until September 1965 of the launch of the main Cathedral appeal had increased the cost of the project by £1,000 per month. In January 1967 Jack Young tried in vain to convince the Cathedral Board of the advisability of finalising the contract for the rebuilding of the organ directly at a fixed price of £25,400. When the Board at last consented to accept a fixed-price agreement a year and eight months later, the amount had increased to £27,940.

By early 1967 the cathedral organ, which had received little attention other than routine maintenance over the six decades since its installation, was the worse for wear with its action becoming increasingly unreliable. Those repairs which were essential to enable it to remain in use until June of the following year, when it was due to be dismantled, were carried out. We fervently hoped and prayed that our live broadcasts in particular would not be marred by the unpredictable ciphers which were recurring with increasing frequency.

After a number of years during which Belfast Cathedral had not been heard in the prestigious weekly BBC Choral Evensong series on Radio 3 we received an invitation to sing a service live on Wednesday 8 March 1967. Largely unaccompanied music seemed appropriate because the date fell in the season of Lent, and advisable given the current state of the organ which would be used only to accompany a hymn and to supply the closing voluntary. With the broadcast only a matter of weeks away it would be necessary to rehearse intensively to achieve the high standard expected by the discriminating listeners who regularly tuned in. To encourage the choristers to become thoroughly familiar with the text of the three psalms for the eighth evening (i.e. nos 41, 42 and 43) I offered a prize to any boy who could recite the words of all three accurately from memory. In this way I hoped to ensure that I would have the complete attention of the choristers when they sang the psalms.

This broadcast was one of the most significant during my eleven years at the Cathedral for it brought the choir to the attention of a nationwide audience many of whom had never previously heard it. We were extremely well served by the BBC engineer who, without any fuss, had made sure that everything came across with the utmost clarity. Listeners expressed their delight at hearing every syllable, especially in the psalms, the singing of which had clearly made a very favourable impression. A former succentor at Salisbury and Exeter Cathedrals asked for permission to use for demonstration purposes a recording which he had made of our performance of the anthem, Byrd's *Bow Thine Ear* (*Civitas sancti Tui*) because, he said, it was 'such a splendid example of good singing'.

Mr E H Powell, writing from Devon, was one of a number who considered that the broadcast was one of the best that they had heard for many months and that the singing bore comparison with that of the choir of King's College, Cambridge. Incidentally, Mr Powell, who had been the founder-chairman of the Old Choristers' Association in Cork, told me that he had met Captain Brennan when they were both stationed with the Royal Irish Fusiliers at Newtownards in 1917.

It was interesting and pleasing to see that the majority of our correspondents, among them some very experienced church musicians, assumed that they had been listening to an all-male choir. A counter-tenor lay clerk at Peterborough Cathedral even began his congratulatory message: 'Dear Gentlemen and Boys'. (I am not sure what the remaining ladies in the choir made of that!) Roy Massey, at that time Warden of the RSCM and later Organist at Hereford Cathedral, sent his comments together with those of his colleagues and students for whom the weekly broadcast of Choral Evensong was, as might have been expected, required listening: 'We were most impressed with the general balance of the choir and noted especially the clarity of the diction and of the top line. We were particularly impressed with the excellence of the chording throughout, and we had difficulty in telling whether you had females in the treble and alto lines. We should, in fact, be most interested to know what the constitution of the choir is as many of our students listened with considerable interest and wondered what forces you were actually using. Altogether I think you are to be congratulated on a broadcast of a very high standard indeed.'

Writing independently at a later date, Dr Gerald Knight was equally complimentary: 'We were tremendously thrilled by a broadcast you and your choir did on a [recent] Wednesday. It was quite incredible to hear Belfast sounding so fine. I do congratulate you. You must have sweated blood to get so good a result. May it continue to flourish.'

I was touched by one brief message, written in a shaky, elderly hand. It came from Sir Harry Verney in Bletchley, Buckinghamshire and read as follows: '8.3.67 . . . 4.46p.m.[i.e. one minute after the end of the transmission]. . . Thank you for the beautiful & moving rendering of the Psalms.'

With this broadcast the Cathedral Choir regained its place on the roster of choirs invited by the BBC to contribute to this important series. From now on Choral Evensong on Radio 3 came regularly from Belfast one or two times a year although, once the building of the south transept at the Cathedral was under way, we had to transfer to one of the city parish churches, none of which, of course, possessed such a splendid acoustic.

On the first Sunday in June each year a special service, organised by the Friends of the Cathedral, is held to mark the anniversary of the consecration of the nave in 1904. There is a notable guest preacher and suitably celebratory music. In 1967 the anthem was Vaughan Williams's wonderfully evocative setting of verses from Psalm 90: *Lord, Thou hast been our Refuge,* which climaxes in a stirring passage of choral counterpoint surrounding the tune *St Anne,* traditionally associated with Isaac Watts's paraphrase of this text, played as a trumpet obligato. We were fortunate to be able to call on the assistance of trumpeters from the band of the Devon and Dorsetshire Regiment, which was still based at Holywood, Co. Down, and the total effect of choir and organ together with the trumpeters, sited high above in a gallery in the triforium, was simply stunning.

H F Selwood Lindsay with his father, Canon Herbert Lindsay, outside their home at Stranmillis

In an effort to make the annual Past Choristers' Association Service something more of an 'occasion' for all concerned, I suggested that we should invite the members attending to join with the choir in as much of the music of the service as possible in keeping with the tradition at most other cathedrals. Such anthems as S S Wesley's *Blessed be the God and Father* and such settings of the evening canticles as that in D minor by T A Walmisley, with their passages for unison lower voices, are appropriate choices when a preponderance of tenors and basses is present. With the prospect of participation resulting in a greatly increased turn-out of members of the association at this particular service, this practice has been followed ever since.

I took advantage of the Harvest Thanksgiving Festival in October to extend further the range of music performed at the Cathedral. At Evensong some of my friends and colleagues kindly agreed to come together, on a purely voluntary basis, to form an orchestra led by Alan Kimberley, to enable the Cathedral Choir to sing the sixth of Handel's Chandos Anthems: *O praise the Lord with one Consent.* With a harpsichord played by Philip Cranmer and portative organ played by John Boal, both instruments lent by the Lord Dunleath, the original orchestral accompaniment gave our performance authenticity and was evidently to the liking of the *Belfast Telegraph's* music critic who was also impressed by the Choir's singing of Bryan Kelly's engaging setting of the Magnificat and Nunc Dimittis: 'From the forcefulness of "He hath shewed strength" to the rapt stillness of "Lord, now lettest Thou Thy servant depart in peace" both canticles are rich in evocative harmonies and rhythms and were given performances of convincing and attention-holding quality.' I was delighted that through the participation of three members of its staff (Professors Philip Cranmer and Raymond Warren, cello, and Alan Kimberley) the University Music Department continued its association with and interest in the work of the Cathedral Choir.

The publication by OUP of the first two volumes in the series, *Carols for Choirs,* had made widely available much of the music heard in the annual Christmas broadcasts from King's College, Cambridge where David Willcocks, the editor of this series, was for many years Director of Music. Every self-respecting choir in the land had purchased a set of copies of at least the first volume in the series, the famous 'Green Book' which first appeared in 1961, and there were soon few carol services anywhere which failed to closely follow the 'King's' pattern with regard to both order and content. Because the carol service at Belfast Cathedral was also broadcast, it was essential that we offered the listening public something different. In order to give our carol service a distinctive character, I decided to include music by locally-based composers. While

Captain Brennan's *Annunciation* and *The Virgin's Hush-song* kept their rightful place in the scheme of things, they were joined in time by new carols and arrangements by George Gibson, H F Selwood Lindsay, John McDowell, Havelock Nelson, the Revd Frederick J Powell, Keith Rogers, Raymond Warren and me.

In the meantime the Cathedral Consort had gained an additional soprano. This was Heather Loane to whom I had become engaged at Christmas 1966. I had first become aware of Heather when, as a pretty little girl of nine or ten, she had boarded the bus from Bangor to Newtownards each morning with her younger brother, Barry. The Loane children, like the Grindles, went to Regent House School. To me, a young man of twelve or thirteen she was then, of course, a mere child! In the fullness of time the pretty little girl became a lovely young woman and a close relationship developed between us after our meeting at one of the musical evenings which Henrietta Moran occasionally organized for her young friends at her home. Henrietta, who later admitted that she had been match-making, observed our developing romance with more than a passing interest and was very happy when Heather and I announced our engagement. We planned to marry in August 1968, a year which was to prove to be momentous for anything but happy reasons in the history of the province.

Whether or not Heather's advent had anything to do with it, 1967 saw the Cathedral Consort rapidly establishing itself on the local musical scene as the group's growing reputation resulted in an increasing number of engagements in various places. The year began with an appearance at the Laharna Hotel in Larne where, in 'An Evening of Music' under the patronage of the Countess of Antrim, we were joined by the talented young local pianist, Roy Holmes. There were concerts for the Music Societies at Queen's University and Stranmillis College as well as at the Cathedral where a programme of Passiontide music was presented on Maundy Thursday with Brenda Claney (Contralto) and Peter Gibson (a Cathedral Chorister) as soloists respectively in 'Have mercy, Lord, on me' from Bach's *St Matthew Passion* and 'Pie Jesu' from Fauré's *Requiem*. Huston Graham gave a superb performance of Bach's great *Fantasia and Fugue in G Minor (BVW 542)* while I contributed a sequence of chorale preludes from the *Orgelbüchlein*. Writing in the *Belfast Telegraph*, the music critic, *Rathcol*, commented on the 'impressive way in which the Consort had adapted itself to the Cathedral's acoustics'. He went on: 'A small and compact body of singers, it is a beautifully balanced ensemble, well disciplined, technically very competent and with a musicianly sense of style. Its pianissimo singing is outstanding and the performance of Byrd's *Ave verum* was of a breath-catching loveliness that will remain in one's memory for a long time.'

We readily accepted an invitation from Michael Emmerson, the Director of the Belfast Festival at Queen's, to give the first performance in Northern Ireland of a work by the noted contemporary Dublin-based composer, James Wilson, at Festival 67 in November. Born in London in 1922, Wilson settled in Ireland in 1948, becoming an Irish citizen in 1999, six years before his death. As a composer he was largely self-taught. His considerable output included 7 operas, 3 symphonies, 12 concertos and several ballets. *Tom o'Bedlam,* the composition selected for performance at Festival 67, is a setting of verses from the critically-acclaimed anonymous poem written c1600 and it is scored for mixed voices, piano, harp and percussion. The deranged behaviour of the eponymous hero, begging for charity while pleading insanity, is startlingly depicted by James Wilson in a work which deserves to be better known.

For this concert the Cathedral Consort was joined in the Harty Room at Queen's by Derek Bell, the prodigiously talented local musician, who was, for the latter part of his career, the harpist in the celebrated traditional music group, *The Chieftains.* The piano and percussion parts were played by students from the University's music department. As well as *Tom o'Bedlam* , the programme also included a group of Tudor anthems and motets, Palestrina's *Stabat Mater* and *Five English Folk-songs* arr.Vaughan Williams as well as music for solo harp. Derek Bell, famed for his eccentric behaviour almost as much as for his musical prowess, took it upon himself to make sure that the members of the audience were in good spirits before the concert began by circulating among them and, in a highly theatrical manner, kissing the hand of any lady he knew or who took his fancy. Thus the success of the concert was assured!

Some time in the mid-1960s the chorus of the Grand Opera Society of Northern Ireland undertook a tour of a number of the provincial towns. This was sponsored by the Arts Council in association with the borough councils of the towns concerned. The programme which consisted of excerpts from *Carmen, Il Trovatore, Nabucco, Prince Igor, The Flying Dutchman* and *Die Meistersinger* was accompanied by Derek Bell and me playing two pianos. The Society's Chorus Master, Douglas Armstrong, suggested that Derek and I should meet him, prior to the first rehearsal with the chorus, for a preliminary discussion about tempi, etc. A suitable venue with two pianos at exactly the same pitch being difficult to find, we adjourned one evening to Hart & Churchill's Music Shop of which Douglas was the Manager. Our rehearsal took place in the shop window where two pianos were located on a platform in full view of the public. With Douglas conducting and singing while Derek and I played, a sizeable crowd soon gathered outside on the footpath to enjoy this unusual entertainment and to applaud our efforts. It occurred to us afterwards that we should have passed round a hat.

Early in 1967 I submitted to Dr Hans Waldemar Rosen, Head of Choral Broadcasting at Radio Éireann in Dublin, a tape-recording of the Consort's singing of a varied repertoire together with a request for a formal audition. With typical Germanic efficiency he replied promptly saying that a choir as good as the Consort did not require an audition. He enclosed a contract for the recording of our first broadcast which he arranged for personnel from BBC Northern Ireland to make on his behalf. Shortly afterwards the Consort was invited to make its BBC début.

In April 1967 I paid two visits to Ballywalter Park, the stately home of Lord and Lady Dunleath. On 8 April 'An Evening of Chamber Music' was presented by The Society of Professional Musicians in Ulster (SPMU), the proceeds going to a local charity. Apart from the running of his estate, Lord Dunleath's passions were vintage cars and organs, on both of which subjects he was an acknowledged authority. He was particularly generous in his promotion both of the organ as an instrument and of its music as well as in his encouragement of promising young players. His spacious residence housed a collection of valuable keyboard instruments including a chamber organ built by Henry Holland (London) in the 1770s. The property of Major H E Montgomery of Greyabbey, this organ had been restored by Noel Mander on the recommendation of Lord Dunleath. Also belonging to the eighteenth century was a Broadwood fortepiano, the restoration of which had been completed only two months previously. A neo-classical harpsichord built in 1960 was a fine example of the craftsmanship of Alec Hodsden.

Following the restoration of the Holland organ, Lord Dunleath had received many requests to borrow it for use as a continuo instrument. After a couple of excursions, however, it was decided that the risk of damage to this venerable organ was too great. Conscious of the need for a compact instrument of this sort in the musical life of the province, Lord Dunleath, in a truly philanthropic gesture, commissioned from Noel Mander a portative organ having a specification similar to that of the older organ with the addition of one of his beloved mixtures. Belfast Cathedral was one of the venues where this new instrument could sometimes be seen and heard, Lord Dunleath kindly arranging for its transportation by specially-adapted trailer as well as for its dismantling, reassembly and tuning.

These instruments featured prominently in the course of the concert in question given by a chamber ensemble from the BBC Northern Ireland Orchestra under Terence Lovett and the Queen's University Singers conducted by Philip Cranmer together with a number of members of the SPMU. As well as playing the first movement of a Haydn concerto for organ on the new Mander portative instrument with the orchestra, I joined with seven colleagues in a special arrangement by Philip Cranmer for sixteen hands of Bach's *Prelude and Fugue in D major (BWV 532)* for organ. This unusual performance, which brought the concert to a triumphant conclusion, was thoroughly enjoyed by artists and audience alike. It gave no one more pleasure than Lord Dunleath who was delighted to see and hear his precious instruments being put to such effective use.

A further demonstration of the quality of these instruments took place later that month when the USOC visited Ballywalter Park where the music heard included a concerto for two organs by the eighteenth century Spanish composer, Antonio Soler, played by Donald Davison and me. In the course of the afternoon visits were also paid to the charming little church at Balligan and to Ballywalter Parish Church where, over a period of some ten years, Lord Dunleath organised a series of celebrity organ recitals in the early summer. Entitled 'Music in May', these attracted large crowds of people, some of whom undoubtedly came not only for the excellent music but also to gain access to Lord Dunleath's imposing residence where the post-recital hospitality was dispensed.

The varied nature of the engagements which were coming my way made for a very interesting life. In February 1967 I took part, playing the organ, with three of the Cathedral Choristers appearing as 'The Pickled Boys', in a rare performance of Britten's *St Nicolas* in Fisherwick Presbyterian Church, Belfast. This was organised and conducted by Dr Michael Swallow, a leading neurologist, who has made an important contribution to the musical life of the city over many years. Later in February, at the invitation of the Revd Cecil Kerr, Church of Ireland Dean of Residences at Queen's University, I directed the student choir in a Festival of the Christian Year. It gave me great pleasure to return in September 1967 to Willowfield Parish Church to participate in a recital to mark the completion of the rebuilding of the organ. Also taking part were the choirs of Grosvenor High School and St Bartholomew's Parish Church under their conductor Ronald Lee whose remarkable record of success as a choral-trainer is his enduring memorial. In October I was back at the Cathedral playing music by Howells (the *Rhapsody in C sharp minor* and one of the *Psalm Preludes*) and Simon Preston (*Alleluyas*) in the annual composite recital given by members of the USOC.

Ulster Opera, which lasted for but one glorious season, mounted productions of Rossini's *La Cenerentola* and Offenbach's *La Grande Duchesse de Gerolstein* for Festival '67. It seemed that no expense would be spared in order to ensure that both productions would be of the highest possible standard. Leading soloists were imported from Great Britain and abroad to sing to the accompaniment of the Ulster Orchestra conducted by Antonio de Almeida and Walter Susskind. Thomas Davidson and I acted as chorus masters for the two productions which were impressively lavish. It proved to be such an exciting experience to be part of so ambitious an enterprise that, like many others, I was very disappointed that Ulster Opera was destined to have no future.

Archdeacon Samuel Crooks, Rector of Shankill Parish Church in Lurgan and with whom I would have a close association following his appointment as Dean of Belfast in 1970, invited me to lunch one day early in 1967 to discuss the annual Choral Festival for the choirs of the Dromore Diocese, to be held in Magheradroll Parish Church, Ballynahinch in June. Sponsored by the Lurgan Clerical Union, this annual event, in the opinion of the Archdeacon, would benefit from a change of conductor and the selection of more challenging repertoire. He had very definite ideas about what should be sung and persuaded me, against my better judgement, to include a setting of the Te Deum in what was essentially a service of Evensong with two or three anthems and settings of the Magnificat and Nunc Dimittis. The Archdeacon asked me to see to the ordering of the music and to send him the bill. Miss Maisie Fee, the formidable manageress of Tughan-Crane's Music Shop, was amazed when I gave her my shopping list. Three hundred copies of each item were required!

These were duly distributed throughout the diocese to the church organists who were expected to make sure that the members of their choirs were thoroughly conversant with all of this music in advance of district rehearsals which I was to conduct in Lurgan, Banbridge and Ballynahinch. As these rehearsals approached, it was rumoured that some of the country choirs and their organists were finding much of the music beyond them and that they might consider withdrawing from the Festival.

At the first rehearsal it was soon obvious that little preliminary work had been done by most of those present and that a strong dose of 'note-bashing' was going to be necessary. After a good hour of this and with perspiration pouring down my face, I took the opportunity of a short break in proceedings to say a few words by way of encouragement. Having remarked that, if we were to have a rehearsal every night for the next two weeks, I might succeed in teaching them the music, I overheard one of the ladies, who was clearly horrified at the thought, muttering to her neighbour: 'Heaven forbid!'

Some urgent stocktaking was called for. I reported back to the Archdeacon strongly recommending that we adopt the more realistic approach which was essential at this eleventh hour. He reluctantly accepted my advice. The list of music for the Choral Festival underwent major revision with the copies of the setting of the Te Deum and one or two other items being collected for return to Tughan-Crane's. It was with some trepidation that I approached Maisie Fee, requesting a refund. Indeed, I thought that the Archdeacon might well have undertaken this particular mission as an act of penance! In the event, perhaps bearing in mind that I brought her a great deal of custom on behalf of both the Cathedral Choir and the Cathedral Consort, she subjected me to a comparatively mild admonition before undertaking to negotiate with the publishers concerned.

As regards the Choral Festival itself, it went very much better than might have been predicted some few weeks previously. The headline over a report in the *Church of Ireland Gazette* proclaimed that it had 'surpassed all expectations'. The combined choirs gave very creditable performances of Stanford's *Magnificat and Nunc Dimittis in C* as well as a group of anthems which were within their capabilities. I hope that they found my talk on the History of English Church Music, delivered from the pulpit, to be of some interest. At the Diocesan Choral Festival at Gilford, Co. Down in 1968, I again directed the music and gave an address which was published in its entirety in the *Church of Ireland Gazette*. In addition, an extract from the address appeared in the October 1968 issue of the *RSCM News*.

After such a rewarding year's music-making of various kinds and in various places, it was with a keen sense of anticipation that I looked forward to the challenges and opportunities which 1968 would bring. As Heather and I happily prepared for our married life together, we were blissfully unaware of the first stirrings of the political unrest which was to have such devastating and long-term implications for the future of Ulster.

CHAPTER SEVEN

1968-70 | BELFAST CATHEDRAL,
DEAN SAMUEL CROOKS

Following the success of the Cathedral Choir's Choral Evensong broadcast in 1967 the BBC gave us two further dates in this series during the following year. Sadly, the first of these broadcasts, in March 1968, was to be the last in which my dear friend and colleague, Huston Graham, would take part. A very busy professional architect who was now a senior partner in a leading city firm, Huston's business travels took him at times as far away as Scandinavia. While he was delighted to be involved in the exciting musical developments at the Cathedral, it was proving impossible for him to attend rehearsals and to find the time for adequate personal practice. It was with the greatest regret on both his part and mine that he decided to resign as Assistant Organist. With typical generosity he offered to continue to be responsible voluntarily for the music at the 7.00p.m. Sunday evening service to allow the modest salary which he had been paid to go towards the provision of an aspiring young musician in a newly-created post. The first appointee was Howard Fee, then a medical student at Queen's University where he would one day become Professor of Anaesthetics.

In June 1968 the organ was dismantled for removal to the Harrison & Harrison factory in Durham and work began on the erection of a great wooden screen cutting off the nave from the eastern end of the Cathedral which would shortly be taken over by the building contractors. For the second of our Choral Evensong broadcasts on 12 June, therefore, we were obliged to move to St James's Parish Church on the Antrim Road. Here the choir had to hastily adjust to a quite different acoustic with much less resonance than that to which we were accustomed at the Cathedral. The church's fine Organist, Norman Walker, a former Cathedral Chorister (under Captain C J Brennan) and an FRCO Limpus prize-winner, was happy to act as our accompanist. The high quality of Norman's playing was recognised by those who subsequently wrote to us, with all being agreed that the two broadcasts had been in every respect on a par with the best they had heard. Naturally the choristers were elated to learn that their singing had been accorded special praise.

It always makes for a particularly pleasant surprise to hear from someone who has had an association with one of the great names of the past. Mr George Everard of Glan Fadryn in North Wales informed me that, as a Cambridge undergraduate, he had been the principal tenor in the Chapel Choir of Caius College under Dr Charles Wood. Now, in his retirement, Mr Everard played the organ in the little church in the village where he lived.

Another broadcast which was well received was of an Evensong sung one Sunday evening in March 1968 on Radio 4 by the Cathedral Consort. The service was conducted by the Revd Brian Harvey, the Canon Theologian at St Anne's Cathedral, who also gave the address. The canticles were sung to Tallis's setting in the Dorian mode and the anthems were Purcell's *Remember not, Lord, our Offences* and part of Bach's beautiful motet: *Jesu, priceless Treasure (Jesu, meine Freude).*

In July, with Michael Swallow playing the Mander portative organ kindly lent by Lord Dunleath, the Cathedral Consort gave a concert of music from the sixteenth and seventeenth centuries in the Chapel of the Resurrection on the Antrim Road near to Belfast Castle. Consecrated in 1869 as a memorial to the Earl of Belfast who had died at the age of 25 while on holiday in Naples, it was the resting-place for the remains of the Donegall and Chichester families. A century later, the building, although structurally sound, was in urgent need of refurbishment and the provision of both an organ and adequate toilet facilities. A heating system had been installed during the previous year. Our concert was one of a series arranged to promote the further use of the chapel as well as to raise the funds necessary for its restoration. Despite its dilapidated state this building had genuine atmosphere, that all-important feature, which Donald Cairns noted in his critique of this concert in the *Belfast Newsletter* : 'Occasionally one encounters something close to the ideal. The right performers, the right music and the right place coalesce to produce something which is more essentially satisfying than many a much-publicised, eagerly anticipated "big attraction"'.

Prior to the commencement of the building work at the Cathedral, the communion-table, choir stalls, reading-desks, etc. were transferred to the nave where worship would be confined for the next six years. It would be 1975 before the installation of the rebuilt and enlarged organ could at last be achieved. Delays in the construction of the south transept and crossing meant that the new instrument had to be stored for a time, first of all at the Harrison & Harrison factory in Durham and then in the crypt of the Cathedral. In its place initially we had the use of the small, extension

Cosgrove organ designed and made by the Irish Organ Company. With the recently-erected wooden screen reflecting its sound into the nave, this little organ, despite the limitations imposed by its mere four ranks of pipes, proved to be just about adequate for hymn and psalm accompaniment. Lacking the tonal range demanded by a large proportion of the repertoire of anthems and canticle settings sung in a cathedral, it severely restricted the choice of music which could be performed satisfactorily. From a teaching perspective, although it could be a useful instrument on which to give introductory lessons to a beginner, more advanced students (and their mentor) were frustrated by its shortcomings.

Being dependent on my teaching for much of my income, I was obliged to seek to gain access to a larger instrument on which to give lessons to those pupils who were preparing for grade and diploma examinations in particular. Through the good offices of my friend, the late Ian Maxwell, a bank official, who was the Organist at St Mary's Parish Church on the Crumlin Road, I was granted permission by the Select Vestry to have regular use of the organ in that church for as long as might be necessary. (Little did any of us then know just how long that was going to be!) Every effort was made to facilitate me and my pupils who, of course, required extra practice on the organ prior to their examinations which were also held in the church. My prayers had been well and truly answered.

One of the youngest of my pupils at that time was Stephen Hamill from Larne in Co. Antrim, who came for lessons in 1966 when he was about ten years old. An exceptionally gifted boy who could play from memory and with a high degree of accuracy substantial excerpts from music he had previously heard only once, Stephen made rapid progress, achieving high distinctions in all grades of the examinations of the Associated Board of the Royal Schools of Music over the next two to three years. In each examination he chose to do the optional keyboard harmony rather than the normal aural tests which he found to be 'too easy'. Likewise, because he considered that the Ulster Boys' Springboard Diving Championship was not sufficiently challenging, he entered the Men's competition, duly winning it and beating his coach among others into the bargain. Examiners were unanimous in their praise of his musicianship with Michael Head, the well-known composer, describing him as a 'Wonder-child'. In June 1968, having been awarded the Norman Hay Scholarship for Musicianship earlier in the year at the Belfast Musical Festival, Stephen came second out of over a thousand candidates in the Associated Board grade eight examination with a mark of 145 out of a possible 150. This entitled him to compete for a scholarship to one of the leading London conservatoires. However, his father persuaded Stephen to follow in his footsteps by taking an engineering degree at Queen's

University in preparation for entry to the world of industry. He has held a number of church organist posts and has given recitals, sometimes featuring impressive improvisations, in various places including St Paul's Cathedral. In 1999 he co-founded the firm Phoenix Organs, now a well-known name in the UK and North America. Stephen is also Organist and Choir-master at St Peter's Parish Church, Belfast where he has been responsible for the rebuilding and enlargement of the organ (from two to four manuals) together with a radical revision of its specification.

Methodist College, Belfast, (familiarly known as 'Methody'), one of the largest co-educational grammar schools in the British Isles, has long been noted for its flourishing musical tradition. The installation in the school chapel of the old organ from Corpus Christi College, Cambridge (acquired through the good offices of Lord Dunleath) gave rise to a lively interest in organ-playing at Methody and there was a flood of enquiries about lessons. In 1967 I was very pleased to accept an invitation from Mr William McCay, Head of the Music Department, to become the school's first organ tutor and to be part of its exciting musical life until I was appointed to a full-time post in another school in the city some years later. The Foundation Organ Scholar at Methody was Maurice Maguire who, in the course of his subsequent career in broadcasting, has become well known as the producer of the popular BBC television programme, *Songs of Praise*. In 1975 the post of Organ Scholar was held jointly by Barry Douglas, who was later to become world-famous as a concert-pianist, and David Graham, now Professor in Charge of Organ at the RCM and Director of Music at Farm Street Church, Mayfair in London.

Because of the increasing number of candidates in the Junior and Senior (O and A level) Music Examinations, it had been found necessary in 1967 to appoint someone to assist Mr Tim Turner, the Schools Inspector and his colleague, Mr James Creighton, with the conduct of the practical tests. I was happy to accept an invitation from the Department of Education to act as the additional examiner, visiting schools throughout the province hearing playing and singing of what proved to be a variable standard. Performances were memorable for different reasons. The finest were given by young people who, in some cases, have continued to distinguish themselves in the course of their subsequent musical careers. At the other end of the scale was the Junior Certificate candidate who counted every beat aloud while she played her piano pieces. As a teacher, my instinctive reaction was to stop her, but, remembering that I was her examiner, I allowed her to continue. When she had finished, I asked her whether this practice had her teacher's approval. She said that her teacher had encouraged it and that it was now a well-established habit.

Tim Turner told me that on one occasion he had given a piece of sight-reading to a boy during a practical examination. While Tim was writing some comments he asked the boy to name the key. The answer came promptly, 'F, Sir.' Tim looked up to find that the piece was entitled 'Minuet in F'. Realising that, in his efforts to keep pace with his tight schedule, he had slipped up, he produced another piece without any such label. This time the same question was met with silence. Eventually the lad replied dejectedly, 'It doesn't say, Sir!'

I always looked forward to my visits to convents where standards were consistently high and the hospitality was excellent. Everything was done to ensure that the examiner was comfortable and at lunch-time one was treated to a meal worthy of a five-star hotel. This was sometimes served in a room in which one's sole company might be a life-size statue of the Blessed Virgin Mary.

Since I did not drive in those days, Heather (who would take the odd day off from her work as a social worker for the purpose) or my father would chauffeur me to those places which were not so readily accessible by public transport. I think that we all enjoyed these excursions in the spring of each year and in the course of them we made many new friends. The nuns of the St Louis Order, with whom I should later have a close association, were always welcoming especially when, in a few years' time, I was accompanied on some of my visits by both Heather and our baby daughter, Hannah.

Heather and I had arranged our wedding for Tuesday 6 August 1968

Harry and Heather on their wedding day, 6 August 1968, with their parents at Ballyholme Methodist Church in Bangor where Heather's parents were living in retirement. Heather's sister, Lindi and my younger sister, Norma, were the bridesmaids. The Revd Cecil Kerr, was my best man and Dr Raymond Reynolds, my groomsman. The Revd Herbert Irvine, Minister of Newtownards Methodist Church, to which Heather's family had originally belonged, officiated. Henrietta Moran mustered an *ad hoc* choir to lead the congregation in the hymns, Brenda Claney, a close friend of Heather's, sang a solo and Professor Philip Cranmer played the organ - a simple but nonetheless special service.

After a couple of days at 80 Stranmillis Gardens, Belfast, our new home, we set off for Donegal where we were to spend our honeymoon. We stayed for a week at Ardmore Guesthouse, Portnoo, situated on a cliff-top overlooking the Atlantic Ocean and the magnificent Naran Strand. The charge, all meals included, was £9 each which we paid separately. In our innocence we had assumed that in such a remote place as Donegal we would be able to find some privacy. However, we were soon to discover that that particular part of the county, with its superb beach, attracts large numbers of holiday-makers from Northern Ireland. Throughout our stay, therefore, we were constantly bumping into acquaintances.

People in general made the most of the sunshine of the summer of 1968 for they were very conscious of the dark cloud taking shape on the horizon with the first stirrings of political unrest in the province. On 5 October a Civil Rights march in Londonderry, resulting in a serious confrontation with the police which was probably its objective, is regarded as the beginning of the notorious 'Troubles'. These were to last for the next thirty years during which 3,523 people would be killed in a campaign of wanton carnage and destruction. All aspects of life would be seriously affected.

At the end of our short break in Donegal Heather and I returned to our house in Belfast. Friends had advised us to try to find a suitable property in the Stranmillis area because it is within easy reach of the centre of the city. Consequently, I am afraid that we had allowed this consideration to weigh too heavily in our hasty selection and, with hindsight, we realised that we should have been altogether more thorough in our researches and more balanced in our judgement.

Stranmillis Gardens, a cul-de-sac, is on a slope abutting on the Botanic Gardens, one of Belfast's public parks. Number eighty, the last house on the left-hand side, was separated from the park by a hedge. Although the previous owners were careful not to admit to it when we called to view the house, it is fairly certain that their reason for selling was that they had learnt that a huge recreation centre for the use of students and staff at Queen's University was soon to be built a short distance away in the Botanic Gardens. Presently a legion of workmen took over the site, a transformer parked on the other side of the hedge opposite our kitchen window ran noisily from 8.00a.m. each week-day and somewhere in excess of seven hundred piles were driven into the ground in the process of laying the foundations. At each blow of the huge hammer our little house shook. The vibrations also caused some subsidence in the locality. Once, in the course of a lesson, one of my piano pupils, a middle-aged lady, unable to contend any longer with the mighty metronome in the park, fled the house in great distress.

When, after a few years, the recreation centre was opened, users would frequently park their cars outside our house across the gateway. On returning home in the course of the evening and finding my access blocked (I was now driving), I should have to go to reception at the centre and request that the car-owners in question be called to move their vehicles. Some of these people, when they eventually appeared, would be quite abusive because I had dared to interrupt their recreation.

Nor was that the extent of our personal troubles. After persistently heavy rainfall we would find ourselves without gas due to the flooding of the old, porous pipes of the ancient system. This was a frequent occurrence. While a phone-call to the City's gas department would in due course bring someone to pump the water out of the system, it was some considerable time before the necessary repair was effected. Frustrating experiences of this sort forced us to conclude that our stay at 80 Stranmillis Gardens would be a temporary one and that we should have to seek our long-term home elsewhere in the city. In the meantime we decided to save Heather's monthly salary in the hope that when we moved in due course to a larger house we would avoid having to increase our mortgage.

Heather's membership of the Cathedral Consort gave the two of us the opportunity to participate jointly in an activity from which we derived great pleasure both musically and socially. Although it was never my intention to enter the Consort for competitions, the offer in 1968 of a prize of £1,000 (a very considerable amount in those days) by the Peter Stuyvesant Foundation to the winning choir in a major choral competition which it was sponsoring proved to be too attractive to ignore. Accordingly one Saturday afternoon the Consort was in the Wellington Hall in Belfast competing against thirteen other choirs from various parts of Ireland. Although the standard was high, I was convinced that our performance of Debussy's technically challenging *Trois Chansons de Charles d'Orléans* was such that the Consort would be among those contestants recalled to sing in the final of the competition that evening. In the event and to my dismay, the adjudicator, while recognising the quality of the Consort's performance, said that he was obliged to dismiss it from his reckoning on account of the significance of the contralto solo element (superbly sung by Isabel Moran) in the second song. This decision served only to reinforce my misgivings about competitions in which there is a single adjudicator. The winners in both 1968 and 1969 were the excellent Lindsay Singers from Dublin under the skilled direction of Ethne Barror who, forty years on, continues to inspire those choirs which are in her charge.

Some time later the Consort was invited to represent Northern Ireland in the Mixed-Voice Class of *Let the Peoples Sing*, an international choral competition organised and broadcast by the BBC. In the second round, we had the misfortune to come up against the ultimate winner, the Blackburn Bach Choir, conducted by John Bertalot who was then the Organist at Blackburn Cathedral. Since this admirably disciplined choir, with a membership of almost thirty, was twice the size of the Cathedral Consort, the contest was perhaps somewhat unequal. At any rate, the Consort gave a very good account of itself in a rousing motet, *Cantantibus Organis,* by Peter Philips, despite its lack of the tonal resources ideally required, and Gustav Holst's masterly arrangement of the old Cornish folk-song, *I love my Love.* The Consort's 'beautiful, natural' performance of the latter, an exceptionally difficult piece, evidently appealed to the panel of adjudicators (Sir Thomas Armstrong, Alan Percival and David Willcocks). It was encouraging to learn that the result had been close, a fact which confirmed that the Consort could hold its own at this exalted level.

It was in 1969 that the Ulster Orchestra began its association with the Cathedral and its choirs. Founded three years earlier as a full-time professional body to replace the City of Belfast Orchestra, the Ulster Orchestra's first conductor was Maurice Miles. Janos Fürst, its first leader, later became Associate Conductor. From 1967-69 the post of Principal Conductor was held by Sergiu Comissiona, a Romanian-born American. One of the world's most widely-travelled conductors, he was a welcome guest with orchestras around the world. Comissiona was renowned as an orchestra-builder. During the time that he was in charge of the Baltimore Symphony Orchestra, from 1969 to 1984, he raised its status to 'world class'. In the opinion of Stephen Cera, the music critic of the *Baltimore Sun*, Comissiona was 'a tremendously gifted, "born" conductor with a decidedly unorthodox technique … his acute ear for subtly nuanced orchestral sound distinguished his finest performances. [He had] an almost alchemical ability to transform the dry ink of musical notation into bewitching sound images'. This ability was manifest in a performance of Vaughan Williams's *Flos Campi*, given by the Cathedral Consort, the Ulster Orchestra and Brian Mack (viola) under Comissiona's direction in the course of a concert in the Ulster Hall on 23 January 1969. It was fascinating to see and hear this magician conjuring from the Orchestra sounds which seemed to be beyond the powers of most other conductors to achieve.

On Maundy Thursday, the Ulster Orchestra conducted this time by Janos Fürst, was back at the Cathedral. As well as singing Palestrina's *Stabat Mater* (under my direction), the Consort also joined the Orchestra and two local soloists, Norma Armstrong (soprano) and Eileen Gavin(contralto) in Pergolesi's setting of the same text. In a third concert at the Cathedral in December, the Consort combined with the Ulster Orchestra, under Edgar Cosma who was making his first appearance as Principal Conductor, in Bach's *Cantata No. 140 : Wachet auf!* and Vaughan Williams's *Fantasia on Christmas Carols.* The Consort also sang a group of unaccompanied carols including the delightful sixteenth century Spanish *Riu, riu, chiu,* John Gould's haunting setting of the *Sans Day Carol* and John Gardner's infectiously rhythmic *When Christ was born of Mary free.*

One of the special events organised in 1969 to mark the centenary of St Mary's Parish Church was an organ recital given by Christopher Dearnley, the Organist of St Paul's Cathedral in London. The Cathedral Consort was asked to contribute two groups of unaccompanied choral items to the programme. Afterwards, Mr Dearnley, who was also the current president of The Incorporated Association of Organists, invited me to take one of the four rehearsals of the Congress Choir at the Association's Annual Congress in London the following year.

The Consort shared a BBC Northern Ireland broadcast in the *Music Making* series with the distinguished Ulster flautist, James Galway who, accompanied by Havelock Nelson, played Hindemith's Sonata for flute and piano. The choral items were Palestrina's *Missa Brevis* and the *Five English Folk-songs* arr. Vaughan Williams. We also included the Palestrina in our first public recital in Dublin on 25 April 1969 at Christ Church, Leeson Park. In this, the second of three recitals devised by David McConnell, the Organist of the Church, under the general title: *Et Resurrexit - Music after Easter,* the Consort also sang a group of Tudor anthems and motets as well as music by Purcell accompanied by David Lee, the Organist of St Bartholomew's Parish Church, Clyde Road, Dublin who was to give the final recital of the series. Writing in the *Irish Times,* Charles Acton, the doyen of Irish music critics, complimented the Consort on 'its accomplished performances, the blend and balance of the voices and the excellence of the diction throughout'. Another critic, mindful of the trying conditions currently being experienced by those of us living north of the Border, commented thoughtfully, 'The background of recent events lent a poignant quality to the music and one could only wish that the day will come when we and our compatriots in the north-east will find unity at least in warm friendship'.

The onset of the 'Troubles' in 1968 had a marked effect on my recruitment of boys for the Cathedral Choir. In the prevailing conditions it was to be expected that some parents would be unwilling to allow their sons to come to the Cathedral which is situated in an area of the city where explosions and other terrorist outrages were not infrequent occurrences with damage to the stained glass windows being unavoidable. In an effort to preserve our tradition, therefore, I was sometimes obliged to accept boys who were not as musically responsive as I should have wished. As a result, the maintenance of the high standards we had set ourselves required even greater effort on my part. Throughout those gloomy years the members of the choir, boys and adults, were the very epitome of loyalty. Nor must one forget the wonderfully supportive parents who made every effort to have their sons at the Cathedral punctually for rehearsals and services.

Few people in Great Britain can have had even the remotest idea of how difficult life was in Belfast at that time. Indeed, the younger generation of Northern Ireland residents would know little or nothing about it. The flow of traffic could often be held up several times a day because explosions or bomb-scares, of which there were hundreds, had entailed diversions away from the affected areas. Traffic was also liable to be halted by the security forces for random checks. Attendance at rehearsals frequently suffered. If a bomb-scare occurred while we were rehearsing in the Cathedral we usually took refuge in the Stygian depths of the crypt where we endeavoured to continue to the accompaniment of a low G sharp drone emitted by a transformer housed there.

One Saturday morning in winter, with an ABC film unit due to record Matins the following day for distribution in the USA, the boys and I were forced to spend the whole of our precious rehearsal time in a snow-covered street nearby while we awaited the all clear. When, after a considerable delay, this had still not been given, we adjourned to a café where we consoled ourselves with the chorister's favourite delicacy - sausages and chips. One could multiply instances of this sort of frustration. Apart from the problems posed by civil disturbances, the situation was compounded by the upheaval caused at the Cathedral by the protracted building of the south transept. Although, at times, the sheer multiplicity of the adverse conditions threatened to overwhelm, one continued to go forward resolutely in faith. There was nothing for it but to 'keep on keeping on', as one of my friends neatly put it.

As far as possible our normal schedule was maintained, with the choristers' rehearsals on Tuesdays after school and on Saturday mornings when the probationers and the Young Men's Choir also met. For a time, when the level of violence was particularly high, the weekly full rehearsal on a Wednesday evening was brought forward to an earlier hour to enable everyone to return home before the bombers and gunmen went into action under cover of darkness. Anyone then on the streets of Belfast at night was putting his or her life in peril.

Belfast Cathedral was one of the first churches in Ireland to adopt the Choristers' Training Scheme which had been introduced by the RSCM in December 1965. This scheme provided boys (and girls) with a structured course calculated not only to improve their musical skills but also to increase their understanding of the liturgy. Beginning at Probationer level, the chorister could gain promotion to the levels of Junior and then Senior Singing Boy. At each level, a boy had to pass a series of tests, with his successes being recorded on a card, before he could graduate to the next level. The best candidates aspired to the achievement of the ultimate goal, the St Nicholas Junior Award. On Saturday mornings the Cathedral was a hive of activity as eager boys arrived early to try to notch up another pass or two, the head choristers testing those at Probationer level, while those at the higher levels came to the Assistant Organist or to me. The Vicar Choral dealt with the liturgical aspect of the course.

The quite advanced examination for the St Nicholas Junior Award was conducted by an external examiner who issued a detailed report. Some members of the Young Men's Choir who had gained this Award were successful in the examination for the St Nicholas Senior Award which was introduced later by the RSCM. By January 1976, when I left the Cathedral, boys and young men had gained between them a total of nineteen St Nicholas Junior and Senior awards which, I believe, was something of a record at that time.

Most of our choristers always attended the RSCM residential courses, directed by Mr Donald Leggatt, which were usually held in Armagh, the first of these being at Easter 1969. Over the years a number of both boys and young men were selected to take part in RSCM cathedral courses at Westminster Abbey, Coventry, Wells, Canterbury and York. John Bertalot and Paul Hale, now Director of Music at Southwell Minster, have told me how delighted they invariably were with the enthusiastic participation and responsiveness of our representatives.

Boys always relish responsibility and it seemed to me important that our choristers be given their heads. At first this meant an anthem for trebles only occasionally at Matins or Evensong, but later their ever-growing confidence allowed them to essay Evensong entirely on their own and it gave them great pleasure to do this from time to time.

The year 1970, which was to prove to be significant in the history of Belfast Cathedral, began with the service of consecration of our Dean,

Dean Crooks (right) with the Revd John Nolan, Harry and three of the Cathedral Choristers: (from the left) Michael James, Stephen Geoghegan and Adrian McCartney

Cuthbert Peacocke, as Bishop of Derry and Raphoe, and Archdeacon George Quin, Rector of Bangor Parish Church, as Bishop of Down and Dromore. With the building project well behind schedule and in dire need of reappraisal, it was imperative that the appointment of Dean Peacocke's successor should not be delayed. Never had it been more important that the right man be chosen to occupy this key position.

The Venerable Samuel Bennett Crooks who, as the first Rector of the new St John's Parish Church, Orangefield in Belfast had overseen its construction, was, for the seven years before he came to Belfast Cathedral, in charge of Shankill Parish, Lurgan which was then reputed to be the largest in Ireland. He therefore brought to his latest appointment considerable and valuable experience as well as abundant energy and Churchillian courage. As indicated earlier (Chapter 6), his radical and realistic approach to the exceedingly difficult situation which he inherited proved to be decisive. Indeed Bishop Arthur Butler's apt choice of title for his funeral tribute to Dean Crooks at the service in the Cathedral in 1986 elegantly encapsulated what was a truly outstanding achievement against all the odds: *Si monumentum requiris, circumspice* ('If you seek [his] monument, look around you').

Prior to Dean Crooks's arrival, I had had some misgivings about how he, with his rather forthright manner, and I might interact. After Matins on his first Sunday at the Cathedral, he made what appeared to me to be a rather derogatory comment with regard to some aspect of the music at the service. Having discussed the matter with Heather over lunch, I decided to phone the Dean and arrange a meeting with him after Evensong. I went to see him in his office where I expressed my hope that he and I would have a good relationship. However, I felt that I ought to make him aware that I had found his comment that morning hurtful because, as he would discover, I was totally committed to the maintenance of a worthy musical tradition at the Cathedral. His reply was typical of the man: 'Harry, I am going to say two things to you: firstly, never pay any attention to what I say and, secondly, you will find that I will be the best friend you ever had'. We shook hands and from that moment onwards we never had another contretemps.

When I was learning to drive the Dean said that he knew ideal places where one might practise the various manoeuvres. He selected the steepest gradient in the countryside for hill-starts and for three-point turns he recommended the open area at the entrance to the Roselawn Crematorium. Passing the Crematorium one day after I had passed the test, I noticed that, in the interim, some large, concrete flower containers had been strategically placed to discourage other learner-drivers from following my example.

Dean Crooks fully understood the importance of music both as an aid to worship and, in its wider context, as a means of promoting the Cathedral at a time when he was trying to raise the vast sum necessary to complete the building. He gave me virtually a free hand to continue to develop the programme on which I had embarked at my appointment and was unfailingly supportive and encouraging. Among other things, he arranged for the construction of a tiered platform which could be erected at the west end of the Cathedral to accommodate the choir when choral and orchestral concerts were being presented. Whenever I needed anything, I had only to ask. I cannot recall any of my requests, which I hope were always reasonable, being refused. Apropos of anthems with Latin texts, he was wholly in favour of them and agreed that we should print translations on the service sheets for the information of the congregation. I asked him what he would say to those who said that they did not approve of Latin anthems. His response was immediate, 'I shall simply say: " There are, of course, those who do!"'

Although we were both contending with a considerable amount of stress in the course of our work, we enjoyed one another's company and indulged in a fair amount of banter. The Dean was amused to discover that our exchanges were sometimes misinterpreted by visiting clergy as being indicative of a mutual disrespect!

As far as the Cathedral Choir was concerned, the major musical event of 1970 was the performance of Bach's *St John Passion* given in conjunction with the Ulster Orchestra in the Cathedral on 26 March. This was my first opportunity to conduct the Orchestra and I made sure that I was thoroughly prepared. The soloists were Norma Gray-Wilson, Valerie Boulard and Harold Gray with Paul Taylor, a former Choral Scholar at King's College, Cambridge as the Evangelist. (Paul, a charming fellow with a mellifluous tenor voice, had sung with the King's Choir in its recording of the work under David Willcocks.) He told me that when, at our full rehearsal, he heard the Cathedral Choir's first chord, he knew that the performance would be a good one. Reviews of the concert would suggest that this prediction was borne out, with Evan John, in *The Irish News*, declaring that it had been 'the most consistently professional and agreeable-sounding performance of the *St John Passion* to be given in Belfast in recent years.'

I also conducted the Ulster Orchestra later in the year when it combined with the Cathedral Consort in a concert of Christmas music at the Cathedral in mid-December. The programme included Parts 1 and 2 of Bach's *Christmas Oratorio,* Philip Langridge (tenor) taking the role of the Evangelist, and Vaughan Williams's ever-popular *Fantasia on Christmas Carols.* The Orchestra was heard on its own in Corelli's *Christmas Concerto* while the Consort sang a group of unaccompanied carols.

In October 1970 the Consort appeared as the 'Harry Grindle Chorale' in a concert in the Ulster Hall with the soprano, Marion Studholme, and the Ulster Orchestra conducted by Eric Robinson. This concert, entitled *Music for You,* after Mr Robinson's radio and television series, attracted a large audience to hear a selection of favourite items from the light classical repertoire. The Consort sang a selection of part-songs including Aaron Copland's *I bought me a Cat* and Stanford's *Shall we go dance?* and *The Blue Bird* as well as arrangements à la Ward Swingle. I note that patrons were invited to 'come early in order to avoid queuing' and that the admission charges ranged from £1 to 7/6 (i.e.37½p). As 'The Singers in Consort' we took part in a live broadcast of *Friday Night is Music Night* on BBC Radio 2 with the BBC Northern Ireland Orchestra (conducted by Kenneth Alwyn), the Band of the Irish Guards *et al* in the Town Hall, Ballymena. This time the Consort sang *Dance to your Daddy* arr. David Stone, *My Lagan Love* arr. Philip Cranmer and *Polly wolly doodle* arr. Stanford Robinson.

The Consort also shared a programme in the BBC (network) choral series, *Sing we at Pleasure*, with The Lindsay Singers from Dublin and gave a performance of James Wilson's Tom *o'Bedlam* as well as of a group of madrigals in the *Music at Night* series on BBC Northern Ireland. The accompaniment in *Tom o'Bedlam* was provided by Derek Bell (harp), Edward Teare (percussion) and Havelock Nelson (piano). Other engagements undertaken by the Cathedral Consort in 1970 included a concert in the lovely council chamber at Bangor Town Hall, a programme of music for Lent and Passiontide (with Donald Davison, organ) which included Bach's motet *Jesu, meine Freude* at Bangor Abbey, and at Down Cathedral a recital of Music for Advent which afforded me the opportunity to play some pieces on the fine Harrison organ in one of my favourite locations.

There were two further Choral Evensong broadcasts, in January and October 1970, from St Mary's Parish Church by the Cathedral Choir. Correspondents, as well as commenting appreciatively on what they had heard, would sometimes express a particular interest in a new piece. A lady wrote from Didcot in Berkshire after the first of these broadcasts requesting a copy of my arrangement of *Love came down at Christmas* which the Choir had sung as an introit. In another kind letter after the second one she said, 'We are all in St Peter's Choir looking forward to singing your lovely harmonies this year in *Love came down at Christmas*. It will also be sung by St Frideswide's Secondary Modern Girls' School. They learnt the soprano and alto lines last week - I put in the tenor (yes, my voice is rather low - a change from my teens when I could sing [top] B flat - am now 61!). I believe the school caretaker will put in the bass eventually...'

Mr Bernard Kedge, at one time a colleague of Donald Leggatt's on the teaching staff at St Edmund's School, Canterbury was always keen to add some of my Anglican chants to the hundreds of others which he had collected over the previous fifty years. 'I never cease to marvel that human ingenuity can *still* produce new musical gems of such variety in the space of 14 bars!'

The threat by the BBC authorities to discontinue the *Choral Evensong* series of broadcasts gave rise to an angry protest on the part of its numerous devotees. My friend, Victor Henry and I decided that, in support of this campaign, we would organise the collection of signatures to a petition for presentation to the BBC. On St Patrick's Day, 17 March 1970, therefore, when the streets of Belfast were crowded with shoppers (despite the efforts of the terrorists), a stall and large notice, bearing the slogan: **SAVE CHORAL EVENSONG,** were set up at the entrance to the Bank Buildings. Throughout the day, relays of choristers, dressed in their cassocks, Eton collars and bows, were on duty to supervise and, indeed, encourage the signing of the petition. It gave us all a great deal of satisfaction to learn later that our effort had helped to secure the future of what is, for many listeners, one of the highlights of the week's broadcasting.

In the course of 1970 the Dean and I had discussions with Professor Raymond Warren about the possible creation of an Organ Scholarship by the Queen's University and the Cathedral acting jointly. Apart from establishing a link between the two institutions, such a scheme would provide the Cathedral Organist with an assistant. Tenure of the scholarship would be for a period of three years with the holder's salary being paid by the Cathedral Board. No doubt the increasing preoccupation with fund-raising for the completion of the building caused this project to be abandoned.

It was Dean Crooks who promoted the concept of the Cathedral as belonging to the entire city - 'Belfast Cathedral' rather than 'St Anne's Cathedral, Belfast', as it had hitherto been generally known. He was always happy to make the building available for such events as school carol services and major concerts which must have brought many thousands through its doors over the years. Above all he was very proud of the standing of the Cathedral Choir and he heartily endorsed the continuing extension of its role on the local and national musical scene.

CHAPTER EIGHT

1971-72 | BELFAST CATHEDRAL, ST LOUIS SISTERS' CHOIR

Far from curtailing our musical activity at the Cathedral, the 'Troubles' seemed to have the effect of spurring us on to greater efforts. Whereas the Cathedral Choir had previously given a short recital of appropriate church music on certain special occasions e.g. Palm Sunday, Easter Day, Harvest Thanksgiving, etc. it was decided, with the enthusiastic encouragement of the Dean, that, from the beginning of 1971, such a recital should replace the sermon at Evensong on one Sunday in the month. Billy Adair introduced this new series in an article in the *Church of Ireland Gazette* setting out the plan for the coming year and both he and Victor Henry kept this latest development in the Cathedral's music programme before the public in their regular reports in the *Gazette* and the *Cathedral Magazine*.

As it happened we did have a speaker, who had already been booked, on 31 January when the choir sang a group of Epiphany anthems after the third collect. This was The Right Revd Trevor Huddleston CR, the Bishop of Stepney and a leading anti-apartheid campaigner. The presence of such a famous figure no doubt added to our congregation. The music of Lent was featured in February and March. A sequence of penitential readings and anthems, among them S S Wesley's affecting *Wash me throughly,* was scheduled for 28 February, while on Sunday 21 March the service was preceded by performances of a Handel Sonata and a work by Edmund Rubbra given by James Middleton (recorder) accompanied, on Lord Dunleath's harpsichord, by Keith Rogers. The choral music included Allegri's *Miserere, The Ways of Zion do mourn* by Michael Wise, and Herbert Howells's *Like as the Hart,* in many respects the quintessence of the composer's individual style. The soloist in the Allegri was Stephen Geoghegan whose astonishing ability to probe accurately the vocal stratosphere allowed him to produce the top Cs with ease. The service on Palm Sunday took the form of a devotion for choir and congregation entitled *The Cross of Christ* and Easter Sunday was celebrated appropriately with the seasonal music from Handel's *Messiah*. In the absence of an Assistant Organist on these occasions, I was fortunate to be able to avail myself of the expert services as accompanists of Victor Henry and Donald Davison, a leading businessman and senior academic respectively. (Both were, in addition, organists in important city churches.) Indeed, I had hoped that Donald might be able to join me at the Cathedral on a regular basis but with his university and other musical commitments he was not in a position to do so. However, I think that he derived some satisfaction from his association with the music of the Cathedral for he was always ready to help us when he was available. Donald was the organist for several of our Choral Evensong broadcasts and listeners were very appreciative of his playing, especially of his sensitive and imaginative accompaniment of the psalms.

Music for Whitsunday included anthems by Tallis, *The Wilderness* by S S Wesley and Raymond Warren's *Come Holy Ghost*. Similarly varied selections of items were also presented on 27 June and 19 September. For the Harvest Festival in October Maurice Greene's popular anthem *Thou visitest the Earth* (in Francis Jackson's edition) was followed by John Travers's rarely-heard *Ascribe unto the Lord*, *Oculi omnium* by Charles Wood and finally Gustav Holst's suitably climactic setting of Psalm 148: *Lord, Who hast made us for Thine own*. With the Advent Carol Service now a familiar feature of the Cathedral calendar in November and the Carol Services at Christmas, devotees of church music could hear in the course of a year a conspectus of the entire repertoire. Depending on the security situation in the city attendances could, naturally, vary to some degree but it was heartening that, on Christmas Eve, despite the lack of public transport, military checks and an explosion in the vicinity, a congregation of about 900 people gathered in the Cathedral.

The launch of a new series of Ulster Orchestra concerts entitled *Music in the Cathedral* was, in itself, recognition of the significance of the building as a concert venue. With the audience facing the west end where the orchestra and, on occasion, the choir were sited, the west wall was an effective reflector of the sound. Although it has to be admitted that the acoustic poses problems as far as the achievement of a good orchestral balance is concerned, it does enhance the quality of choral sound which must nevertheless be well projected with very clear enunciation if the words are to carry.

With Havelock Nelson's Ulster Singers having established proprietorial rights, as it were, to Bach's *St Matthew Passion* through their tradition of annual performances of the work, I opted for the *St John* again at the Cathedral in April 1971. This time two members of the Cathedral Consort, Frieda Graham and Isabel Moran, were the female soloists with

Paul Taylor and Harold Gray repeating their successes of the previous year.

Another concert in which I conducted the Ulster Orchestra took place in the Cathedral in November. The programme consisted of Haydn's *Symphony No 100 ('The Military')* and Mozart's *Divertimento (K 136)* for strings, with the Cathedral Choir joining the orchestra in Purcell's verse-anthem, *O sing unto the Lord* and Handel's stirring *Zadok the Priest*. The Choir also sang a group of unaccompanied anthems which included Gibbons's jubilant *Hosanna to the Son of David* and *O clap your Hands* as well as the intensely moving *When David heard* by Tomkins and *Justorum Animae* by Byrd. Evan John, *The Irish Times* music critic, summed up this concert as follows: 'Music of high quality, efficiently performed, left a pleasing impression on a large audience.'

Since Kodaly's *Psalmus Hungaricus* has been rarely performed in Northern Ireland, it was disappointing that more people did not take the opportunity to hear the work when it was given by the Cathedral Choir and the Ulster Orchestra conducted by Janos Fürst in the course of a concert in the Ulster Hall in May 1971. John Minchinson, was the tenor soloist.

As a statement of solidarity with my colleague, Martin White, at Armagh (Church of Ireland) Cathedral and his loyal choir, the choir of Belfast Cathedral and I visited Armagh in March 1971 for an Evensong in which the two choirs joined forces. The choirs each sang three anthems before combining in Parry's setting of verses from Psalm 122 : *I was glad*, which, with the large number of singers taking part, sounded especially thrilling on this occasion. A collection was taken for the RSCM to which both choirs are affiliated.

For a number of years the Ulster Orchestra was led by Meyer Stolow, a Canadian-born musician who had previously been co-leader of the London Mozart Players. Through our collaboration in various concerts we discovered that we shared similar artistic ideals and we became firm friends. One day early in 1971 Meyer and I met with James Allaway, the manager of the orchestra to discuss a proposal which Meyer had put forward. This was the setting up of a choral and instrumental body expressly for the performance of Baroque music. The suggestion was that the Cathedral Consort would combine with an ensemble of interested musicians drawn, as required, from the ranks of the Ulster Orchestra. It was evident to us all that there was a role for such a specialist group on the Northern Ireland musical scene and we eagerly looked forward to its exciting and fulfilling future. Unfortunately, shortly afterwards, Meyer Stolow was appointed to the post of co-leader of the Orchestra of the Royal Opera House, Covent Garden and with his departure went any likelihood of the realisation of our cherished dream. Alas, too, at about the same time, a serious disagreement about policy arose between the men of the Cathedral Consort and me. After a considerable investment of time and effort (voluntarily) on my part over the previous five years during which the Consort had enjoyed great success, I was left with no option but to resign as the group's conductor.

Donald Leggatt, the RSCM's Northern Ireland Commissioner and chairman of its regional committee on which I had served for a number of years, took a kindly interest in my well-being, giving me every encouragement and support. He asked me whether, after the past seven very demanding years at St Anne's Cathedral and in view of the ongoing 'Troubles', I had given any consideration to a move 'across the water.' The route to the post of Director of Music, as it is now generally known, at an English cathedral has traditionally been via an Oxford or Cambridge organ scholarship and/or a cathedral assistantship. At thirty-five and without a foot already on that particular ladder, I reckoned that it was probably unrealistic to harbour further ambitions in that field. At any rate, being married and with Heather expecting our first child, I would no doubt be better advised to seek a position offering a decent salary and the prospect of being able to spend some precious 'quality' time with my family. The lot of a cathedral organist's wife can be a very lonely one.

Consequently, I applied for the post of Director of Music at a public school which, in view of what transpired, had better remain nameless. The Headmaster contacted me to say that he intended to interview another applicant and me before coming to a decision and asked me to come with Heather to the school the following week. We hurriedly arranged flights and Victor Henry willingly agreed to look after my Sunday duties at the Cathedral. On the Saturday morning I received an exceedingly apologetic phone call from the Headmaster. He explained that he was due to retire at the end of the current school year when he would be succeeded by a senior house-master at another public school. This gentleman, overriding the official selection process, had taken it upon himself to appoint one of his friends. The incumbent Headmaster told me, that if it were any consolation, he had every intention of appointing me, as the strongest candidate, to the post. I am still puzzled by that episode and have often wondered whether the incoming Headmaster was within his rights to act as he did.

At about this time I had also applied for the new post of Music Officer with the Arts Council of Northern Ireland (ACNI). At the interview I was asked whether I thought it likely that ACNI would appoint to this purely administrative post someone who was as actively involved on the local musical scene as myself. I replied that I had assumed that it might be possible to hold the post of Cathedral Organist and this new one simultaneously. When it appeared that I was not being regarded as a serious contender for the post of Music Officer, I withdrew. The following day I received a phone call from the chairman of the panel at the previous day's interview who said that, after further deliberation, he and his colleagues would be prepared to discuss with me the possibility of an arrangement which would enable me to hold both posts. However, having given the matter further thought and having come to the conclusion that I already had more than enough administration to do, I declined the offer.

Janos Fürst, Associate Conductor with the Ulster Orchestra, had attended the International Summer Course for Orchestral Conductors held at Monte Carlo and, having derived a great deal of benefit from it, he strongly recommended that I should follow his example. With a grant from ACNI to cover my expenses, I spent September 1971 in the company of about sixty other aspiring conductors who had come from all corners of the world to learn more about their craft from the famous naturalised Italian maestro, Igor Markevich and his professional staff. Markevich's Russian birth was manifest in his characteristically rigorous approach which guaranteed that all aspects of the course, based at the Monte Carlo Opera, were highly organised and that the training was thorough. The opening days were dedicated exclusively to theoretical matters and technique by way of preparation for the practical sessions with the Monte Carlo Opera Orchestra which were to follow.

Like many other great conductors Markevich emphasised the importance of economy of movement, with each gesture having an extremely precise meaning. He was insistent that when we took our turns to face the orchestra we would do so without a score. We had all noted that no desk had been provided! Access to the podium was denied those who were not prepared to conduct from memory. Bearing in mind that the course syllabus covered a range of music from overtures and other shorter orchestral works to Beethoven's Ninth Symphony, it was hardly surprising that the really serious students found themselves with little time for either socialising or sight-seeing.

For one hour every morning we had to submit ourselves to the equally strict régime of the quite extraordinary Dr Mosche Feldenkreis. I can do no better than translate the description of him which appeared in a Monte Carlo newspaper: 'A crown of unruly hair like Ben Gurion on a small but sturdily-built and incredibly agile body, the sparkling eyes of a Rubinstein, a harsh-sounding voice but an assured delivery in almost any language.' In the course of a colourful and varied career, Feldenkreis had been, among other things, a builder, a guerrilla, a physicist, a secret agent and a judo practitioner. In his book, *La Conscience du Corps* ('Body-awareness') he advances the startling theory that we are making use of a mere five per cent of both our mental and physical resources. He was a hard task-master, whose exercise routine was designed to help us to realise more of this dormant potential. His polyglot swearing left a lasting impression on everyone!

Like Sir Adrian Boult, Maestro Markevich regarded as anathema any undue flamboyance on the part of a conductor. He put faithfulness to the score and a mastery of its details at the top of his list of priorities. When some of his protégés were in danger of being carried away on a surge of youthful exuberance, he was quick to intervene with a reminder that, while this sort of display may appeal to the gallery, it has little effect on experienced orchestral musicians. All those who attended this course were of the opinion that we had been fortunate to sit at the feet of such a master of the art of conducting whose practice was informed not only by the breadth of his international experience in this field but also by his earlier activities as both a concert pianist and a composer.

Early in 1971, in the course of my travels as an examiner for the Department of Education, I had visited the St Louis Grammar School in Ballymena. Here, the music teacher, Sr Mary Finan, sought my help in the implementation of a proposal which was currently before the governing body of the St Louis Order. The Order's Secretary-General, Sr Paul Byron, had just returned to Ireland after a period of service in the USA where she had taken part in some of the choral workshops which are such a popular musical activity there. Sr Paul was keen to introduce this concept to the St Louis nuns because it would bring them together from time to time from their far-flung convents as well as giving their meetings a specific focus. While providing recreation for all, it was thought that those nuns who were music-teachers would derive benefit from singing under the direction of an experienced choir-trainer.

Hence, one Saturday in October 1971, I joined a company of about a hundred nuns at the St Louis Convent at Rathmines in Dublin. This was to be the first of many such meetings, with rehearsal sessions on both Saturday and Sunday. Hospitality was, as usual, of the highest standard. At each convent I was accommodated in the room set aside for the use of any priest who came to officiate at Mass. Beside the bed there was always a table stocked with every imaginable form of liquid refreshment.

Our repertoire consisted of an attractive, tailor-made Mass for three-part upper voices, strings and two horns by Michael Haydn, a younger brother of Joseph, Pergolesi's *Stabat Mater* and a selection of motets and anthems. It was expected that the work done at our rehearsals would be supplemented by private study on the part of the nuns. Our first goal was a concert, a purely domestic affair, at the convent in Monaghan some months later and for this a scratch orchestra was assembled with peripatetic instrumental teachers among others being pressed into service. In addition to choral music, the programme included an organ concerto by J G Walther and Boëllmann's *Suite Gothique* played by the distinguished Dublin organist, Gerard Gillen on an Allen Computer Organ which we had hired for the occasion. The choir gave such a good account of itself that I felt it deserved a better orchestral accompaniment. I therefore approached Beaty Cromie, the Ulster Orchestra's current manager, to ask if the orchestra might be prepared to collaborate with us. We found a vacant slot in the orchestra's schedule in February 1973 and duly organised a concert to take place at St Macartan's Roman Catholic Cathedral in Monaghan. This time, in addition to the music performed at the choir's debut, the programme included Bach's *Brandenburg Concerto No. 3 in G* and Handel's *Organ Concerto in F Op. 4 No.4* in which the soloist was Gerard Gillen who again played an Allen Computer Organ. The soloists in the Michael Haydn *Mass* were Mary Sheridan and June Croker both of whom were from Dublin.

People came from far and wide to fill the cathedral, the audience totalling well over a thousand. Robert Johnson, the music critic of the *Irish Press*, in his column the following day hailed the concert as 'a milestone

The St Louis Sisters' Choir in rehearsal for their concert in St Macartan's Cathedral, Monaghan in February 1973 with Gerard Gillen at the organ

in the history of music in Ireland outside Dublin'. Gerard Gillen was so impressed by the event and its obvious success that he urged me to try to arrange for a repeat performance in the capital. This took place in October 1973 in the Examination Hall at Trinity College where it was enthusiastically received by another capacity audience which included a number of Dublin's leading musicians. The nuns were particularly proud that the soprano soloist on this occasion was Ann Murray, one of their former Monaghan school-pupils, who was at that time at the beginning of what was to prove to be a highly successful career on the operatic stage. In fact she was destined to be created a DBE by the Queen in 2002. For this concert we had the use of a positive (pipe-) organ made by the Dublin organ-builder, Kenneth Jones. A beautiful example of Mr Jones's superb craftsmanship, and a joy to both eye and ear, this instrument was one of the concert's 'stars', with Gerard Gillen making the most of its resources particularly in his performance of the Handel concerto.

Charles Acton, in *The Irish Times*, could scarcely have been more complimentary: 'I have never heard a choir with such marvellous diction - and that means real care to project the whole work. Their intonation was impeccable. The phrases rose and fell, harmonically and melodically, with a musical delight. Their tone was sweet and lively and yet full. They deserved the highest praise and, if they are spread throughout the country teaching, we may be full of hope. The repertory of good, suitable works for female choir is limited: I hope they will put us further in their debt by commissioning music from such as Bodley, Potter, Sweeney or other Irish Composers.'

I was very sorry indeed that my later appointment to a full-time teaching post meant that I had to resign as the conductor of the St Louis Sisters' Choir. Our association had been an exceedingly happy one from a purely social point of view as well as being fulfilling musically. My successor, Eric Sweeney, the noted Irish composer, would extend the range of the choir's repertoire to include more modern works among them some of his own compositions.

The fact of my being a Protestant and, indeed, the son of an Orangeman, had not in any way affected my relationship with this large group of Roman Catholic nuns who regarded me as a friend, showing me every kindness and consideration. The elderly Sisters, who came to look on me as a surrogate nephew, were especially solicitous for my welfare, insisting that I take adequate rest during our week-ends of concentrated rehearsal. We all shared a Christian faith and a love of music and it is evident from the many letters which I received from members of the choir following my resignation as its conductor that they felt that their lives had been enriched by the experience which they had enjoyed over the previous two years.

Meanwhile, back in Belfast, it was a case of 'business as usual'. In June 1971 there was another broadcast of Evensong by the Cathedral Choir from St Mary's Parish Church with Donald Davison playing the organ. We were all again greatly encouraged by the response of listeners many of whom wondered how such standards were maintained without a choir-school and in the prevailing circumstances. We were moved to learn that they sympathised with us in our plight and that they joined their prayers to ours for 'a happy issue out of all our afflictions'.

In May, Ian Maxwell arranged a concert by some of 'Ulster's 1971 Young Music-Makers' in St Mary's Parish Church, where he was the Organist, to provide a platform for the Choir of Campbell College, Belfast, conducted by Donald Leggatt and four of my organ pupils who were currently having the use of the organ in the church. The centrepiece of the programme was a fine performance of Byrd's *Mass for Five Voices* by the Campbell Choir. A wide range of music was covered by the four organists. Rosemary Collins, who was then reading Spanish and Music at Queen's University and who already held an LTCL Performer's Diploma for organ, opened the concert with a chorale prelude by J L Krebs and Bach's *Fantasia in G (BWV 572)*. Incidentally, in due course, Rosemary married Peter Hunter who had been one of my choristers at Belfast Cathedral in the mid-1960s. Peter has been for a number of years Organist and Choirmaster at St Mark's, Dundela, Belfast, where Rosemary acts as his assistant.

Brendan O'Hare played Bach's chorale prelude, *O Mensch, bewein' dein' Sünde gross (BWV 622)('* O Man, thy grievous Sin bemoan'*)* and Hindemith's *Sonata no. 3*. Having graduated with 1st Class Honours in Physics at Queen's University the previous year, Brendan was then engaged in PhD research in Atomic Collision Physics. Brendan's brother, Michael, a medical graduate of Queen's University, and a Resident House Physician at the Mater Infirmorum Hospital in Belfast, held an FTCL diploma for organ. Michael played Franck's *Choral no 3 in A minor*.

The other organist was David Bryant, at that time a sixth-former at Inst. He played Bach's *Prelude and Fugue in A (BWV 536)*, two chorale preludes from Brahms's Op.122: *Schmücke dich, O liebe Seele ('*Deck thyself, O my Soul'*)* and *Es ist ein' Ros' entsprungen ('* Behold, a Rose is blooming'*)* and *Processional* by William Mathias. At the 1971 Belfast Musical Festival David had won both the Under-18 and Open Organ classes as well as the Norman Hay Scholarship for Musicianship.

David later studied at London University (King's College) where he graduated with a PhD in Musicology in 1981. He currently teaches at the University of Venice and is Director of the Documentation Centre for Music History at the Fondazione Giorgio Cini. An acknowledged authority on the history of Medieval and Renaissance Church Music, he has edited several volumes of the complete works of the Venetian composer, Andrea Gabrieli and is the author of studies on the function and sounds of music in St Mark's, Venice and other churches in the Venetian territories.

In March 1971 I gave the opening recital on the rebuilt organ in Hamilton Road Presbyterian Church in Bangor where my dear friend, Henrietta Moran, was the Organist, and in July, at the invitation of Rick Battersby, a post-graduate student at the University of Ulster, who was having organ lessons from me at that time, I gave a recital at Agherton Parish Church in Portstewart. This was one of a series by Irish Cathedral Organists. In 1970, I had given a recital at the church on Thursday 21 May. This being one of the practice evenings for the annual North-West 200 Motor-Cycle Race, the start of the recital was put back until 9.15p.m. because the course then used for the race went past the church. That morning, on the BBC Northern Ireland News Programme, one of the presenters, Larry McCoubrey, a friend of mine, when he was announcing both the race and the recital could not resist making something of the juxtaposition of two such disparate events. The possibilities offered by an overlap, were the race practice to finish late, simply had to be exploited and he duly played a recording of part of Bach's best-known organ work, the *Toccata and Fugue in D minor (BWV565)* liberally punctuated by the roars of motor-cycle exhausts. It was all good fun - and good advertising. However, I was interested to find that the Cathedral Choristers were not at all amused. They were offended that a broadcaster had, in their estimation at any rate, dared to make their leader the butt of his humour.

By September 1972 it was possible to broadcast Evensong from the Cathedral even if we would be without the rebuilt Harrison organ for a further three years. We had to continue to make do with the Allen computer instrument which served us well despite the fact that its tonal shortcomings could be all-too-evident in louder passages. Choral Evensong was broadcast from St Anne's on both 6 and 13 September. Writing to the Dean after the first of these, the Vicar of South Shields, Canon Gordon Berriman, himself a former chorister at Durham Cathedral and currently Chairman of the Federation of Cathedral Old Choristers' Associations, said that he had enjoyed the broadcast 'tremendously' and that he had been 'positively swept up into joy by the sheer verve and panache of the anthem which is itself a thrilling piece of writing.' This was Bryan Kelly's *O be joyful in the Lord*, which the composer had dedicated to the Choir of Belfast Cathedral and me. Clearly a companion-piece to his *Magnificat and Nunc Dimittis in C*, which are also based on Latin-American rhythms, this setting of the *Jubilate* was meat and drink to the eager young members of the Cathedral Choir who projected it tellingly backed by Donald Davison's equally vital organ accompaniment. We were delighted to discover that this particular Choral Evensong was mentioned in the 1973 Annual Report of the Friends of Cathedral Music as being one of the outstanding broadcasts of the previous year.

For the broadcast on 13 September, the choir was joined by Edwin Gray, who had been appointed Assistant Organist at the Cathedral in the autumn of 1971. Among our correspondents this time was Mr David Johnston, a professional singer who occasionally came to Northern Ireland to take part in operatic productions. 'As a former chorister and lay-clerk of Salisbury [Cathedral] I suppose I know a bit about the business and am fairly used to hearing a good sound. But it's a long time since my attention was so arrested as it was by the sensitive and musical singing by your choir yesterday'.

The Ulster Orchestra's concert series, *Music in the Cathedral*, continued to attract sizeable audiences on occasional Sunday afternoons. A few people objected to paying for entry to an event which took place at what was the normal time of Evensong, i.e. 3.30p.m., although I am not sure that they were all, in fact, regular attenders at this service. The Cathedral Choir took part in three of these concerts, two of which I conducted. The first, on 26 March, included the young Mozart's delightful *Symphony No 29 in A (K201)*, Ravel's *Pavane pour une Infante défunte*, at once beautiful and sad, and Fauré's ever-popular *Requiem*. In this, the eloquent soloists, both members of the Cathedral Choir, were Ellen Rainey and Cyril Willoughby. The second concert, on 10 December, began with Mendelssohn's *Ruy Blas Overture,* choir and orchestra combining in Pergolesi's *Magnificat*, all the soloists being again from the choir, and Vaughan Williams's *Fantasia on Christmas Carols* in which Cyril Willoughby gave an impressively authoritative account of the important baritone solo part. The programme also included Gerald Finzi's delectable *Dies Natalis,* a cantata for high voice and strings consisting of settings of three poems by the seventeenth century mystic, Thomas Traherne. One of our young tenors, Ashleigh Rodway, rose to the challenge of the taxing vocal line with considerable aplomb. Corelli's charming *Christmas Concerto* played by the strings of the orchestra and two unaccompanied carols sung by the choir added further variety to what, I think, was an attractive selection of seasonal music. On 1 October the Cathedral Choir sang Vivaldi's *Credo* accompanied by the Ulster Orchestra in the course of a concert under the direction of Edgar Cosma, the Orchestra's Principal Conductor.

Like other cathedrals, St Anne's, because of its size and its role in the religious life of the city it serves, is in the course of each year, the chosen venue for a number of civic and other 'special' services. There is no doubt that in 1972 one of the most colourful and most significant from a musical perspective was a Service of Thanksgiving held on Sunday 3 December to mark the centenary of the foundation of Trinity College of Music, London. To Victor Henry, then an invaluable member of the Cathedral Board, and himself a Licentiate of Trinity College, must go the credit for proposing this event and for willingly undertaking most of the considerable amount of administration which its organisation entailed. The College's Director of Examinations, Mr Ernest Heberden, came from London to read the Act of Thanksgiving and the Revd Donald Cairns, the Music Critic of the *Belfast Newsletter* read one of the lessons. Dr E W J Boucher, Head of Music for BBC Northern Ireland, resplendent in his DMus robes, gave an illuminating address in which he traced the history of the College, emphasising its Church connections both through its motto: *Gloria in excelsis Deo ('*Glory to God in the Highest*')* and through its name: *Trinity College.* Many diploma-holders from across the province accepted our invitation to attend and to take part in the choir procession wearing their academic attire.

The service was preceded by a programme of organ and orchestral music played by Michael McGuffin and the Ulster College of Music Orchestra under my direction, while Victor Henry accompanied on the organ the music of the service which took the form of Evensong sung by the Cathedral Choir with the large congregation joining heartily in appropriate well-known hymns. The Responses were by Bernard Rose, the Canticles were sung to Howells's *Collegium Regale* setting and the Anthem was Purcell's *Rejoice in the Lord alway,* complete with its string 'symphonies'. Despite the fact that the east end of the building was still hidden behind a massive, unprepossessing wooden screen, the service had been a wonderfully uplifting occasion.

Given his business acumen, drive and flair, Victor Henry was destined to become a leading figure in the commercial life of Belfast. An accomplished organist and pianist, he characteristically also found time to pursue with conspicuous success his keen interest in church music. During his presidency of the USOC (1978-79) he generously presented the Society with a handsome presidential badge of office which he had had specially designed in consultation with the committee. He was a very worthy recipient of an Honorary Fellowship of Trinity College of Music, London both for his services to church music in Northern Ireland and for his tireless promotion of the College's interests. Later Victor left Belfast for London on his appointment to the Board of Directors of Harrods.

Another centenary being celebrated in 1972 was that of St Enoch's Presbyterian Church in Belfast where a number of special services and other events had been arranged. One of these took place on Sunday 4

June when the Cathedral Choir sang Evensong. This being the first time in the church's history that such an Anglican act of worship had taken place within its walls, there were doubtless some in the congregation for whom such a sung service was a new experience. Everyone listened attentively to Wood's setting in D of the Canticles, and anthems by Monteverdi, Tomkins, Gibbons, Stanford and Parry. The Vicar Choral, the Revd John Nolan, acted as Cantor and Dean Crooks read the lessons. The ladies of the congregation were, of course, greatly taken with the Choristers who, as usual, did full justice to the delicious supper which was laid on afterwards.

As indicated earlier (in Chapter 7), Heather and I regarded 80 Stranmillis Gardens as a temporary home and had been looking forward to the day when we might be able to purchase a house in a more peaceful part of Belfast. We had managed to save just enough to avoid having to increase the mortgage on our present home in Cairnburn Crescent to which we moved with our small daughter, Hannah, in May 1972. Nevertheless we had to borrow from a kind friend the money necessary to pay the solicitor's fees. After the vicissitudes of life in Stranmillis Gardens, this lovely part of the eastern suburbs of the city offered an altogether more pleasant prospect. There are probably few residents who have cause to appreciate it quite as much as we do.

Like her late mother, Heather has a keen interest in gardening. Whereas at Stranmillis Gardens there had been a lawn about the size of a postage stamp and no flower-beds, Heather was delighted to have now a much larger area at her disposal and she was soon planning a revision of its layout. In the autumn of 1974 she and a neighbour, Mrs Esdale Johnston (affectionately known as 'Jono'), rather over-ambitiously, as it turned out, decided to rent an allotment. The onion sets which they planted initially yielded a crop of such superb specimens that even seasoned male allotment-holders were envious. By the following spring, however, when it was necessary to prepare the ground for the planting of the other vegetables, Heather, who was then expecting our second child, was in no condition to undertake such heavy work.

A few of our friends from the Cathedral Choir: Valerie Ireland, Tom Agnew, Alan Boyd and Cyril King joined me, therefore, one very wet Saturday afternoon at the allotment armed with spades and digging forks. When the task had been accomplished all repaired to our house to have a wash prior to tucking into fish and chips from our local 'chippy'. Although Heather's career as a vegetable-grower had been short lived, she still remembers those magnificent onions with a sense of pride – and so does Jono.

We had decided that after Hannah was born in October 1971 Heather would not return to work but would stay at home to look after her. Because this meant that we were now entirely dependent on my income, Heather had to be very resourceful in her household management and her degree in Economics was to prove to be a great blessing! Nevertheless, although we had done our sums with the utmost care, there were times when it was difficult to find the money to pay all the bills. Indeed, I recall that now and then, if funds were low, Heather would purchase a bone for 5p at the local butcher's to make soup to see us through the week-end.

In 1972 I applied for the post of Assistant Director of Music at Solihull School in Birmingham, at that time an independent school for boys, and was called for interview. As well as teaching and other duties, the successful applicant would be in charge of Chapel Music, an aspect of the job which I found especially attractive. In the course of my visit to the school I taught a class of second-form boys, who, when they learned that I was from Belfast, bombarded me with questions about the terrorist campaign. I think that they were somewhat disappointed that I had not, so far, come face to face with IRA personnel. At the end of the day I was offered the post at a top-of-the-scale salary of £2,900.00 per annum plus accommodation.

On my return home I telephoned the Dean who called to see Heather and me forthwith. Preoccupied as the poor man had been with the raising of a further £200,000 to complete the construction of the south transept and crossing at the Cathedral, it had not occurred to him that the Organist's salary was in urgent need of review. He had no idea that Heather and I were finding it difficult at times to make ends meet and he was very sorry to learn that this was the case. Consequently he called an emergency meeting of the Cathedral Board. The members were fully aware that, given the daily worldwide television coverage of the appalling scenes in Belfast and elsewhere in Ulster, it would be exceedingly difficult to attract applicants from outside the province for the post of Organist at St Anne's Cathedral were it to become vacant. In an effort to induce me to stay, the Board decided to increase my salary from £900.00 to £1,350.00 with the Board, in addition, offering to be responsible for the payment of the premium of £50.00 on the Contributory Insurance Policy to which consideration was to have been given eight years previously. Although the relentless strain under which I was working was causing me to have weekly migraine attacks, out of loyalty to Dean Crooks, who pleaded with me not to leave the Cathedral at what was one of the most difficult times in its history, I agreed to remain for the present. Nevertheless, while my work at the Cathedral meant everything to me, it was becoming increasingly clear that I was going to have to give serious consideration to my long-term future and that a decision could not be postponed indefinitely.

CHAPTER NINE

1972-74 | Belfast Cathedral, Choir's first commercial recording

Periodic invitations to adjudicate at competitive musical festivals in the Republic of Ireland offered welcome respite from the ongoing 'Troubles' and, when I could make myself available, they were always gladly accepted. At Sligo in the west of Ireland and at Arklow in the south-east because the standard of performance in the senior piano classes was invariably very high it was often difficult to select a winner from a number of accomplished entrants. Most of these gifted young people were studying with leading teachers in Dublin where there has always been a strong piano-playing tradition. It is a pity that the instrumental classes, which were usually held during the day, did not attract larger audiences for they often offered some of the finest music-making of the festival. On the other hand, the participating choirs in the choral classes which mostly took place in the evenings, filled the hall, generating an expectant and appropriately competitive atmosphere. The climax of the festival or *feis,* to give it its Irish name, was the prize-winners' concert which took place on the final evening.

I am full of admiration for all those good people who give generously of their time and energy to mount these annual musical events which have over the years played a vitally important role in the identifying and fostering of emerging musical talent. It is very interesting to note that a small, country town such as Arklow has been able to maintain a thriving *feis* through good times and bad whereas similar festivals in such large centres of population as Belfast and Bangor, Co. Down have long since ceased to function through lack of support. It is pleasant to record, on the positive side, however, that, due to the enterprise of a group of musicians in the locality, the festival at Holywood, Co. Down has been revived in recent years and is flourishing once again.

Another invitation which I accepted with alacrity was to act as chorus-master for a Glyndebourne-influenced production of Handel's *Acis and*

Galatea at Campbell College in May 1972. The members of the audience were required to come in formal dress and dinner was served during the interval which lasted one-and-a-half hours. Prices of admission were: £3.00 (including dinner) and £1.50 (opera only). The Ulster Orchestra was conducted by its Associate Conductor, Alun Francis and the soloists included Ian Urwin, a former member of the Cathedral Choir and Consort, who, with Jack Smith was to be a co-founder of Castleward Opera which staged its first production (Mozart's *Cosi fan Tutti*) in 1985.

In December 1972 the Cathedral Choir made a number of television appearances. The first of these, on BBC 1 in the *Sunday Gallery* series, was to recognise the achievement of the eight choristers who had gained the RSCM's St Nicholas Award, a record number in one choir at that time. John Barnes and Alan Boyd, who were among the first in the United Kingdom to receive the Senior Award, were presented with their medals by Dean Crooks in the course of the programme.

The other television work came about through an imaginative initiative on the part of Victor Henry in his capacity as Managing Director of the Bank Buildings. Victor, whose son Paul was one of our choristers, engaged the choir to take part in a video recording of a commercial to be shown several times on Christmas Day and Boxing Day on Ulster Television to promote the store's post-Christmas Winter Sale which was due to begin on 27 December. The various 'punchlines' were to be sung by the choir to an Anglican chant (reproduced below) which I had written for the purpose and which could be adapted as necessary to accommodate the text.

The fee which the choir earned for this, its first foray into the world of commerce, went towards the cost of funding a visit to London in August 1973 to sing the services for a week at St Paul's Cathedral during the 'resident' choir's summer vacation. It is perhaps worth stating that while such duties at English cathedrals are now undertaken quite regularly by choirs from this country, the residency by the Choir of Belfast Cathedral in 1973 at St Paul's is believed to be the first by a Church of Ireland choir in that magnificent building. In order that the cost to each individual choir member would not be excessive, a committee, consisting of representatives of the choir and choristers' parents plus the Vicar Choral and me, was appointed to organise a series of fund-raising events.

Having set ourselves a target of £2,000 we launched our appeal with a sponsored eight-mile walk in Tollymore Forest Park, Newcastle, Co. Down in November 1972. The enthusiastic participation in this of Miss Sheila Regan and some of her secretarial colleagues from the Diocesan Office together with the Bishop of Connor, the Rt Revd Arthur Butler, all staunch supporters of the choir, was a great encouragement to us. A resounding success from every point of view, this very happy event brought in a most welcome sum of £600. By May 1973 we were well on the way towards our target.

It was fortunate that one of our tenors at that time was Clive Scoular, a Divisional Welfare Officer. With his professional management background and superb organisational skills he willingly accepted the responsibility for making all the travel, accommodation and other arrangements in connection with our London visit. He made a first-class job of it and, I believe, derived a certain measure of satisfaction from doing so. Clive had hired a double-decker bus for the duration of our stay in London. This met us at the docks in Liverpool, took us everywhere we needed to go during the week and, at the end of our stay, returned us to Liverpool to catch the boat back to Belfast. Being the International Scout Commissioner for Northern Ireland, Clive was able to book accommodation for our entire party of almost seventy people at Baden-Powell House, the headquarters of the Scout Movement, on the Cromwell Road in London. He also saw to it that appropriate recreational activities were provided for the choristers.

The choir sang Evensong at St Paul's each day (Monday - Saturday 13 - 18 August) preceded by an hour's rehearsal with the organ in the Cathedral. A preliminary rehearsal was held every morning after breakfast at Baden-Powell House. On Sunday 19 August the choir sang all the services at St Paul's where the congregations included large numbers of overseas visitors. Throughout the week the organ was played by Edwin Gray, the Assistant Organist at Belfast Cathedral, who was at St Paul's early each day in order to practise for an hour or two before the building was opened to the public. Edwin quickly came to terms with the organ and the acoustic and, was thoroughly prepared for each service. He was thrilled to have the opportunity to play such a famous instrument and he showed himself equal to all the demands made on him in the course of what was a very busy week. A heat-wave then over London caused day-time temperatures to rise to about ninety degrees Fahrenheit. Since this had an enervating effect on everyone, we had to be careful to conserve our energy in order to be able to discharge all our duties. Many gallons of water were drunk in the course of the week.

Belfast Cathedral Choir at Westminster Abbey, August 1973

On Wednesday 15 August the choir was welcomed at Westminster Abbey by Canon Ronald Jasper, the Precentor, well known as the Chairman of the Liturgical Commission, who would later become Dean of York. The nave of the Abbey was packed for our lunch-time recital of Tudor Church Music. This was unaccompanied except for Gibbons's *This is the Record of John* in which the alto soloist was Brian Hunter with the organ being played by Timothy Farrell, the Assistant Organist at Westminster Abbey.

One day during our stay in London, our party was entertained to tea by the monks of the Anglican Order of St John the Evangelist or 'The Cowley Fathers,' as they are better known, at St Edward's House which is situated quite close to the Abbey. The choristers, who had been among the first to arrive, scoffed most of the delicious food which the monks had provided, leaving little for the adults. By the time Heather and I reached St Edward's House all of the plates had been cleared!

As an expression of his personal appreciation of the work of the Cathedral Choir and its role in the life of the province, Mr William van Straubenzee, the Minister of State for Northern Ireland, received our party at the Houses of Parliament and conducted us on a fascinating tour of those historic buildings. He congratulated the members of the choir on the high standards which they were maintaining in Belfast in the most trying of circumstances and on being such admirable ambassadors for Northern Ireland.

Similar sentiments were expressed by members of the public in writing to the press. The following is a typical extract from a letter to the *Belfast Telegraph* from Mr Gordon Claney of Bangor, Co. Down, who with his wife Brenda, an occasional soloist at Cathedral Consort concerts, had attended Matins at St Paul's on Sunday 19 August: 'Nowadays when so many unfavourable things are being said about Northern Ireland, it was an inspiration for us to hear the extremely high standard of music from our own beloved country and to realise that we can be represented in such a worthy manner'.

Another important project in 1973 was the making of the Cathedral Choir's first commercial recording by the Dublin-based, New Irish Recording Company. It was decided that this would be of a programme of Christmas music including a number of items composed for the Choir and Organist by locally-based composers. Among these was *Away in a Manger* by Dr H F Selwood Lindsay, sometime Director of Music at St Bartholomew's Parish Church, Belfast and a devotee of cathedral music, who was a well-known GP in the Stranmillis area of the city. Also included was a setting of Dr Lindsay's text, *Hush thee to sleep*, by the Revd Frederick J Powell, a music graduate of Durham University and a Church of Ireland clergyman who, prior to his ordination in 1929, had held Organist posts in Carrickfergus and Belfast. *In the bleak mid-Winter* and a chorale prelude for organ on *Corde natus ex Parentis* ('Of the Father's Heart begotten') were composed by Keith Rogers, then Head of the Music Department at Belfast Royal Academy. Captain Brennan was represented by his two best-known pieces, both of which maintain their places in the Cathedral Carol Services and in the affections of those who attend them. These are *The Annunciation* and *The Virgin's Hush-song*. We were fortunate that the dedicatee of the former, Canon Graham Craig, having retired from parish ministry, was in 1973 serving as Dean's assistant on the clerical staff of the Cathedral where he had once been Vicar Choral. His beautifully-controlled singing of the solo part to the accompaniment of a chorus of upper voices is one of the highlights of the recording. Indeed, Brian Kay, the well-known broadcaster and foundation member of the King's Singers, who had made Canon Craig's acquaintance in the course of the group's visits to Belfast, played this recording later during one of his radio programmes. He commented that he would be very pleased indeed if, when he himself reached the age of sixty-seven, he were capable of singing as well. Equally memorable is Ellen Rainey's exquisite performance of the soprano solo in *The Virgin's Hush-song*. One of our local radio presenters regards this as so exceptional that he has regularly selected it for inclusion in his Christmas programmes.

What with military helicopters on reconnaissance patrols overhead and the risk of an explosion in the area at any time in addition to the unremitting traffic noise in the busy surrounding streets, conditions at the Cathedral were hardly conducive to the making of a recording. A phone call from the Dean to the police officer in charge of traffic-control resulted in neighbouring streets being sealed off for periods of time to facilitate us. With the other disruptive elements beyond anyone's control, there was nothing for it but to proceed in faith that all would be well. A number of retakes were necessary because of extraneous noises and my organ solos were not recorded until about 4.00a.m. on one of the days.

Attractively packaged in a folder which opens to reveal the texts of all of the carols and hymns sung, together with a photograph of the choir in 1973, the twelve-inch long-playing record reflects great credit on the producer, Bill Somerville-Large, who, in far-from-ideal conditions, achieved a result which, I think, surpassed our expectations. Reviews were unanimously positive. Among the most enthusiastic was that by Basil Ramsey which appeared, rather later than the others, in the Spring 1975 issue of *The Organists' Review* of which he was then the editor: 'I've been thrilled to receive a record of carols made a year ago in Belfast Cathedral. The singing by the choir of 50 men, women and boys is a joy to the ear. Tone, diction, blend, balance and rhythmic impetus charge every piece with a life-force. The strife-torn city outside might as well be a thousand miles away. Some of the carols are the product of local talent; the rest from standard repertory. I shall not forget the magnificence of *Personent hodie* as sung by the men. Here *is* gravitational pull.' Our performance of *Personent hodie* also appealed to Charles Acton (*Irish Times*) who was very impressed by the clarity of the Choir's enunciation and its phrasing. 'It is good that in all Ireland there is now a good record of Christmas music made by an Irish Choir and an Irish company'.

Alan Maitland in his review in the April 1975 Annual Report of The Friends of Cathedral Music said that it was 'a pleasure to welcome the first commercial recording to be made at Belfast Cathedral. No cathedral anywhere in Britain is working under greater difficulty than Belfast, and the continuance of such high standards by this big choir is a tremendous achievement.' The mainly very positive critique in the RSCM's magazine *Promoting Church Music* (July 1974) included the following somewhat enigmatic remark: 'I must confess to more than a sneaking liking for Mr Grindle's arrangement of *When the crimson Sun had set*.' In the opinion of an anonymous *Belfast Newsletter* columnist the versatility of the Allen Organ was one of the features of the album. Canon O V Marshall of Paignton in Devon in a letter to Bishop Arthur Butler, thanking him for a copy of the recording which he had sent, said how favourably impressed he had been by the sound of the Allen Organ and wondered why it should be considered necessary to raise and spend a large sum of money on rebuilding and enlarging the Harrison instrument. Keenly interested in church music, Canon Marshall's collection of recordings made by leading English cathedral choirs was one of his most treasured possessions. His 'league table', he said, had hitherto been headed by Chichester Cathedral, followed by St John's College and King's College, Cambridge. After hearing our recording of Christmas music, he had decided that the Choir of Belfast Cathedral should now occupy the premier position!

An invitation was received from the Shallway Foundation, Connellsville, Pennsylvania, USA to send one or more choristers on a three-week exchange visit as 'singers-in-residence' with American boychoirs (as they are known in the USA), all expenses being paid apart from trans-Atlantic air fares. Had we not been obliged to put all our efforts into raising the funds for our visit to London in August 1973 I am sure that we should have tried to make it possible for at least one of our senior choristers to take advantage of this attractive offer. Our American correspondent enclosed with his letter a sheet of adhesive stamps on each of which was reproduced a picture of the Belfast Cathedral Choristers singing on the steps at the entrance to the Cathedral. This picture had originally appeared in the RSCM's magazine, *Promoting Church Music* in October 1972.

Since the Choir had an important role in the promotion of the Cathedral, we did our best to fulfil as many additional engagements as we could. Sometimes this could result in periods of fairly intense activity. On Sunday 6 May 1973, the Choir having sung the statutory services at the Cathedral, went on to sing a further Evensong at 6.30p.m. at St John's Parish Church, Malone which included a performance of Vaughan Williams's *Five Mystical Songs* with organ accompaniment provided by Dr Donald Davison, the Organist of the church. On Sunday 20 May Choral Matins was broadcast from the Cathedral on Radio Telefís Éireann and on the following Saturday, 26 May, the Choir sang Evensong at another joint meeting of the Ulster and Leinster Societies of Organists and Choirmasters. The canticles were sung to Herbert Murrill's setting in E and the anthem was Byrd's magnificent 5-part motet, *Laudibus in Sanctis*, the text of which is a free paraphrase, in Latin elegiac verse, of Psalm 150.

I was bitterly disappointed that illness prevented me from conducting a concert in the Ulster Orchestra's series *Music in the Cathedral* on 4

February, 1973 when the programme, which I had chosen, included some of my favourite music: Mozart's *Serenata Notturna in D (K 239)* for strings and timpani; Handel's Chandos Anthem No.6, *O praise the Lord with one Consent* and Bizet's *Symphony in C*. At the last moment my place was taken by the young Scottish conductor, Alasdair Mitchell. Fortunately, the Cathedral Choir had performed the Handel work before and was thoroughly conversant with it. I was told that the concert went well despite the minimum amount of rehearsal under a different conductor.

I had recovered in time to take preliminary rehearsals of Haydn's *Creation* with the Linenhall Choir for a performance with the Ulster Orchestra on 7 April in the County Hall in Ballymena. The soloists were Hazel Holt, Paul Taylor and Stewart Haslett. Stewart had been one of the two head-choristers appointed on my arrival at Belfast Cathedral in 1964 and he had later been a bass soloist in the Cathedral Choir. After studying singing at the RAM he embarked on a successful career as a recitalist and concert artist which was, alas, cut short by his early, tragic death.

In April, 1973 the Cathedral Choristers took part as usual in the Ulster Singers' annual performance of Bach's *St Matthew Passion* and later in the year joined me in a recital at Drumbeg Parish Church in a series called *Music in Church*. At the Cathedral itself our monthly recitals of church music continued, that on 15 April including Allegri's *Miserere*, Palestrina's *Stabat Mater* and Bach's motet: *Jesu, priceless Treasure*. A sequence of Christmas music under the title, *Ding, dong merrily* was recorded at the Cathedral for broadcasting on BBC Radio 4 Northern Ireland in December 1973. This consisted of items sung by the choir with organ solos played by me. On 2 September the BBC broadcast a recital which I had previously recorded on the organ of Hamilton Road Presbyterian Church, Bangor. The programme included chorale preludes by Janacek and Flor Peeters as well as the *Three Preludes on Welsh Hymn tunes* by Vaughan Williams.

The Irish Church Music Association (ICMA) was founded in 1969 to provide training for church musicians in the furtherance of its aim to improve standards of performance and the effectiveness of music in the liturgy of the Roman Catholic Church. Each year a National Summer School is held at which a number of leading practitioners, both clerical and lay, act as tutors, sharing their expert knowledge with and giving encouragement to the large number of students who attend from all parts of the country. I was very pleased to accept an invitation from ICMA to be the Course Choirmaster at the Summer School in 1973 which took place at the Redemptorist College in Mervue, Galway in the west of Ireland. Whenever it was possible for me to do so, I attended the tutorials of some of my colleagues. Particularly memorable were the classes on plainchant. Here the charismatic Fr Tom Egan from Killarney held his audience in thrall as, with eloquent hand-gestures, he directed the singing of those wonderful, timeless melodies which constitute the fundamental repertoire of the Christian Church.

All the while I had been giving much thought to the future. Although I very much enjoyed the diversity of the free-lance work which I undertook to supplement my cathedral salary, the income from this tended to be variable. Long-term security was another serious consideration. Heather and I decided, after lengthy discussions, that the solution might be for me to seek a position as an assistant music teacher in a Belfast school. I should be able to spend a little more time at home, the regular monthly salary would be very welcome and I might be enabled to continue to serve the music of the Cathedral, my real *raison d'être*.

I was appointed to a post at Ashleigh House School for Girls in Windsor Avenue in Belfast where I joined the staff in September 1973. Peter Harris, the Head of Department and a very able all-round musician whom I already knew, made me feel at home in my new surroundings and was a most agreeable colleague. Held in the highest esteem by both pupils and colleagues, Peter was the possessor of an utterly unflappable temperament which was an invaluable asset particularly in the run-up to and during school operatic productions. In addition to class-teaching, we each prepared candidates for GCSE Music and gave individual piano lessons.

With one exception the classes were a pleasure to teach. Miss Cochrane, the school's rather eccentric Headmistress, had ordained that the sixth form should have a weekly dose of culture in the form of a period of music appreciation and I was appointed to administer it. The reaction of these sophisticated young ladies to something which they saw as an imposition was very interesting. They entered the room in silence, sat in silence throughout the lesson looking steadily straight in front of them and left the room in silence when the bell rang. I soon discovered that there was no point in trying to engage them in any discussion. They had clearly decided to mount a silent protest. For me it was a novel if rather unnerving experience.

One Monday morning, at the end of a recorder lesson with a small group of pupils from the preparatory department, a little girl approached me. She said that at the week-end her uncle David, who played the recorder, had visited her family. When this information failed to elicit the response which she had expected, she added that her uncle David appeared from time to time on television playing the recorder and other instruments. I was now paying attention. Her uncle was, in fact, David Munrow (1942 -76), the world-famous early music specialist and one of the most influential musicians of his generation.

Nineteen seventy-four, which was to be the busiest year to date at the Cathedral, began with a broadcast of Choral Evensong on 16 January. The introit was *Hush thee to sleep,* by the Revd Frederick J Powell which was published in the 1960 edition of the *Church of Ireland Hymnal* and I subsequently received a number of enquiries from church organists about this lovely piece. I was very pleased to hear from Mr Powell himself who had been an appreciative listener. He had been particularly impressed by the pointing and treatment of the Psalms (Nos 82-85). The last of these had been sung to a very appealing chant by Edgar Day, a former Assistant Organist at Worcester Cathedral. By chance, Mr Day had spotted his name in the notice published in *Radio Times* giving details of the music and was very interested to see that his chant, written many years previously for the Worcester Chant-book edited by Sir Ivor Atkins, had crossed the Irish Sea. He said that he had greatly enjoyed the service and asked me to pass on his thanks to the choir for their beautiful singing of his chant.

In March the Cathedral Choir took part with school choirs from North Belfast and the North-East Ulster Schools' Symphony Orchestra in a special television *Songs of Praise* programme for St Patrick's Day which was recorded in the Wellington Hall in Belfast. The Cathedral Choir's particular contribution consisted of the accompanied chorale, 'Jesu, lead my Footsteps ever', from Bach's *Christmas Oratorio* and Keith Rogers's setting of *In the bleak mid-Winter.* Many viewers in Britain were moved, in some cases to tears, by this programme in which school choirs from both sides of Ulster's notorious religious divide combined happily in a celebration of their common patron saint.

For many years it had been the tradition at Belfast Cathedral, as at numerous other major churches, for the choir to sing the Easter music from Handel's *Messiah* on Easter Sunday. Dean Crooks, always trying to think of new ways of raising badly-needed funds, suggested, with his usual boyish enthusiasm, a performance of the whole work on Easter Sunday afternoon to be given by the Cathedral Choir and soloists from Northern Ireland some of whom were pursuing high-profile singing careers in Britain and further afield. In order to keep the performance to a reasonable length, it was decided to omit a number of the central items while including some of those near the end which are less frequently heard. Norma Burrowes, Jean Allister, Uel Deane, a former Belfast Cathedral Chorister, and Paschal Allen all readily accepted our invitation to take part although, in the event, Eileen Gavin, a well-known local contralto, had to deputise for Jean Allister who was, unfortunately, indisposed. Professor Philip Cranmer, who had left Queen's University in 1968 on his appointment to the Chair of Music at Manchester University, kindly agreed to undertake the Herculean task of accompanying the work on the

(Allen) organ. Despite the fact that many people were away on holiday over the Easter week-end, the Cathedral was packed for the performance on 14 April 1972 when the admission charges were £1.00 and 75p.

There can be little doubt that many people had come specifically to hear Norma Burrowes and they were not disappointed. As the music critic, *Rathcol*, reported in the *Belfast Telegraph*: 'this was the kind of inwardly motivated and vocally immaculate singing that has placed this excellent soprano far above most of her rivals. And there was a radiance about "I know that my Redeemer liveth" that brought home the message of Easter as few sermons I have heard have done'. The other soloists, while perhaps lacking Miss Burrowes's 'star' quality, nevertheless gave a very good account of themselves and Professor Cranmer was throughout a veritable tower of strength as the accompanist, his vast experience in this field and his great musical skill enabling him to make the most of the rather inadequate instrument at his disposal. The members of the Cathedral Choir, provided with a rare opportunity of singing to a capacity congregation/audience, excelled themselves, the choral lines coming across clearly in the resonant acoustic.

On Sunday 12 May 1974 the Cathedral Choir sang a group of three anthems by Henry Purcell at Evensong. A string ensemble from the Belfast School of Music provided the accompaniment in two of the composer's extended verse anthems, the well-known *Rejoice in the Lord alway* and *My beloved spake* which is perhaps less familiar. The choir also sang Purcell's wonderful setting of Psalm 102 v 1, *Hear my Prayer, O Lord*, a full, unaccompanied anthem for eight parts which, with its overwhelming climax in its final bars, ranks among the greatest achievements in the Anglican church music repertoire. Later that same day, the Choir sang a second Evensong at Belmont Presbyterian Church, the music this time including John Ireland's Magnificat and Nunc Dimittis in F and a group of six anthems by Gibbons, Tomkins, Purcell, Stanford and Wood. The congregation, for its part, proved that when it comes to hymn-singing, Presbyterians yield the palm to no one.

The consecration of the south transept and the dedication of the new Chapel of Unity, which it housed, had originally been scheduled for Friday 30 November 1973, St Andrew's Day. However, it was found necessary to postpone this important event in the history of the Cathedral's evolution until Thursday 20 June 1974. On one of his visits to Liverpool's Anglican Cathedral, Dean Crooks had been impressed by its team of vergers, all past-choristers, dressed in colourful robes, which took part in the choir procession. Belfast Cathedral soon followed suit with its own team of young vergers playing an important ceremonial role particularly at special services such as this when civic and church dignitaries including the Archbishops of Armagh and Dublin were present.

In his compelling sermon, the Bishop of Coventry, the Rt Revd Cuthbert Bardsley sought to answer a question which is frequently asked: 'What is the purpose of a cathedral?' Taking as his text Genesis Chapter 28 v 19 which describes Jacob's vision of God at Bethel, the Bishop's address, which was later published in full in the *Church of Ireland Gazette,* was truly worthy of the occasion. Also worthy of the occasion, I hope, was the music which included Vaughan Williams's *Te Deum in G* and the specially-commissioned anthem, *Behold, the tabernacle of God* by the noted British composer of South African origin, John Joubert. The anthem was later published by Novello. This powerful setting of words, selected by Dean Crooks, from the Sarum Antiphon for the Dedication of a Church, made a deep impression, its hushed coda for double choir of divisi voices being especially effective. Mr Joubert expressed himself very pleased with the recording which I sent him afterwards: 'I was very struck by the quality of the performance, particularly as it is not an easy piece to do. Please convey my congratulations to the members of the choir on the way in which they have mastered it'.

Our monthly recital of music at Evensong on Sunday 30 June 1974 marked Petertide and consisted of settings of *Tu es Petrus* by Palestrina and Byrd together with Britten's *Hymn to St Peter.* The canticles were sung to the gloriously spacious setting which Herbert Howells composed for St Paul's Cathedral, London in 1951. All of this music was being sung by the Cathedral Choir for the first time at this service.

On Friday and Saturday 5 and 6 July, the Choir visited Tuam, a small provincial town in the north of Co.Galway about twenty-two miles from Galway itself. The purpose of our visit was to take part on the Saturday in the service held annually for the Friends of St Mary's Church of Ireland Cathedral, a building dating from the fourteenth century, which was by the 1970s in a very poor state of repair. After a civic reception in Tuam on their arrival at 7.30p.m. on the Friday evening, the adult members of the Belfast Cathedral Choir participated individually and collectively with local artists in a concert in St Jarlath's College Hall at 9.00p.m. to raise the funds necessary to cover the cost of the choir's stay. To encourage as large an attendance as possible at this event the charge for admission was a mere 50p. On the following day at the Friends' Service at the Cathedral the congregation included many Roman Catholics who, by their presence, were expressing their continuing support for the small Protestant community striving to maintain the dilapidated old building as a place of worship.

In 1974 a series of popular television programmes entitled *Sounding*

Voices was broadcast by BBC Northern Ireland. The Cathedral Choir's contribution to the programme devoted to 'The Music of Religion' broadcast on 9 July was Bach's *Jesu, Joy of man's Desiring;* 'O for the Wings of a Dove', the second part of Mendelssohn's *Hear my Prayer*, in which the soloist was Stephen Geoghegan; the chorus, 'He that shall endure to the End' from the same composer's oratorio *Elijah,* and the hymn *Be still my Soul* sung to the tune *Finlandia.*

We were sorry that we were unable to accept an invitation to undertake a residency at Bangor Cathedral in Wales during August 1974, but on Saturday 28 September two buses conveyed a party consisting of the Choir of Belfast Cathedral and a number of parents and friends to Dublin where the Choir was due to sing Evensong at 4.00p.m. at St Patrick's Cathedral. A large number of people, most of whom had not previously heard the choir 'live', attended the service at which the introit was Tallis's beautiful motet, *O nata Lux de Lumine*, the other music being Bernard Rose's Responses, Howells's *St Paul's Service* and Byrd's *Laudibus in Sanctis.* Edwin Gray, although unfamiliar with the organ and building, was an excellent accompanist throughout. At tea afterwards the Dean of St Patrick's, the Very Revd Victor Griffin, warmly welcomed the choir on its first visit to sing at his Cathedral. He also spoke in glowing terms about the choir's heroic efforts to maintain its musical tradition in a strife-torn city.

The choir was asked to take part in another television recording of *Songs of Praise* to be broadcast on the BBC network from Belfast Cathedral on Sunday 3 November. Perhaps because 1974 marked the 50th anniversary of broadcasting in Northern Ireland the producers may have considered that it would be appropriate to include a few substantial musical items in addition to the usual hymns. The Cathedral Choir therefore sang Stanford's *O for a closer Walk with God,* based on the tune *Caithness* and Vaughan Williams's *Lord, Thou hast been our Refuge*, accompanied by the organ and trumpeters from the Salvation Army Lurgan Citadel Band. With the distinguished Dublin contralto, the late Bernadette Greevy as the soloist, the men of the choir took part in a performance of the final section of Brahms's *Alto Rhapsody.* Choirs drawn from the rural deaneries of the dioceses of Down, Dromore and Connor joined the Cathedral Choir in the singing of the hymns.

One correspondent who had enjoyed the programme had noted that our choristers were wearing Eton collars and bows. I have personally always preferred these to the more-commonly-worn ruffs which look very well when they have been newly starched but are soon drooping forlornly. This gentleman, a member of a Manchester church choir in which the choristers also wore Eton collars, said that he was having great difficulty finding replacements for the studs as they either wore out or disappeared down the heating grids in the vestry.

I was very pleased to receive a congratulatory letter from Dr Lionel Dakers who had succeeded Dr Gerald Knight as Director of the RSCM in 1972. Dr Dakers said that this *Songs of Praise* programme had been the most musical and interesting which he had seen for a long time. Earlier in the year he had invited me to direct the RSCM's Annual Course for Amateur Organists and Choirmasters to be held at Addington Palace, the headquarters of the RSCM, in June 1975. Because I would then be preoccupied with preparations for the Cathedral Choir's residency at Westminster Abbey in August 1975, I had to decline.

As part of BBC Northern Ireland's 50th anniversary celebrations a series of thirteen programmes, with associated talks, had been devised to present a survey of Irish musical life over the previous four centuries. One of these programmes, recorded before an invited audience in the Cathedral for broadcasting in December, was advertised as *An eighteenth Century Benefit Concert*, its form and content being typical of concerts given at that time in Dublin in aid of Mercer's Hospital. The Cathedral Choir accompanied by the BBC Northern Ireland Orchestra conducted by Havelock Nelson, sang the setting of the *Jubilate* which Handel had composed for the Peace of Utrecht as well as his better-known coronation anthem, *Zadok the Priest*. The programme also included orchestral music by Boyce and Geminiani.

Another large audience responded to the BBC's invitation to attend the television recording of a further concert at the Cathedral on 10 December for broadcasting ten days later. This was a performance of excerpts from Handel's *Messiah*, including the Christmas music and the *Hallelujah* Chorus, in which a section of the Ulster Orchestra with Edwin Gray (organ) and Keith Rogers (harpsichord) joined the Cathedral Choir and some leading local soloists: Irene Sandford (soprano), Margaret Maguire (contralto), Ian Urwin (tenor) and Eric Hinds (bass), under my direction. Thankfully we were spared any interruptions due to terrorist activity in the vicinity, and the resulting production was considered to be a great success from both visual and musical points of view.

Although another phase of the Cathedral building had been dedicated in June 1974 steadily rising costs meant that, in order to finance the completion of the construction work, the Dean found it necessary to make a further public appeal in the autumn. This appeal was launched at a special service in the Cathedral on 15 September 1974 at which the address was given by Mr Malcolm Muggeridge, the renowned journalist, author and media figure. A convert to Christianity, Muggeridge was rather a controversial person but his presence guaranteed a crowded congregation and maximum press coverage.

As indicated earlier (in Chapter 6) Jack Young had made due provision for the rebuilding of the Harrison organ which had been delayed by the work on the south transept where the organ was to be sited above the Chapel of Unity. We all now looked forward to the day in 1975 when, enlarged and tonally improved, it would further enrich the worship of the Cathedral and take its rightful place among the finest instruments in the country.

CHAPTER TEN

1975-76 | BELFAST CATHEDRAL, REBUILT
ORGAN, FIRST CATHEDRAL FESTIVAL

Heather and I never regretted for one moment our decision that she should stay at home to look after our two children, Hannah (b. October 1971) and Rachel (b. December 1975). In later years, when the girls were at school, Heather undertook some part-time jobs such as examination administration and invigilation for various bodies as circumstances allowed. While the Cathedral Board had increased

Hannah (aged six)

Rachel (aged three) with Heather and tin whistle

my salary in 1972, faced with a crippling debt due to the on-going building programme, the Board was regretfully unable to pay, during that distressing period in the history of the Cathedral, the sort of amount to which the holder of such a demanding and responsible post might have been entitled. In years to come the Director of Music at Belfast Cathedral would be paid a much more substantial, full-time salary, to make it possible for him to concentrate on his service to the Cathedral and to the wider Church.

In normal conditions, I could probably have continued to fulfil the roles of both school-teacher and Cathedral Organist despite the exacting nature of each. However, with the 'Troubles' at their height in the early 1970s, it was with the greatest difficulty that one managed to maintain musical standards at the Cathedral. The strain at times was such that it was beginning to have an adverse effect on my health and I was forced to the inevitable conclusion that I had no option but to resign from the Cathedral post, a decision which was taken with the utmost reluctance. I was appointed to a lectureship in the Music Department at Stranmillis College, a teacher-training institution in Belfast, with effect from September 1975. In order to give the Cathedral Board time to appoint my successor, I remained in the Cathedral post until January 1976 doing both jobs simultaneously for three months.

Nineteen seventy-five had begun with two Choral Evensong broadcasts from the Cathedral on 1 and 8 January. The Choir's reputation was now such that a growing number of listeners made a point of tuning in when they saw the announcements in *Radio Times* of further contributions from Belfast to this weekly series. It was good to hear again from David Johnston whose two sons, following in their father's footsteps, were now choristers at Salisbury Cathedral. David had brought one of the boys with him when he had come to St Paul's Cathedral in August 1973 to hear and meet the Belfast Cathedral Choir during its residency. Cyril Willoughby, one of our former basses, wrote from Birmingham where he was then living and working. Cyril had joined the choir of Birmingham Cathedral. Another correspondent was a lay-clerk at Bradford Cathedral. A Miss Neale in Bristol said that her thoughts were 'with us all in our troubled country and city' because her nephew, Michael Baguley, whom I know very well, was working for the BBC in Belfast at that time.

The following extract from a letter dated 2 January from a listener in Staffordshire summarises the comments which were expressed by others:

> I have found it a very moving experience to hear this fresh, vigorous singing; superb articulation of words in the psalms; intelligent and sensitive phrasing; great artistry in giving the music time to breathe in the acoustics of the Cathedral; a feeling of youthful vitality and enthusiasm in everything. The Stanford B flat Evening service was a joy. So was the very musicianly performance of the *Shepherd's Cradle Song* [arr. Macpherson]. But the remarkable clarity of the Psalms is a memorable pleasure. Bravo! Keep it up!

The main work in our monthly recital of church music on Sunday 16 February was Tallis's *Lamentations of Jeremiah*. This sublime, extended piece, scored for an unaccompanied five-part choir of men's voices (ATTBB), is considered to be one of the composer's masterpieces. On this occasion it was sung by 12 men standing in an arc on the chancel steps in order to project the sound into the nave. The complete choir sang a group of appropriate motets and anthems from the same period while I played three of Bach's Lenten chorale preludes as an interlude. Critical comment was very positive, Donald Cairns concluding his review in the *Belfast Newsletter* as follows: 'If anyone needed proof that music is more, much more than an entertainment, that hour in St Anne's [Cathedral] surely provided it'.

On Saturday 8 March, the Cathedral Choir and I were in Dublin to take part in the opening concert of the 1975 Dublin Arts Festival in St Patrick's Cathedral with the New Irish Chamber Orchestra conducted by André Prieur. The Cathedral was packed for this major event, the audience including the President of the Irish Republic, Cearbhall Ó Dálaigh. A symphony by J C Bach was followed by Palestrina's unaccompanied *Stabat Mater*, sung by the choir under my direction in the choir stalls as the antiphonal nature of the music demanded. The remaining two works were by Haydn: the *Symphony No. 48 in C* and the *Theresienmesse* composed about thirty years later in 1799. Incidentally, modern research has proved that this work, one of the greatest of Haydn's late settings of the Mass, was dedicated to the Princess Marie Hermenegild, wife of Nicholas II Esterhazy, Haydn's patron rather than the Empress Marie Thérèse as had originally been assumed.

The most impressive of the four soloists was undoubtedly the late Bernadette Greevy, the distinguished Irish contralto. Ms Greevy had participated in the famous 1965 Argo recording of the work with the choir of St John's College, Cambridge and the Academy of St Martin-in-the-Fields under George Guest. In fact she made a significant contribution to the success of the performance, singing her thrilling solo passages with great authority and effect while, in the ensembles, exerting a steadying influence on her less experienced colleagues who, as a result, all rose to the occasion. At the conclusion of the concert the enthusiastic audience accorded the participants a standing ovation.

In the estimation of Judith Segal, music critic of the *Evening News,* 'the Haydn Mass proved to be an unadulterated pleasure. The choir faced the audience, divulging its full power artistically and splendid diction dramatically.' Fanny Feehan, writing in the *Evening Herald*, considered that 'the performance of the Mass was one of which any country might be proud.' In fact she was of the opinion that RTÉ had 'missed the boat' by not having cameras present to film the concert for showing both at home

Cearbhall Ó Dálaigh, President of the Republic of Ireland, (foreground, second from the right) with Harry, Mary Gallagher (leader of the New Irish Chamber Orchestra) and André Prieur (conductor) *(Photo: The Irish Times)*

and abroad. Charles Acton, in the *Irish Times*, said that in both its items, the choir had shown that its reputation was fully deserved. He commented on its 'firm, full tone, admirable balance, [its] rich bass line [and] a lovely treble line that avoids the Anglican hoot and the continental tendency to stridency, and inner parts that blend beautifully. They have the good diction that shows real care for their music and an artistic flexibility. All this is the more remarkable since St Anne's has no choir-school'.

By Palm Sunday 23 March the installation of the Harrison organ at Belfast Cathedral had progressed sufficiently to allow Edwin Gray, the Assistant Organist, to contribute a group of chorale preludes by Bach and Brahms to our monthly recital. The programme included Palestrina's *Stabat Mater* and Byrd's *Three-part Mass* sung by six male voices, two to a part.

A large audience was attracted to the Cathedral for our second annual performance of Handel's *Messiah* which took place on Easter Sunday 30 March at 3.00p.m. with an admission charge of £1.00. Once again the outstanding soloist was Norma Burrowes 'who displayed her lovely vocal quality (and, more important, her ability to colour it at will) in the finely sung soprano solos.' (*Rathcol* in the *Belfast Telegraph*.) The contralto soloist, 'Bernadette Greevy is a frequent visitor to the North and, as usual, she performed with all the polish and artistic authority befitting her artistic stature.' (Norman Finlay in the *Irish Times*.) 'The Cathedral Choir gave us a clean sound with precise runs and great security of intonation. Obviously much attention had been given to clarity of diction and most of the words came across despite the resonant acoustic.' (Gerard O'Rawe in the *Irish News*.) Seated at the console of the still only partly-playable Harrison Organ, behind and some distance from both the choir and soloists whom he was accompanying, Philip Cranmer was deserving of the highest praise for his masterly discharge of his vitally important role.

A number of my friends had been trying for some time to persuade me to form a choir to take the place of the Cathedral Consort in the Cathedral's music programme. Hence the Cathedral Singers, a sixteen-voice chamber choir, similar in size to the Consort, made its first appearance in a recital of music by William Byrd on Sunday 13 April 1975 singing the *Mass for Four Voices* and a group of motets and anthems. The Belfast Baroque Consort, a very efficient and fine-sounding recorder quartet directed by Keith Rogers, played some of Byrd's music for this ensemble. The music critic of the *Belfast Telegraph* commented favourably on the new choir's flexibility, balance, tuning and diction, concluding that it had made a 'highly promising' début.

At the monthly recital on Sunday 11 May the Cathedral Choir was joined by an instrumental ensemble in the performance of two of Bach's church cantatas: No. 106 (*Gottes Zeit ist die allerbeste Zeit* - 'God's Time is the best of all') and No. 25 (*Es ist nichts gesundes an meinem Leibe* -'There is no Health in my Body'), both of which were sung in German. The programme also included a *Suite for two treble recorders and continuo* by Bononcini played by Robert Frost, Keith Rogers and Norman Finlay, and two movements from Bach's *Suite in G* played by Jeremy Adair, a very talented seventeen-year-old cellist. Jeremy went on to study at the RCM in London. He died in tragic circumstances in 1982.

The balance of the programme met with the approval of Alfred Burrowes, the music critic of the *Irish Times*, who evidently enjoyed what he heard. 'The listener derived pleasure not only from the music itself, but also from the high standard of both the singing and the playing …The boy choristers sang well with a uniformity of head-tone, managing the difficult semi-quaver groupings with a marked rhythmical assurance . . . In their correct setting, the Bach cantatas had a real feeling of authenticity, the building enhancing and mellowing everything it heard'.

The very fine Band of the Royal Artillery (Woolwich), which was on tour in Northern Ireland at the time, visited the Cathedral on Trinity

Sunday 25 May to give a recital with the choir. The Band played music by Frescobaldi, Charpentier, Handel (movements from the *Music for the Royal Fireworks*), Beethoven (*'Egmont' Overture)*, Weber (two movements from the *Clarinet Concert No 2* with an excellent soloist), Saint-Saëns and Grieg. The choir sang Tschaikovsky's *Hymn to the Trinity* and Charles Wood's *Hail! gladdening Light* as well as combining with the string-players from the band and organ in Purcell's *'Bell' Anthem*.

On Sunday 1 June the seventy-first anniversary of the Consecration of the Nave of the Cathedral was marked by a special recital by the Choir and Organists entitled: *Five Centuries of English Church Music* which began with Gibbons's *O clap your Hands* and ended with Vaughan Williams's setting of the same text composed some three hundred years later. The programme was as follows:-

16th and 17th Centuries

Choir: *O clap your Hands* - Orlando Gibbons (1583-1625)
         When David heard - Thomas Tomkins (1572 -1656)
         O Lord, give Thy Holy Spirit - Thomas Tallis (1505 -1595)
         Prevent us, O Lord -William Byrd (1543 -1623)
         Rejoice in the Lord alway -Henry Purcell (1659 -1695)

18th and 19th Centuries

Organ: *Voluntary No.9 in G minor* -John Stanley (1713 -1786)
Choir: (Boys' voices) *O praise the Lord* - Maurice Greene (1694 -1755)
         O where shall Wisdom be found? - William Boyce (1710 -1779)
         Thou wilt keep him in perfect Peace - Samuel Sebastian Wesley (1810-1876)
         O Saviour of the World - Sir Frederick A G Ouseley (1825 -1889)
         I saw the Lord - Sir John Stainer (1840 -1901)

20th Century

Organ : *Psalm Prelude (Op. 32 No. 2)* - Herbert Howells (b 1892)
Choir :   *O for a closer Walk with God* - Sir Charles Villiers Stanford (1852 -1924)
         My Soul, there is a Country -Sir Hubert Parry (1848 -1918)
         Greater Love hath no Man - John Ireland (1879 -1962)
         Let all mortal Flesh keep Silence - Sir Edward Bairstow (1875 - 1946)
         O clap your Hands -Ralph Vaughan Williams (1872 -1958)

Organ : (Recessional) *Rhapsody in C sharp minor (Op. 17 No. 3)* - Herbert Howells

Evan John, in the *Irish News*, described this programme as 'an admirable conspectus of the period ending with this century' adding that, in his estimation, 'St Anne's is certainly a fine custodian of the "English tradition"'. He went on: 'The whole thing, in fact, was a nostalgic delight, from the opening organ voluntaries onwards. And it was great to hear the organ, now reinstalled after many years of silence, an instrument of the highest quality when it was built about seventy years ago and breathtakingly right for this sort of situation.'

From left: Kenneth James, Harry, and Henry James at the console of the rebuilt organ at Belfast Cathedral, 1975 *(Photo: Belfast Telegraph)*

When Kenneth James, Harrison & Harrison's head-voicer, came to Belfast to carry out the tonal finishing of the rebuilt organ at the Cathedral in early June, he was accompanied by his eighty-seven-year-old father, Henry, who acted as his assistant. In order that they could cram as many hours of work into the day as possible, it was essential for them to live on the site. To enable them to do this, the Cathedral Hall was temporarily turned into a 'bedsit' with a few basic items of furniture. Despite the far-from-satisfactory nature of their accommodation, the two men appeared to enjoy their stay. For Henry James it revived the happiest of memories.

The veteran craftsman first came to Belfast in 1907 as part of the team from Harrison & Harrison's factory in Durham to install the original organ in the Cathedral. While he was here, he stayed in lodgings in Carlisle Circus with a Mrs Donovan whose daughter, Ellen, he married in 1911. Their wedding took place in the Cathedral. After his wife's death in 1972 he went to live with his daughter. Even at eighty-seven he was not contemplating retirement and it gave him great pleasure to assist Kenneth, the only one of his three sons to have followed in his footsteps as an organ-builder. 'Why should I retire when I can still do my work?' was his dismissive response to anyone who might dare to suggest that, at his advanced age, he should take life easy.

Professor Gerard Gillen

The opening recital on the rebuilt organ was given on 29 June 1975 by the renowned Dublin organist, Gerard Gillen, who has been a leading figure on the Irish musical scene for many years. He was appointed Titular Organist of Dublin's Pro-Cathedral in 1976 and held the Chair of Music at the National University of Ireland, Maynooth from 1985 to 2007. Professor Gillen has an international reputation as an organist, having given, to date, over nine hundred recitals throughout Europe, the Middle East and America. He was founder- chairman of the Dublin International Organ and Choral Festival of which he was Artistic Director from 1990 to 2000. In 1984 he was conferred with a Knighthood of St Gregory by the Vatican and in 2006 was created a Chevalier des Arts et des Lettres by the French Government. He has also been awarded a doctorate *(h.c.)* by the Pontifical University.

For his recital at Belfast Cathedral he selected music which allowed him to demonstrate a range of the enlarged instrument's tonal resources. With Bach's great *'Dorian' Toccata and Fugue (BWV 538)* as its centrepiece, his programme included a *Dialogue in C* by Louis Marchand, Samuel Wesley's *Prelude and Fugue in C minor* and a *Voluntary in D* by William Boyce. The other works were *Postlude for the Office of Compline* by Jehan Alain and César Franck's *Grande Pièce Symphonique* which brought the recital to a triumphant conclusion. Further recitals were given by me on 27 July, by Edwin Gray on 24 August and by Desmond Hunter, at that time Organist at Lisburn Cathedral, on 14 September.

The Cathedral Choir visited London for the second time from Tuesday

5 to Sunday 10 August 1975. This time it was based at Westminster Abbey where, in addition to singing Evensong each week-day, the choir sang all of the Sunday services. Two recitals were also given. The first of these was at the Abbey at lunch-time on Wednesday 6 August and the other on the following evening at Westminster Cathedral. The press naturally made much of the fact that this would be the first time that a Church of Ireland choir from Northern Ireland had sung at London's major Roman Catholic Church.

In the middle of such a busy week we were glad to accept an invitation to a reception given for our party at the Ulster Office, Berkeley Street, Westminster by Sir Harry Jones, Agent for Northern Ireland in Great Britain, and Lady Jones. Lord Donaldson, Parliamentary Under-Secretary for Northern Ireland was also present. Temperatures being in the nineties, as was the case in 1973 when the choir had previously visited London, Sir Harry and Lady Jones must have wondered whether, faced with the choristers' seemingly unquenchable thirst, their supplies of chilled fruit juice would hold out.

With Clive Scoular once again in charge of all the travel and accommodation arrangements everything went according to schedule. However, our arrival at Westminster Cathedral on the Tuesday evening for our rehearsal, surprised the sacristan who, due to an internal breakdown in communication, had not been informed. The consequent late start of our rehearsal resulted in the loss of much valuable time and the telescoping of our preparations for the recital on the following evening. Nevertheless, the recital itself went well with our programme of music by Byrd, Palestrina, Monteverdi, Fauré and Duruflé giving evident pleasure to the audience which was perhaps not as large as we might have expected.

In spite of the enervating effect of the subtropical weather conditions and their many commitments in the course of their week in London, the members of the choir were agreed that it had been an altogether memorable experience. We had been warmly welcomed at Westminster Abbey by the Chaplain, the Revd Neil Collings who was always available, during our residency, to advise and help. A charming and very kind young man, Neil was soon regarded as a friend by everyone in our party, his enthusiastic participation in a choir table-tennis tournament endearing him to the choristers in particular. At one point during the week he gave us a very interesting talk on the history of the Abbey and on Sunday, after our final Evensong, he and his clerical colleagues entertained us to refreshments in the beautiful garden in Little Cloister.

One of the 'characters' at Westminster Abbey at that time was the Head-Verger, Algernon Greaves who was invariably the very epitome of solemnity as he led the choir procession or conducted clergy to and from their places in the course of services. Off duty, he was pleasant and friendly, with a winning sense of humour. The walls of his office at the Abbey were covered with bold headlines culled from the sports pages of various newspapers about the exploits of a famous English footballer who was also called Greaves e.g .'HAT TRICK FOR GREAVES,' ' GREAVES SCORES FOR ENGLAND', etc.

On my return home I was distressed to discover that my father had taken ill during my absence. Shortly afterwards he was transferred to hospital where he died on 28 August. Dad had been a leading member of the Orange Order in the Bangor District and he enjoyed the fellowship of Commercial Temperance Lodge No. 447 in which he mixed with other men who were involved in the business life of the town. Dad regarded his lodge as a sort of men's club and he would always refer affectionately to his fellow-members as 'the Boys'. Scores of Orangemen attended Dad's funeral in Bangor Abbey and afterwards, wearing their sashes, walked behind the hearse as the long procession, en route to the cemetery, wended its way through the respectfully silent streets of the area in which he had lived and worked for the greater part of his life.

The exploitation by Nationalists of such situations as that at Drumcree in Portadown resulted in confrontations between some Orangemen and the security forces which, through widespread media coverage, did considerable damage to the image of the Order and brought great sadness to all its law-abiding brethren. To brand Orangemen 'a tribe of bigots', as one misguided clergyman has done, is to gravely insult the majority of the membership.

My father was quite simply one of the finest people I have ever known. He was a thoroughly decent, hard-working man who gave loyal service to his church and to the community in various capacities throughout his life and who was revered by all those who were in any way associated with him. None respected him more for his integrity than the many Roman Catholics among the regular customers at our small grocery shop, some of whom made him, rather than their own kin, their confidant and even their executor. My father was certainly no bigot. He is remembered with love, gratitude and great pride.

September found me settling into a new sphere of activity at Stranmillis College, about which more later, while continuing to discharge my various duties at the Cathedral. On 28 September, the monthly recital consisted of two choral works, Palestrina's *Missa Brevis* and Britten's *Hymn to St Cecilia*, which were sung by the Cathedral Singers and organ works by Bach including the great *Fugue on the Magnificat (BWV 733)*, played by me.

The Dean and I were agreed that a Cathedral Festival, the first of its kind, would be a suitable way in which to celebrate the completion of the South Transept and the rebuilding of the Harrison Organ. This major event, which had the Cathedral Board's whole-hearted approval and support, ran for a week, from Sunday 5 October 1975.

The opening concert, given by the Cathedral Choir and the BBC Northern Ireland Orchestra, Havelock Nelson and I sharing the conducting, was broadcast 'live' on Radio Ulster. A recording was also transmitted later on Radio 3. The varied programme began appropriately with the rousing *Overture for an Occasion,* originally composed to a BBC commission for the Festival of Britain in 1951 by Howard Ferguson who was born in Belfast in 1908. In the course of his long career, during which he was based in England, Ferguson achieved great distinction as a pianist, composer and musicologist. This opening work was followed by Stanford's *Three Motets Op. 38*, Philip Cranmer's *Teach us, good Lord* and Raymond Warren's *Come, Holy Ghost,* its accompaniment specially arranged for strings by the composer. The other orchestral music was a *Suite in A minor* by Bach. The climax of the concert was a performance of Vaughan Williams's *Five Mystical Songs* in which the choir and orchestra were joined by the outstanding baritone soloist, Brian Raynor Cook.

On Monday 13 October the King's Singers, making their third appearance at the Cathedral in recent years, gave great pleasure to the large audience which they regularly attract. One of their many encores was *Green-shield Stamps.* Sung to the melody of the English folk-song, *Greensleeves,* this was a particular favourite of Dean Crooks who always requested it. The King's Singers kindly agreed to give a twenty-minute recital in the course of a special Diocesan Festival Service held in the Cathedral the following evening.

We had originally hoped to have an organ recital on the Wednesday evening by the world-renowned Italian organist, Fernando Germani. Unfortunately, Signore Germani's British tour was cancelled due to his ill-health and we were obliged to find a substitute. The brilliant young American organist, pianist and harpsichordist, Daniel Chorzempa, who was giving recitals in Britain at the time, was available on that date and he consented to play for us. His CV was certainly impressive. At eighteen years of age the youngest-ever graduate at the University of Minnesota, Chorzempa won the Organ Prize at the J S Bach International Competition at Leipzig in 1968. His definitive performances of the music of Liszt gained him further important awards and established him as an artist of the first rank. Chorzempa is a genuine virtuoso, playing the whole of his wide-ranging repertoire from memory.

Prior to his visit to Belfast he had been in Dublin where he had been preparing for a recital on the magnificent Willis organ in St Patrick's Cathedral towards the end of that week. His railway journey north on

Wednesday morning was disrupted by an IRA bomb explosion on the line, a fairly frequent occurrence in those days, causing him to arrive in Belfast later than he had planned and severely reducing the amount of time available for practice. Nevertheless he gave a masterly recital that evening of music by Buxtehude, Pachelbel, Bach, Reger and Messaien. In view of the fact that playing of this very high calibre was rarely heard in Belfast at that time, a much larger audience might have been confidently expected.

Concerts on Thursday and Friday 16 and 17 October gave the young people of the city opportunities to demonstrate their instrumental and vocal abilities. The first of these concerts was given by the City of Belfast Youth Orchestra, conducted by Leonard Pugh and in the second, some of the leading school choirs performed both individually under their own conductors and collectively under the direction of Douglas Armstrong.

For the many people who participated in it, the final event, which took place on Saturday 18 October, was undoubtedly one of the highlights of the Festival. The music critic of the *Belfast Telegraph* reviewed it as follows:

> In the morning and afternoon much musical activity was centred on the grand finale of the St Anne's Cathedral one-week Festival, a highly successful event that reflects much credit on the Dean, Organist and all involved.
>
> Another celebrity, this time the revered David Willcocks, of King's College, Cambridge fame, prepared a gigantic choir of anything up to 500 singers from local parish church choirs for Choral Evensong.
>
> The service itself was an inspiring experience, displaying the Anglican tradition at its best. Stanford's setting in C of the canticles and Charles Wood's *O Thou the Central Orb* came over with tremendous impact backed by Mr Grindle's effective organ accompaniment. The choral tone was of splendid quality, rich and firm, and producing a thrilling sound at climaxes.
>
> Four solid hours of rehearsal showed why Mr Willcocks's reputation was so well deserved. With great economy of words and almost deceptive ease he overcame problems like the ever-present singer who never watches the conductor and the almost universal variations in chanting. The singers responded superbly to his lead.
>
> With excellent balance, and a surprising array of men's voices, this was a service to remember, while the seemingly never-ending and dignified procession of choristers in robes of various colours was in itself a sight to behold.

This report specifically mentions the way in which Mr Willcocks dealt with a singer who was not paying any attention to his conducting. From my position at the organ console I had an excellent view of the choir and the quite dramatic effect of the ploy which he used. Without identifying the person in question he said, 'There is a lovely lady over here on my right who isn't looking at me.' The key-word was 'lovely'. With one accord *all* of the ladies in that area immediately looked up at him.

In the course of the Festival many hundreds of people had come to the Cathedral to enjoy the music and to inspect the latest addition to the building. From Friday 10 until Sunday 12 October there was the added attraction of a Flower Festival entitled *A Vision of Peace*. The beautiful floral arrangements gave us glimpses of that better future for our province for which everyone earnestly prayed.

The invitation to past choristers to participate in the singing of most of the choral items at their annual service in November had resulted in increased attendances in recent years. Such traditional ceremonies as the induction of a new chorister and the presentation of various awards were usually included in the service, adding a touch of nostalgia to the proceedings for the older generation. On 23 November 1975, when the assembled vocal forces numbered in the region of a hundred, all derived obvious enjoyment from their singing of Noble's setting in B minor of the canticles and that perennially favourite anthem, *Blessed be the God and Father* by Samuel Sebastian Wesley. I am sure that in their performance of the famous passage for trebles only, 'Love one another with a pure Heart fervently', the choristers were always determined to show their predecessors that the tradition at Belfast Cathedral was in very safe hands.

It was the normal practice at this service for individual past choristers to undertake such duties as the reading of the lessons, the lifting of the collection, etc. The Vicar Choral would occasionally invite a fellow clerical member of the Past Choristers' Association to act as Cantor. This gentleman would turn up on the day and sing the service. With my introduction of various sets of responses by Tudor and other composers, our visitor, who was probably a parish clergyman, was now likely to find himself in unfamiliar musical territory. After one particularly disastrous experience, I had to insist that visiting cantors attend the previous Wednesday's full choir rehearsal.

At this service the sermon was usually preached by a clergyman with a musical background. In 1975, at the invitation of the Dean, I gave an address on 'The role of the musician in the worship of the Church.'

My final public concert with the Cathedral Choir and the Ulster Orchestra took place on Advent Sunday, 30 November that year. It gave me great pleasure to be associated with the orchestra's excellent leader at that time, Pan Hon Lee, who in 1980 would be appointed to the leadership of the Hallé Orchestra in Manchester. Pan's thoroughly professional approach to his work was an important contributory factor to the success of this concert. The purely orchestral items were Bach's *Brandenburg Concerto No3 in G* and Purcell's *Chacony in G minor*.

I have always felt that the intimate, chamber-music character of this Brandenburg Concerto is best realised by having one player to each part. Arranged in a semi-circle, the players can readily share with the listeners their delight in the many attractive features of this wonderful music such as the antiphonal interplay of the trios of violins, violas and cellos in the first movement. In Bach's time, one would assume that the two extant quick movements were separated by a contrasting slow one probably improvised at the keyboard. To complete our performance of the work, Keith Rogers, who was our harpsichordist, played a passage from Bach's *Toccata in E minor (BWV 914)*.

The first half of the concert also included Purcell's *Rejoice in the Lord alway* and Pergolesi's *Magnificat*. After the interval the Cathedral Choir sang three unaccompanied anthems: settings by Gibbons and Weelkes of *Hosanna to the Son of David* and Robert Parsons's beautiful *Ave Maria*. Choir and orchestra then combined in the final work, Bach's Cantata No 140 : *Wachet auf! ('Sleepers wake!')* which was sung in German.

The Cathedral Choir undoubtedly added to its laurels with this concert and critiques were extremely positive. An excerpt from the review by Alfred Burrowes in the *Irish Times* includes an interesting reflection:

> It was a splendid occasion, the fine Choir of young men (many of whom are ex-choristers), boys and a few women being a living testimony to a remarkable achievement over a decade of solid patient work that needed adaptation to changing conditions inside and outside the Cathedral.
>
> The Choir is now a potent force in its prime and well equipped in every department, and its confidence is visible in its bearing. It must be a matter of some heart-searching that such a man as Harry Grindle, trained to this specialised work, should find it necessary to relinquish what for many is an ultimate goal.

Because I was due to leave the Cathedral in January 1976, I had handed over the conductorship of the Cathedral Singers to Keith Rogers and it was under his direction that they gave their second recital in the Cathedral on Sunday 14 December when the programme consisted largely of music for Advent. As well as accompanying the Choir in Gibbons's *This is the Record of John* and Britten's *Rejoice in the Lamb,* I played some seasonal chorale preludes by Bach, Brahms, Flor Peeters and Keith Rogers. I made one further appearance with the Singers in March 1976 accompanying their performance of Handel's coronation anthem, *The King shall rejoice* and playing Buxtehude's *Chaconne in E minor* and Vaughan Williams's *Three Preludes on Welsh Hymn tunes.*

The annual Carol Service in December 1975 was notable for the inclusion of two specially-composed items. The first of these, with interpolated English verses by the composer, was Keith Rogers's *Dormi Jesu* which was later published by Banks. This extremely sensitive setting of a traditional text bears very favourable comparison with the better-known one by Edmund Rubbra.

The second novelty was *A Star was His Night-light* by Paul Hoey, the winning entry in a Carol Competition sponsored by the Cathedral Choir. This competition was open to young musicians under the age of twenty who had been born in Northern Ireland. In addition to a cash prize the winner was promised a first performance of his/her composition by the Cathedral Choir. Paul Hoey who was at that time a sixth-form student at Grosvenor High School, as it was then known, recently reminded me that I was the examiner when he sat both his O and A level practical examinations. Since 1975 his winning carol has had a number of further performances, one of them in a cathedral in Australia. Paul was ordained into the ministry of the Church of Ireland in 1981.

Although my contract at the Cathedral terminated at the end of 1975, I had willingly agreed to accept responsibility for the direction of two Choral Evensong broadcasts on 14 and 21 January 1976. In the second of these the canticles were sung to Herbert Howells's *St Paul's* setting and the anthem was 'Let all the World in every Corner sing', the last of Vaughan Williams's *Five Mystical Songs*. Among the many appreciative letters which we afterwards received was one from Herbert Howells which is reproduced below:

Letter from Herbert Howells, January 1976 (Published by kind permission of the Literary Executors of the Herbert Howells Trust)

from
HERBERT HOWELLS
3 BEVERLEY CLOSE
BARNES, S. W. 13
01-876 5119

23 Jan.ᵗ 1976

My dear Harry Grindle:

For two reasons I owe you my affectionate thanks:

one; for your very kind letter — (it touched me so much)

two: Wednesday's broadcast of the "St Paul's" Canticles.

For both I am really grateful. My warm thanks go to you yourself and I want you, in your kindness, to tell your buoyant, keen, enlightened Choir at St Anne's how grateful I am for a performance so secure and moving. I shall remember it in gratitude for (especially) the way you seemed to rebuke those other folk who try to make me believe it's "difficult"! What may be hard is the getting to the heart of it — But that's just what you did, bless you!

I'm so glad I had the chance to listen to the broadcast. And "Let all the world" was thrilling. "Uncle Ralph V-W" would have loved it.

Thank you again.

Yours very sincerely,
Herbert Howells:

The members of the Cathedral Choir, Edwin Gray, who had played the organ accompaniments, and I were, of course, delighted to know that our performance had clearly met with the composer's enthusiastic approval. We also regarded it as something of a compliment that Dr Howells had taken the trouble to write to us, because, as I was to discover, in his latter years he was not given to answering letters.

At what was for me personally an extremely emotional juncture in my life as I took my leave of the Cathedral where I had spent ten very challenging but none-the-less fulfilling years, Dr Howells's kind and encouraging message was all the more welcome. In years to come I would undertake a detailed study of his church music and would have the great pleasure of meeting him at the RCM to discuss this very important aspect of his output.

As I reflect on the eventful decade which I spent at Belfast Cathedral, I can say with the utmost certainty that nothing gave me more satisfaction than my work with the boys. It is, therefore, particularly gratifying to record that a number of those who were choristers during that period have gone on to pursue either full- or part-time careers in music. Among them are the following:

CHRISTOPHER BELL studied music at Edinburgh University. His appointment as Associate Conductor of the BBC Scottish Symphony Orchestra launched a busy and varied career that has taken him to many countries. An inspiring choral conductor, he is Chorus Director of the Grant Park Chorus in Chicago, USA and Chorus Master of both the Edinburgh Festival Chorus and the Belfast Philharmonic Choir. He has been Director of the Royal Scottish National Orchestra Junior Chorus since 1994 and Artistic Director of the National Youth Choir of Scotland since its inception in 1996. Described as 'probably the best-known and most-loved musician working in Scotland today', Christopher Bell has been the recipient of a number of important awards. The most recent of these is the degree of Master of the Open University in May 2009.

STEPHEN BELL (Christopher's younger brother) is a music graduate of Southampton University and also holds a MMus degree in conducting from the University of Surrey. His early association with the Southampton University Light Opera Society as its Musical Director gave rise to a lifelong passion for shows. Stephen combines his musical activities with a career as a Group Training Manager with Mercedes-Benz, Milton Keynes. He has wide experience as a choral and orchestral conductor and played the bassoon in the Northampton Concert Band until his appointment as the Band's permanent conductor in September, 2005. Under his direction the Band has won a number of gold awards at the National Festival of the British Association of Symphonic Bands and Wind Ensembles. In September 2007 he was appointed Musical Director of the St Cecilia Singers in Rushden, Northamptonshire. Stephen's daughters, Rebecca and Hannah, have been violinists in the National Youth Orchestra of Great Britain.

ALAN BOYD has maintained an unbroken association with Belfast Cathedral since his days as a chorister in the 1960s. As a counter-tenor in the Cathedral Choir, as Choir Librarian, as a member of the Cathedral Board, as Chairman and Secretary of the Past Choristers' Association at various times and in his present capacity as Hon. Archivist he has rendered loyal and invaluable service. He studied singing locally with Donald Cairns and Paul Deegan and has attended the Deller Summer School in the South of France. A primary school teacher by profession, Alan has been very actively involved in the musical life of the province. With first-rate counter-tenors in short supply, he has been for many years in great demand as a soloist, particularly in music of the Baroque period, and he has broadcast on several occasions. He has also sung in a number of leading local choirs and vocal ensembles. Alan is currently on secondment as Director of the Pushkin Trust.

MERVYN COLLINS read music at the University of Surrey and studied singing with Arthur Reckless and Mary Thomas. As a member of the Netherlands Chamber Choir (1980-81) he sang under such eminent conductors as Gustav Leonhardt and Nikolaus Harnoncourt. He was a lay-clerk at Guildford Cathedral 1982-84 and at the Queen's Chapel of the Savoy 1984-85. Since 1985 he has been a Vicar Choral at St Paul's Cathedral, London. He has performed extensively as a tenor soloist in many countries, his repertoire ranging from Gibbons to Honneger. Mervyn is particularly noted for his performances of the role of the Evangelist in the Bach Passions. He is also a very experienced session singer, working in both television and film productions with such artists as Tommy Steele, Maurice Jarre, Michael Crawford and Stan Tracey.

BRIAN GORDON won many prizes as a treble at competitive musical festivals including major awards at the Feis Ceoil in Dublin. Later he studied both singing and conducting at the RAM. He was a lay-clerk at St George's Chapel, Windsor (1978-79) and he has at various times sung with the Monteverdi Choir, the Schütz Choir, the Deller Consort, the Sixteen, the Hilliard Ensemble and the BBC Singers. As a concert and opera soloist, Brian has appeared at a number of prestigious European venues including London's South Bank, the Musikvereinsaal, Vienna and La Scala, Milan. A Baroque specialist, he has also taken part in commercial recordings of Handel's *Israel in Egypt* and Purcell's *Ode for St Cecilia's Day* under Sir John Eliot Gardiner. Since 1990 he has devoted himself to voice-teaching (at Eton College and elsewhere), coaching and choir-training.

STEWART HASLETT was a treble and later a bass soloist in the choir of Belfast Cathedral. He enjoyed considerable success at competitive musical festivals and broadcast on BBC radio and television. At the age of twenty he entered the RAM where he studied with the distinguished bass-baritone, Henry Cummings and he was soon appearing regularly at concerts both in London and the provinces. He deputised frequently in the choir of St Paul's Cathedral. For a time he was a lay-clerk in the Choir of Christ Church Cathedral, Oxford under Simon Preston. Stewart's highly promising career was cut short by his tragic death at an early age.

PETER HUNTER studied organ initially with the author and subsequently with Gordon Phillips at the London College of Music from where he graduated in 1974. After his return to Northern Ireland, he was Organist and Choirmaster successively at Donegall Square Methodist Church (1974-75), St Mark's Parish Church, Dundela (1975-76) and Bangor Abbey (1986-89). In 1975 he was also appointed Head of Music at Annadale Grammar School where he himself had been educated. Since 1995 he has been in charge of the Music Department at Friends' School, Lisburn and he has held the post of Organist and Choirmaster at St Mark's, Dundela (for a second time) since 1996. Peter has carried out extensive research into the work of some of the lesser composers of the twentieth century English Musical Renaissance, his specialism being the life and music of Robin Milford (1903-59), of which subject he is at present preparing a study for publication.

CHRISTOPHER JENKINS studied at the RCM (1969-72) with Sydney Campbell and John Birch(organ), Millicent Silver(harpsichord) and Herbert Howells(composition). After serving as Assistant Organist at Southwark Cathedral (1971-72), he held the post of Organist at the Parish Church of St John the Divine, Kennington (1972-73). From 1973 to 1988 he combined the post of Director of Music at Ruthin School in North Wales with that of Organist at the Collegiate Church of St Peter in Ruthin. Christopher was Precentor (i.e. Director of Music) at St Columba's College, Whitechurch, Dublin from 1988 to 2002. Under his direction the school choir travelled widely, singing in France (Chartres

Cathedral and Paris), Italy (St Peter's Basilica in Rome, the Duomo in Florence and Venice) and America (New York and Boston). He has also given organ recitals at Lincoln and Truro Cathedrals, Christchurch Priory and various London churches.

AUBREY McCLINTOCK, having combined a choral scholarship at Norwich Cathedral with his music studies at the University of East Anglia (1977-80), taught and sang in the choir at St Michael's College, Tenbury 1980-81. He subsequently pursued a varied career as a teacher, singer and choral conductor. Under his direction the St Bede's School Chamber Choir won the National Choral Competition in 1988 and was runner-up in 1989. In 1990 Aubrey returned to Northern Ireland where he has built up a thriving private teaching practice. He also founded and directed the Armagh City Junior Choir, the Armagh Girl Singers and various vocal groups. In 1994 he established the Charles Wood Summer School and, until 2000, he directed the Charles Wood Singers. He has appeared as a soloist with many of the province's leading choirs.

HUGH MACKEY holds a first-class honours degree in Drama and English from Manchester University. He studied singing at the Manchester School of Music with John Grierson and Dame Isobel Baillie and at the Guildhall School of Music and Drama. He has also taken part in Master Classes given by, among others, Peter Pears and Galina Vishnevskaya at the Britten-Pears School of Advanced Musical Studies. Hugh was engaged by Hamburg State Opera in 1986 and was the Northern Ireland representative entry in the BBC's Cardiff Singer of the World Competition in 1987. As a soloist in opera and oratorio and as a Lieder singer, he has appeared in a number of European countries. He has recorded, for Chandos, Moeran's *Nocturne* with the Ulster Orchestra under Vernon Handley and has taken part in the filming of Vaughan Williams's *Riders of the Sea* with the RTÉ Orchestra and Chorus conducted by Bryden Thompson .

ROGER MARTIN, after graduating in Modern Languages at Queen's University, Belfast, trained as a chartered accountant in preparation for a career in the world of business. He has been company accountant with a number of firms. As an adult he sang alto and then bass in the Choir of Belfast Cathedral and studied singing with Donald Cairns. While at university he formed a barbershop quartet, aptly called *Five-minus-one,* which performed frequently on BBC Radio and Television. He was for many years a member of the Renaissance Singers who won the first Sainsbury's Choir of the Year Competition in 1984 and he has sung with the St George's Singers and the Priory Singers. Roger particularly enjoys singing in small vocal ensembles. For ten years he was a member of Pavane, a very successful group of ten voices, and he currently sings with Melisma (eight voices). He is also well known locally as a soloist in both oratorio and opera.

RODERICK SMYTH who is a music graduate of Queen's University, Belfast also holds MEd and BTh degrees from the Universities of Ulster and Wales (Lampeter) respectively. Since 1978 he has been successively Head of Music at three of the province's schools and was appointed Head of Senior School at Bangor Academy and Sixth Form College in 2006. Having sung bass in the choirs of St Bartholomew's Parish Church and Belfast Cathedral, he became a church organist in 1978. He has been at St Gall's Parish Church, Carnalea, Bangor for the past seventeen years. Roderick has also been active as an opera and choral conductor and can claim the distinction of directing, while at Queen's, the first reconstructed performance of Luigi Rossi's *L'Orfeo* since 1610. In 1975 he was elected a Life President of the Queen's University Opera Society. He continues to conduct the Gryphon Consort which he founded in 2006.

CHAPTER ELEVEN

1975-85 | Stranmillis College, further studies

Founded by the Northern Ireland Government in 1922, Stranmillis College occupies a magnificent, 46-acre site in the southern part of Belfast, a blend of woodland, meadow and marsh giving the grounds a unique rural quality. By the 1970s there were five other teacher-training institutions in Northern Ireland. These were the so-called 'voluntary' Roman Catholic Colleges, St Joseph's (for men) and St Mary's (for women), the Queen's University Faculty of Education, the New University of Ulster (NUU) and the Ulster Polytechnic. With the gradual reduction over the ensuing years in the intakes of trainee-teachers it was evident that rationalisation and consolidation would be necessary. In 1982 the Higher Education Review Group under the chairmanship of Sir Henry Chilver advocated the amalgamation, on a single site in a new Belfast Centre of Teacher Education, of the three Colleges of Education (i.e. Stranmillis, St Joseph's and St Mary's) and the Queen's University Faculty of Education. This proposed amalgamation found favour with the Stranmillis Board of Governors and Academic Board who, in their submission to the Review Group in 1979, had expressed their preference for an integrated approach to the training of teachers. Despite the obvious advantages of such an arrangement, from both organisational and social points of view, the Chilver recommendations proved to be unacceptable to the two Roman Catholic Colleges. A compromise solution, suggested by the Stranmillis Board, that consideration be given to a federation of the Colleges on a split site seems to have been equally unwelcome. In the face of such opposition the Government decided against the pursuit of an essentially logical and economically desirable aim. The net outcome of what had been protracted and difficult negotiations was the voluntary merger of St Joseph's with St Mary's and the amalgamation of the NUU and the Ulster Polytechnic. This reduced the number of teacher-training institutions in the province from six to four.

A closer relationship between Queen's University, which validates the BEd degree, and the two colleges of education was brought about by the granting of 'university college' status to Stranmillis and St Mary's from September 1998. Academic provision would be henceforth fully integrated into the University's structure while the governing body of each of the colleges would retain its independent control. In his lecture to mark the seventy-fifth anniversary of Stranmillis in 1997 the eminent educationist, Sir William Taylor, sought to inspire his audience with his optimistic vision of the College's future. In reality, for several years, as it strove to maintain its viability despite falling student numbers, Stranmillis had been increasingly attempting to extend its programme of academic diversification. At the time of writing (2009) it would appear that Stranmillis will be amalgamated with the Queen's University Faculty of Education when the latter transfers in due course to the College site. The St Mary's Board will seek to maintain the autonomy of its college.

In the mid-1970s the Stranmillis Campus was a particularly busy place as an academic staff of about 120 prepared some 1500 students for entry to both the primary and secondary sectors of the teaching profession. The promotion of John McDowell to the post of Head of the Music Department in 1975 had created the vacancy which I was appointed to fill. John, a fine pianist and composer, was to prove himself to be a very able administrator. Our experienced colleagues were Daphne Bell who was also the Director of the Ulster College of Music, Michael Richards and Charles Keenan.

As well as giving lectures to full-time students, one might be required to take evening classes (5.00p.m. - 7.00p.m.) attended by in-service teachers some of whom travelled considerable distances to be present. Visits to schools to supervise students' teaching-practice were another aspect of the lecturer's schedule.

Music has always played an important role in the life of the College, many of the activities bringing together students from various subject departments. It was, however, largely due to John McDowell's professional direction that performance standards attracted widespread public attention. The Operatic Society's annual Gilbert and Sullivan productions accompanied by the College Orchestra were always enjoyed by packed houses. The Stranmillis Singers, a chamber choir founded by John in 1970, broadcast regularly and appeared several times on television. They had an impressive record of success at competitive musical festivals. In the 1970s they were three-times winners of the Northern Ireland heat of the BBC choral competition, *Let the Peoples Sing*, and on one occasion were United Kingdom runners-up.

All music students were expected to sing in the College Choir membership of which was also open to students from other departments and to staff. The College Orchestra under Charles Keenan, our string specialist, gave the instrumentalists valuable ensemble experience while the weekly lunch-time recitals, usually given by visiting soloists, sometimes provided a platform for outstanding student performers.

John McDowell assigned to me the direction of the College Choir which in 1975 had about eighty singers, among them nine members of staff. Michael Richards was our helpful and patient accompanist. Rehearsals were on Wednesday afternoons which, in the College time-table, were allocated to recreational pursuits. John rehearsed his Stranmillis Singers later in the afternoon in order to accommodate the graduate members who were serving teachers.

Harry rehearsing the Stranmillis College Choir c1997 *(Reproduced from* Stran *by kind permission of the authors, George Beale and Eamon Phoenix)*

The College Choir normally gave two concerts per year, one in December and the other at the end of the Easter term, in either the College Theatre or Belfast Cathedral or the Harty Room in the University's Music Department. Programmes usually included a substantial choral work with orchestral accompaniment, vocal soloists being almost always undergraduate students. As well as such standard repertoire items as Handel's *Messiah*, Bach's *Christmas Oratorio*, Haydn's *Theresienmesse*, Mozart's *Requiem*, Schubert's *Mass in G* and Fauré's *Requiem*, the choir presented less familiar works from time to time. Among these were Purcell's *Ode for St Cecilia's Day* and Carissimi's oratorio, *Jephte*, which, requiring a SSSATB chorus, was a very appropriate choice for the College Choir with its preponderance of upper voices. Both the alto part of the narrator and the bass solos in *Jephte* were sung by William Thompson, a former King's College, Cambridge choral scholar, who was at that time a post-graduate student at Stranmillis. Another versatile soloist was Valerie Ireland who has been closely identified with music-making at the College since her student days. A founder-member of the Stranmillis Singers and one of the 'stars' of the Operatic Society, Valerie's musical talent has long been recognised. When in March 1979 the student contralto soloist in Pergolesi's *Stabat Mater* was taken ill on the day before the performance, Valerie stepped into the breach at twenty-four hours' notice, learning the music and singing it with characteristic aplomb at the concert the following evening with the minimum of rehearsal. Five years later she delivered the demanding soprano solo part, which includes several top Cs, in Bach's Cantata no. 51, *Jauchzet Gott in allen Landen* with astonishing agility, accuracy and clarity. With Valerie's superb singing admirably complemented by Clifford Lennon's masterly trumpet-playing, this performance, directed from the harpsichord by John McDowell, was a real *tour de force*.

As the number of male students decreased it became more and more difficult to maintain a mixed-voice chorus and this was eventually replaced by a ladies' choir which, too, was capable of achieving high standards. There can be few works for upper voices to compare with Benjamin Britten's *Ceremony of Carols* which this choir sang in December 1981. Like many another creative musician, Britten found mediaeval verse a rich source of inspiration and this delightful work, composed when he was in his late twenties, is an undoubted masterpiece. We were fortunate to have, as our accompanist, the Ulster Orchestra's harpist, Audrey Douglas, whose excellent playing enhanced a performance which must be counted as one of the choir's finest.

Concerts also included contributions from the College Orchestra, the Stranmillis Singers, the College Brass Ensemble or one of the current student chamber music groups. Student instrumentalists of concerto standard were always grateful for the chance to play in public a work of this sort accompanied by a competent orchestra. In March 1976 at a concert in the Harty Room at Queen's University, it gave me great pleasure to conduct a performance of Handel's *Organ Concerto in F Op. 4 No. 4* in which the very able soloist was Edwin Gray, a final-year student, who had been my assistant at Belfast Cathedral.

The polished performance of the Stranmillis Singers was the outstanding feature of the annual College Carol Service held each year in Fisherwick Presbyterian Church. A large congregation, which included many former Stranmillis students and friends of the College, invariably filled the candlelit building, joining lustily in the singing of the hymns and thoroughly enjoying the general atmosphere of this special event. On this and other occasions when the Stranmillis Singers were invited to appear in churches I would act as their accompanist as well as playing some organ solos.

Although I did not now have the freedom that I once had to accept other engagements, when these were either in the evening or at weekends I could usually manage to make myself available. Sometimes, in the process, I renewed acquaintances with old friends or former colleagues as was the case when I gladly agreed to assist Dr Murray Brown, from Durham University, with the adjudication at the1976 Musical Festival in Bangor, Co. Down, my home town. The experience brought back many happy memories of my association with this event in past years. As a small boy I had competed in the Junior Piano Class in the first session of the first day of the very first Bangor Musical Festival, 29 April, 1947. My singular lack of success on that occasion was probably due as much to understandable nervousness as it was to finding myself, the only boy in the competition, up against a group of young ladies for most of whom the prospect of playing in public seemed to hold no terrors whatsoever.

During the time that I served as the Organist of Bangor Parish Church (1962-64) I was a member of the Festival Committee. In 1976, the Honorary Music Secretary of the Festival was Mrs Caroline Jones, née McClune, who, as a girl, almost always won the classes in which she competed. Caroline and her colleagues on the Festival Committee kindly presented me with a suitably inscribed plaque, bearing the coat of arms of the Borough of Bangor, in recognition of the award to me of an Associateship of the Royal School of Church Music (ARSCM). I consider myself fortunate to have one of these attractive plaques which became increasingly rare after Bangor's loss of its borough status in October 1973 when, in a reorganisation of local government, the town was incorporated in the new borough of North Down.

I was honoured to be the first Irish musician to receive this diploma which was presented at a special garden party on 2 July 1977 at Addington Palace, Croydon, the headquarters of the RSCM, to mark the golden jubilee of its foundation. Because Heather had to remain at home with our two daughters, now aged six and two, I had invited, as my guests, Frank and Ellen Freestone with whom I had lodged when I was teaching at Friern Barnet Grammar School in the early 1960s. My personal enjoyment of this splendid social occasion was increased by the surprise arrival of my Belfast friends Valerie Ireland, Geoffrey Blower and Alan Boyd who had decided to come along to lend their support and to join in the celebrations.

In March 1977 the choir of Bangor Parish Church, directed by Ian Hunter, gave a recital of Passiontide music as a tribute to the memory of the great English composer, Benjamin Britten who had died in December of the previous year. An impressive programme, consisting largely of music by Britten, had been arranged. When Dr Havelock Nelson, who was to have given the eulogy, had to withdraw, I was asked to take his place at short notice. I clearly remember that the service was at 8.00p.m. and that at 7.30p.m. I was putting the finishing touches to my script at home in Belfast. Having reached the church just as the choir was entering it, I took my place at the end of the procession!

At the invitation of the organiser, Mr Geoffrey Trory, the Department of Education's Music Inspector, I directed a series of five choral workshops as part of the 1977 Summer Course for Teachers. This was held in the Music Department of Queen's University towards the end of June.

In July 1977 and August 1978 I took part in recitals at Ballywillan Presbyterian Church which is situated on the outskirts of Portrush, a popular seaside resort on the north coast of Northern Ireland. Over a period of thirty years (1975-2004) the enterprising Organist of the church, Adrian Anderson, arranged recitals on Sunday evenings throughout the summer months. While his primary aim was to promote an interest in organ music, Adrian, in an attempt to give the recitals as broad a public appeal as possible, devised programmes which usually included another instrumentalist and either a vocal soloist or choir. In addition to engaging established artists, Adrian gave opportunities to promising young musicians to demonstrate their talents to appreciative audiences which regularly numbered in excess of two hundred.

Other recitals in which I took part in 1977 included one in March with John McDowell's Stranmillis Singers in Strean Presbyterian Church in Newtownards and another with the choir of St Mark's Parish Church, Dundela in November for a visit of the USOC. I also gave solo organ recitals in St Bartholomew's Parish Church, Belfast in the Stranmillis College lunch-time series in February and October. On Christmas Day 1977 a programme of choral music by Buxtehude sung by the Stranmillis Singers was broadcast on BBC Radio Ulster. As well as providing organ continuo, I played two of the composer's seasonal chorale preludes.

In 1976 I had resumed my academic studies which were inevitably neglected during the eventful decade that I spent at Belfast Cathedral. My immediate objective was the completion of the MusB degree at Trinity College, Dublin. In my preparation for the final examinations, I sought the help of Dr Joseph Groocock who was to prove to be both an inspirational mentor and a generous friend.

Born in Croydon, Surrey, Joe was educated at St Michael's College, Tenbury, (a unique Anglican choral establishment, founded in the mid-nineteenth century by the Revd Sir Frederick Gore Ouseley), where he was a Choral Scholar, Rugby School, and Christ Church, Oxford where he read Classics and Music. He came to Ireland in 1935. Over the next sixty years he taught thousands of music students, first at St Columba's College, Whitechurch, then at Trinity College , the Royal Irish Academy of Music (RIAM) and the Dublin College of Music. In the course of his long association with the Trinity College Choral Society as its beloved conductor, Joe touched countless lives. It gave him the utmost pleasure to introduce his largely undergraduate chorus to the great choral masterpieces, in particular those of Bach whom he revered. He was also active as a broadcaster, adjudicator, accompanist and organist. The award to him of a Doctorate in Music *(h.c.)* by Trinity College in 1964, in recognition of his wonderful record of service to the cause of music in Ireland, was richly deserved and widely applauded.

He delighted in sharing his enthusiasm for and vast knowledge of the processes of musical composition with those who were eager to learn from him and he was always at pains to enable his students to realise their full potential, insisting that what was written must be accurately heard by the inner ear. An acknowledged authority on counterpoint, Joe was in his element when dealing with fugal writing. He died, as he had wished, 'in harness', in August 1997. The music of J S Bach figured prominently in the very impressive and moving funeral service in Trinity College Chapel and it was appropriate that we should take our leave of our very dear friend by singing the final chorale from the *St John Passion*. For Joe's sake the members of the choir and capacity congregation struggled to overcome their emotion to give a worthy performance of this touching valedictory text:

'Lord Jesus, Thy dear angels send,
Whene'r my mortal life shall end,
And bear my soul to heaven.
Within its narrow chamber keep
My body safe in painless sleep,
Till Thy last call be given.

And when from death Thou wakest me,
In bliss untold mine eyes shall see,
O Son of God, Thy glorious face,
My Saviour and my Fount of Grace.
Lord Jesus Christ, O hear Thou me,
Thee will I praise eternally.'

Initially Joe had adamantly refused to accept any payment for the periodic consultation lessons which he gave me, saying that he regarded it as a compliment that someone should be prepared to travel so far to seek his advice on musical matters. It was stimulating to be in his company. In order to encourage the quick response necessary when working under examination conditions and against the clock, he would frequently set a contrapuntal problem to be solved on the spot in a few minutes. By the end of the allotted time, he himself had invariably come up with a number of possible solutions.

Because the Trinity MusB was an 'external' degree i.e. open to candidates who were not full-time students of the University, the examinations were held over three consecutive days in June to accommodate those entrants who came from a distance, in some cases from various parts of Great Britain. On the first day one was required to complete a composition for a prescribed medium in the space of six hours. Contrapuntal technique was tested in a three-hour examination on the morning of the second day with a history of music paper in the afternoon while, on the third day, candidates had to write a fugue on a given subject in the morning and make specified orchestral arrangements of given contrasting passages of piano music in the afternoon. On one of the evenings each candidate also had to undergo a *viva*, based on a number of set works, with the external examiner.

After about nineteen hours of examination, much of it calling for intense concentration, I was utterly exhausted and was glad to return home to Belfast in the evening of the final day. Joe Groocock had promised to phone me with the results when they were posted, according to tradition, at midnight on that same day. The news could not have been better- I had graduated with first-class honours and, having come top in the examinations, had been awarded the Stewart and Prout Prize.

Having taken part with the Cathedral Consort in the BBC choral competition, *Let the Peoples Sing*, in 1969, it was very interesting for me to be involved in the adjudication process nine years later. As the outside assessor for the Northern Ireland regional heats in March 1978, I acted as chairman of the panel of judges summarising its comments and announcing the winners in the course of a broadcast of a selection of performances by the competing choirs.

I was pleased to be invited to adjudicate the music classes at the Warrenpoint Feis which was being revived in November 1978 after a lapse of more than twenty years. The Feis, which was held in conjunction with the Newry and Mourne Arts Festival, also included sections, with separate adjudicators, for Speech and Drama as well as Irish Dancing. The hard-working members of the organising committee must have been heartened both by the large number of entries which were received and by the level of public support for the Feis. In the junior violin classes I was very impressed by the promise shown by several of the competitors whose musical and technically-secure playing testified to the excellence of the tuition which they were receiving from a gifted local priest.

It was with some excitement that I learned in the late 1970s of Dr Donald Davison's proposal to establish in Belfast a centre 'with the aim of providing instruction, information, help and encouragement to all concerned with church music,' to quote from its first quarterly newsletter issued in the Spring of 1980. Few have done as much as Donald Davison to further the cause of church music in Ireland.

Donald was educated at Inst, Queen's University, Belfast and Gonville and Caius College, Cambridge. He gained the FRCO diploma at the age of nineteen and has, for much of his life, pursued, with conspicuous success, parallel careers as a mathematician and as a musician. For twenty-one years he was Belfast City Organist, giving hundreds of recitals in the Ulster Hall and playing often with the Ulster Orchestra in concerts and recordings. He has broadcast frequently and has given recitals at such prestigious venues as King's College, Cambridge and St Paul's Cathedral, London. For many years he also held the position of University Organist at Queen's University, Belfast where he was Head of the Department of Statistics and Operational Research. A parish church organist since boyhood, he has occupied his present post at St John's, Malone since 1977. For the Church of Ireland, he was Joint Musical Editor of *Irish Church Praise* (1990), Music Editor of the *Church Hymnal*, 5th edition (2000) and Joint Editor of the monumental *Companion to CH 5* (2004). His compositions include service settings, anthems and responses. The awards of an ARSCM in 2006 and the MBE in 2007 were recognition of a notable record of devoted service.

It was with the enthusiastic support of his fellow-members of the Joint Committee for Church Music in Ireland, who provided generous financial assistance, that the Ulster Church Music Centre (UCMC) was opened in January 1978 with its base at St John's, Malone. For the convenience of those who lived some distance from Belfast, courses were also arranged to take place at other venues across the province. I was glad to be a member of the committee and to assist with the organisation and direction of some of the courses which were offered and for which there was a great demand, as the rapid take-up of places indicated. Those of us who were tutors found it very rewarding to teach such eager students and to help them to develop their musical skills. It was a great pity that a decision was taken to close the UCMC in 1988.

I had become a member of the USOC in February 1954 when I was still in my teens. Since then I have been invited to address the Society a number of times on the subject of choir-training among other things. One of these illustrated talks was given in October 1979 in the Chapel of the Union Theological College, in Belfast. As well as dealing with the preparation and performance of hymns, psalms and anthems, I also discussed the identification and solution of choral problems in a passage of music written for the occasion.

I considered it an honour to be invited by Gerard Gillen in 1979 to contribute to the major series of organ recitals which he arranges each year on Sunday evenings during June, July and August at St Michael's (Roman Catholic) Church in Dun Laoghaire. Large audiences, including a strong representation from the Dublin church music fraternity, come to hear organists not only from Great Britain and Ireland but also from Europe and North America. Gerard Gillen acted as consultant when the organ, constructed by the Austrian firm, Rieger Orgelbau, was installed in 1974 in the modern church which replaced the original Gothic building destroyed by fire in 1968. The spire of the latter, for long a familiar landmark in the town and the only part of the earlier church to survive, has been incorporated in the new building.

The Rieger Organ, something of a novelty in Ireland at the time of its installation, has two manuals, Hauptwerk and Brustwerk, with mechanical key and stop action throughout. The Brustwerk is enclosed, the shutters being, unusually, made of glass. Since, with its 'classical' voicing, the organ is ideally suited to the performance of Baroque works, my programme consisted of music by Bach and the French composer, Clérambault.

After successfully completing the MusB degree at Trinity College, Dublin, I decided to take an MA by examination over two years in Anglican Church Music at Queen's University, Belfast where the Head of the Music Department was Professor David Greer. I sat written examinations in the Church Music of the Restoration Period and the History of Hymnody and I also gave a public organ recital in the Sir William Whitla Hall where the audience included, among others, a number of students from Stranmillis College in addition to members of the panel of examiners. My programme of English organ music, drawn up and prepared with Gerard Gillen's kind assistance, ranged from a fourteenth century *Estampie* through Byrd, Bull, Tomkins, Stanley, Walond, the Wesleys, Vaughan Williams and Howells to Simon Preston's *Alleluias*.

The subject of my dissertation was *The Church Music of Herbert Howells* and I dealt with it under four headings: (i) Style, (ii) The Service Music, (iii) The Anthems and Motets, and (iv) The Role of the Organ. It occurred to me that it might be a good idea to try to arrange to meet Dr Howells and to discuss his music with him prior to the writing up of my work. As I have indicated earlier, in his latter years, Howells became an increasingly reluctant correspondent and, as I had expected might be the case, my letters went unanswered. For help I turned to Sir David Willcocks, now the Director of the RCM, who had a long association with the composer and his music. Sir David kindly arranged for me to meet Dr Howells, then in his late eighties, at the RCM on Monday 17 December 1979 and I went along armed with a small tape recorder, a brief-case crammed full of copies of his church music and a list of questions to put to him. We spent a couple of hours together. He expressed himself in his characteristically deliberate way, choosing his words carefully but with a tendency to wander from the subject under discussion. He seemed to enjoy reminiscing and appeared to be genuinely interested in what I made of his music. When we came to consider the great series of settings of the Magnificat and Nunc Dimittis which he had composed for various cathedrals and Oxbridge college chapels, he picked up the copy of the Gloucester Service, commenting, 'That is the one I like best,' quickly adding: 'But don't tell them that at King's!' Howells's heart had always belonged to Gloucestershire and the city of Gloucester, with its glorious cathedral, makes its own special contribution to the atmosphere of his music, as surely as traces of the regional accent, albeit slight, still lingered in his measured and thoughtful speech. Before we parted he took his pen and, in a shaky hand, inscribed the said copy as follows : 'Warm greetings to Harry Grindle from his friend Herbert Howells (1979)'. 'And that is what you are,' he said, smiling.

Although most of the questions on my list had not been addressed, the interview had been very worthwhile. I was deeply grateful for the opportunity to meet someone who has greatly enhanced the worship of the Anglican Church with a stream of inspired compositions which rank with the finest in the repertoire. It is possible to trace many influences on Howells's style: plainchant, Tudor polyphony and the music of such more recent English composers as Vaughan Williams, Elgar, Delius and Walton. There is also a certain indebtedness to Debussy and Ravel. Howells's style is essentially contrapuntal, the music's wonderfully convoluted lines reminding the listener that the composer was a devoted disciple of the great J S Bach. As an expression of the numinous, Howells's music has few equals.

Even before I had successfully completed this degree I was looking ahead to my next academic objective. Most church musicians are probably familiar with *English Cathedral Music from Edward VI to Edward VII* by E H Fellowes (1870-1951), to whose pioneering work, as an editor of the music of the Tudor period in particular, later generations are deeply indebted. It occurred to me that Irish Cathedral Music might well be a fertile field for research and I went to see Professor Brian Boydell at Trinity College to discuss the matter with him.

Brian Boydell (1917-2000) was born in Dublin. Having graduated with a first-class degree in Natural Sciences at Cambridge, he studied music at the University of Heidelberg, the RCM where his composition teachers were Hadley, Howells and Vaughan Williams (1938-39) and the RIAM in Dublin where he was Professor of Singing 1944-52. In 1959 he was conferred with the MusD degree at Trinity College and held the Chair of Music there from 1962 to 1982 bringing an enlightened approach to the revision of the syllabus and the teaching of the subject. He was later elected a Fellow Emeritus of Trinity College

Throughout his long and very distinguished career Professor Boydell was actively involved in the promotion of music in Ireland as a lecturer, broadcaster, conductor and adjudicator. One of the most important Irish composers of the twentieth century, his output for a wide range of media includes four string quartets, a violin concerto, orchestral, chamber and choral works.

In his retirement Brian Boydell devoted himself to musical scholarship writing two books on the music of eighteenth century Dublin. He also contributed articles to the *New Grove Dictionary of Music and Musicians* (1980). A man of many interests, he had been a surrealist painter in the 1940s and had an enduring passion for cars and photography.

Among the many honours which he received were the degree of DMus *(h.c.)* from the National University of Ireland, *Commendatore della Republica Italiana* in recognition of his services to the music of Italy and an Honorary Fellowship of the RIAM. In 1984 he was appointed to membership of Aosdána, Ireland's state-sponsored academy of creative artists.

With his keen personal interest in the history of music in Ireland and as the author of a number of publications on the subject, Professor Boydell was conscious of the need for a comprehensive account of the development of the choral tradition at those cathedrals of the Church of Ireland where it has at some time flourished. I duly enrolled at Trinity as a postgraduate research student being placed initially on the MLitt register. Over the next five years most of my vacations were spent travelling throughout the country. At each cathedral visited a careful examination was made of all surviving volumes of chapter acts, board minutes, proctors' accounts and other relevant primary source material. This investigation yielded a considerable amount of valuable new information about the various musical establishments. The archives of the two Dublin Cathedrals, St Patrick's and Christ Church, house the best-preserved collections to be found anywhere and I spent much time in each of these places. Every week-day morning I would purchase a bottle of fruit-juice and a sandwich (for my lunch) on my way to the cathedral where, having attended the early service of Holy Communion, I would work throughout the day with a lunch-break at about one o'clock.

I looked forward to my periodic meetings with Professor Boydell, even if I did not share his liking for very strong tea! After his retirement from the University in 1982, these meetings took place either in his rooms in Westland Row or at his beautifully-situated residence at Howth where, from the spacious music-room, there was a superb view of Dublin Bay.

My researches brought me into contact with another very remarkable man, Hugh Alexander Boyd, who spent his entire life in Ballycastle, the town on the North Antrim coast where he was born in 1907. He was educated at Ballycastle High School and Queen's University, Belfast where he graduated with an Arts degree in 1927. During his long subsequent association with the University he served for many years as a member of the Standing Committee of Convocation. He taught history at his old school throughout his career, becoming Vice-Principal in 1957. The acquisition of degrees was something of a hobby with Hugh Boyd. He took an MA at Queen's in 1933, an MLitt at Trinity in 1950, an MEd *(h.c.)* was awarded to him by Queen's in 1980 and he was conferred with an

Hugh Alexander Boyd and his wife, Pearl, with Harry outside their home, Mowbray House, in Ballycastle

MPhil by the University of Ulster in 1983 when he was seventy-six. A large suitcase in his home held a vast quantity of documentary material which he had intended to use as the basis of a thesis on a former Church of Ireland Primate, Lord John George de la Poer Beresford (1773-1862). Occasionally he would point at the suitcase and say, 'There's a PhD in there, you know.' However, I think that he was resigned to the fact that, at his advanced age, this particular goal was beyond his reach.

A committed churchman, Hugh Boyd served as a lay-reader in the Church of Ireland for sixty years from his commissioning in 1932. He was very proud of his unique collection of plaques, some of them specially made, bearing the coats of arms of the all the Anglican dioceses in Great Britain and Ireland. Also on display in his home was the coat of arms which he himself had been granted by the College of Arms in July 1954.

Hugh was an acknowledged expert on academic dress. On graduation days at Queen's in his retirement he was always to be seen in his favourite seat in the gallery towards the front of the Sir William Whitla Hall. From this position he was able to spot any irregularities in the attire of the members of the platform party.

While he was the author of histories of local parishes and of the town of Coleraine, Hugh Boyd's *magnum opus* was undoubtedly his MLitt thesis on *The Cathedral System of the Church of Ireland since Disestablishment*. He was very pleased to hear of my research interest in a related subject and I found his advice, especially with regard to deciding initially on a proper *modus operandi*, to be invaluable. Indeed he even went to the trouble of drawing up a suggested overall plan for my work, which, although it was not ultimately adopted, did nevertheless have a considerable influence on my thinking. His enthusiastic support meant a great deal to me and I was assured of a warm welcome when I periodically called on him to report on my progress. He was always anxious to know whether I had 'struck any oil', as he put it, in the course of my latest researches. Whenever he himself came across any information which he thought might be of use to me he would enclose it with an encouraging letter.

In 1980, with our daughters, who were now aged nine and five, both at school, Heather and I agreed to accept the responsibility for the organisation and conduct of the examinations at the Belfast Centre for Trinity College of Music (London) on the retirement, after many years' service, of Mr and Mrs James Vincent. Although I was officially the Local Representative, it was, in fact, Heather who did most of the work. The three grade and two diploma examination sessions each year were always particularly busy and they naturally gave rise to a vast amount of administration but we were very glad of the extra income. During term-time at Stranmillis I was, of course, able to offer Heather little assistance. It was fortunate that I was at home on the day when, with the diploma practical examinations in full swing, a bomb-scare resulted in the evacuation of all the buildings in that part of Belfast, bringing a mass of people on to the streets and disrupting the bus service. There was nothing for it but to set up a temporary examination centre in our house on the outskirts of the city. The two examiners set off for Cairnburn Crescent by taxi, leaving Heather to seek out the candidates on the crowded pavements and to hail further taxis to take them there also. She told me afterwards that, while those who played orchestral instruments were easily identifiable because of the cases they were carrying, she had some difficulty in finding the pianists and singers.

At Stranmillis and St Mary's Colleges, with the introduction of an honours BEd in 1977, the certificate course had been discontinued. The honours students were taught in combined classes with both staff and students travelling between the Colleges. In the early years of this new course it was possible for me to bring the few Stranmillis students concerned with me when I drove to St Mary's. Later, when the number of students was larger, we might all go by the College minibus, or, if this were unavailable, the students might have to travel by public transport which could sometimes mean that the start of the lecture was delayed. All of this inconvenience and loss of valuable time could, of course, have been avoided if the two Colleges had been combined on the one site as the Chilver Report had recommended.

I played the organ for a broadcast morning service sung by the Stranmillis Singers in St Bartholomew's Parish Church in February 1981 and continued to be the choir's accompanist on such other occasions as the annual Carol Service in Fisherwick Presbyterian Church. Unfortunately, in the mid-1980s, when it was proving increasingly difficult to recruit male singers and to maintain the high performance standards for which the choir was noted, the decision was regretfully taken to disband it. The Stranmillis Singers made their final appearance at the College Carol Service in December 1985. Thereafter their place was taken at this service by the College Ladies' Choir.

Three engagements in 1981 brought about the renewal of old acquaintances, one after many years. In April I played the organ for a performance, in St Mary's Parish Church, of Stainer's *Crucifixion* conducted by David Humphries, the Organist of the church and a former Stranmillis student. David was ordained in 1986 and is currently Rector of St Molua's Parish Church in Belfast. On Sunday, 5 July I was at Kilmakee Presbyterian Church, Dunmurry for the dedication of the new organ, accompanying the morning service and giving a recital afterwards. The service was conducted by the Revd Ruth Patterson, the first woman to be ordained into the ministry of the Presbyterian Church in Ireland. Ruth is the daughter of the Revd Tom Patterson who was the minister at Shore Street Presbyterian Church, Donaghadee in the 1950s when I was the Organist there and she was a little girl. After fourteen years' service at Kilmakee, Ruth Patterson became, in 1991, the Director of Restoration Ministeries, a non-denominational charitable trust at the forefront of the movement to promote peace and reconciliation in Northern Ireland. In 2001 she was awarded a DD degree *(h.c.)* by the Irish Presbyterian Theological Faculty and in 2003 an OBE for public service.

In September I took part with Tom Agnew and William McDonald in the annual recital by members of the USOC held in Down Cathedral, one of my favourite church buildings. It was a pleasure to play Clérambault's *Suite du premier ton* on its fine Harrison organ. Edwin Gray was now in charge of the music at Down Cathedral and I had been looking forward to hearing the Cathedral Choir (accompanied by R A Megraw) under his direction. The beautifully balanced and expressive singing of items by Gibbons, Elgar, Vaughan Williams, Stanford and Quilter made a very favourable impression on the audience.

On Christmas Eve 1982 I was happy to be back at Bangor Abbey to play the organ for the annual *Christmas Chorale,* a 'celebration of Christ's nativity in words and music', which, each year, attracts a large congregation from far and wide. On Christmas Day 1983 an ITV network broadcast of Morning Service, produced by Andrew Crockart of Ulster Television, came from St Molua's Parish Church, Stormont, Belfast which has long been noted for its fine musical tradition. Jim Drennan, the Organist and Choirmaster at that time, asked me to accompany the service while he directed the choir. In the event, we reversed roles for the first broadcast performance of my carol, *What is that Light?,* a setting of words by my sister, Norma, which was later accepted for publication. I also acted as organist for a BBC broadcast service from St Molua's in September 1985.

By 1984 I was ready to begin writing up my work, my research having justified my transfer to the PhD register. The thesis was in two main sections. In the first, the history of the development of the choral tradition at the Irish Cathedrals is traced from the mediaeval period to the twentieth century. Among the topics discussed are the constitutions of the choirs, the conditions of employment of the choirmen, the education of the choristers, the liturgical practices, the repertoire, the organists, the choirmasters and all those other individuals, both clerical and lay, whose gifts and personalities have enriched the scene. In addition to Stanford and Wood whose contribution to Anglican Church music is well known, other significant figures are discussed. The second section deals separately with the organs and the composers and their music.

Mrs Margaret Stevenson, a member of the administrative staff at Stranmillis College, kindly agreed to undertake the typing of my thesis but said that she would require a typewriter with a 'golf-ball' attachment. I turned to my friend, Dean Crooks, for help. He phoned Mr Wesley Parker, the Manager of the Ulster Bank in Waring Street, and arranged for me to borrow such a type-writer for a month. Mr Parker even sent out an engineer to repair the machine while it was on loan. The degree was duly conferred, appropriately for an Ulsterman, on 12 July, 1985.

Commencements (i.e. graduation) at Trinity College, Dublin, July 1985. From left: Harry's sister, Norma, his mother, Professor Brian Boydell, Harry, and Joseph Groocock

A number of my friends, among them Jack Gamble who is a joint director, with his wife Jean, of Emerald Isle Books, advised me strongly to seek publication. The story of this search together with an account of the next stages in my musical pilgrimage are the substance of the next chapter.

CHAPTER TWELVE

1986-2008 | STRANMILLIS COLLEGE, THE PRIORY SINGERS, RETIREMENT

ew cathedrals have a location to compare with that of St Flannan's, Killaloe, Co. Clare. In an idyllic setting at a bend in the River Shannon, this remarkably well preserved twelfth-century building, which has probably always functioned as a parish church, is supported and maintained by the members of the small Church of Ireland community. I was very pleased to be invited by the Dean, the Very Revd Dr Frank Bourke, to give a recital with a local choir on the second evening of the special four-day Festival which took place in July 1985 to mark the octocentenary of the Cathedral. The Festival was officially opened by His Excellency, the President of the Republic of Ireland, Dr Patrick Hillery. The President was to a certain extent upstaged by his *aide-de-camp*, Ciaran Fitzgerald, the captain of the Irish Rugby Team, who, smartly dressed in his uniform as an army officer, was the centre of attention at least as far as most of the younger ladies were concerned. Lt-Col Anthony Galloway, the Cathedral Organist, who, on his retirement from the British Army, had moved to Killaloe, was most hospitable and made sure that I thoroughly enjoyed my first visit to this lovely part of the country.

Many years later I returned to Killaloe to give a lecture to the Friends of St Flannan's on *Music in the Worship of the Church*. Again I was right royally entertained by these charming and kind people with one parishioner inviting me to join a family party on a morning cruise on the River Shannon. No full Irish breakfast has tasted quite as good as that which he cooked and served while we were afloat.

In March 1986 I assisted Peter Sweeney with the adjudication of the Church Music International Choral Festival (CMICF) at St Mary's Cathedral, Limerick. Peter, who was for eleven years Director of Music at Christ Church Cathedral, Dublin, is one of Ireland's foremost organists. In the course of his distinguished career he has given recitals throughout Europe and North America. An outstanding communicator, he is also known as a highly successful presenter of music programmes for children, his effervescent personality guaranteeing a happy experience for his audiences. I was very pleased to return to Limerick in March 1997 as principal adjudicator at the CMICF with Seamus Crimmins, an RTÉ music producer, as my colleague.

In May 1986 there were two visits south of the Border. The first of these was to St John's Cathedral, Sligo to direct the music at an ecumenical service conducted by the Dean, the Very Revd Sterling Mortimer. Sterling had been one of two choristers from Belfast Cathedral selected to sing at the coronation of George VI in Westminster Abbey in 1937. A loyal supporter of the RSCM and chairman for a number of years of its Irish committee, he was awarded the ARSCM diploma in 1985. On the second occasion I was at All Saints' Parish Church, Castleconnell to give a recital in aid of the Organ Maintenance Fund.

As my friend, Jack Gamble, had suggested, I sent a copy of my PhD thesis to Oxford University Press requesting that it be considered for publication and after some time I was asked to come to Oxford to discuss this matter further with a senior official of the firm. He told me that my work had been read by Professor Nicholas Temperley, of the University of Illinois, a renowned church music scholar, who was the editor of a new series called *Oxford Studies in British Church Music*. He allowed me to see Professor Temperley's very thorough critical report which was encouragingly positive and which recommended that, with certain minor modifications, the text would be suitable for inclusion in this series. I returned home elated.

For some unexplained reason these negotiations fell through and when, after several months, I had heard nothing further from OUP, I decided to approach an academic publisher nearer to home. This was the Institute of Irish Studies at Queen's University, Belfast. Professor Brian Walker, having read my thesis, informed me that, although the Institute would undertake to publish a book based on it, I would be expected to pay a subvention of £4,000 towards the cost. When I had recovered from the shock caused by this news, I had no option but to set about raising the necessary funds. Over the next year or so I must have sent out scores of begging letters to various charitable trusts and individuals. I was very grateful to receive donations, both large and small, which eventually amounted to the sum required and publication went ahead. *Irish Cathedral Music*, dedicated to the memory of Samuel Bennett Crooks, Dean of Belfast 1970-85, and with a foreword by Archbishop Robin Eames, appeared in 1989. Mrs Isabel Crooks, the Dean's widow, was a very welcome guest at the launch.

Of the fourteen reviews of the book in various journals, all were favourable except for one from a local critic who did not have too many good words to say about it. However, when scholarly writers of the standing of Watkins Shaw expressed their unreserved approval, I reckoned that I had little cause for concern. Copies of the book sold like the proverbial 'hot cakes' and the original print run of a thousand was soon exhausted. Correspondence would suggest that many students have found *Irish Cathedral Music* to be a very useful work of reference and it is gratifying to find that it is quoted in most of the more recent literature on the subject. .

After a decade during which a great deal of my spare time had been taken up with academic pursuits, attempts were increasingly being made by some of my friends to persuade me to form another choir. On Saturday 30 November 1985, Billy Adair organised and presented an interesting recital of music by former members of the USOC in Rosemary Street Non-Subscribing Church, Belfast. A goodly number of current members of the Society came to hear a range of items, both sacred and secular, by Dr E M Chaundy, Captain C J Brennan, John Vine, Dr E N Hay and the Revd F J Powell. Billy had asked me to recruit a small group of singers to perform those choral pieces which were not already available on record.

In the course of my doctoral research I had made editions of a considerable amount of music, some of it by Daniel and Ralph Roseingrave, members of an influential Anglo-Irish family of musicians active on the Dublin musical scene in the eighteenth century. In March, 1986, for a BBC Radio Ulster recording of a programme of their music, the producer, Dr Joe McKee, suggested that the choral group which had sung at the USOC event in November, 1985 should be reconvened, if at all possible. It was, therefore, basically the same choir, named 'The Priory Singers' for the occasion, which took part in the recording broadcast on Sunday 2 March 1986 with Alan Boyd (counter-tenor) and Dr Donald Cullington (organ) as soloists.

Most of the members of this group were interested in joining the more permanent choir which, by now, I was convinced should be formed and The Priory Singers made their public début on Monday 16 June 1986 at a concert in St Molua's Parish Church, Stormont. Our programme, with Byrd's *Four-part Mass* as its centrepiece, also included some Tudor motets and a selection of pieces by the Roseingraves which had been sung in the course of the broadcast in March. The organist was again Donald Cullington who played Bach's *Prelude and Fugue in F Minor (BWV 534)* and two voluntaries by Ralph Roseingrave. At that time Head of the Music Department at the University of Ulster, Donald had been formerly Assistant Organist at St Mary's Cathedral, Edinburgh.

We were greatly encouraged by the size of the audience at the concert and by the warmth of the reception which it gave to the choir. The following excerpt from a review by Alfred Burrowes (*Irish Times*) is representative of press critiques which were generally very complimentary: 'These talented singers are highly competent, self-disciplined and equipped with a uniform set of pure vowel sounds that ensures a good, even vocal production and blend. Consonants are clearly enunciated without damage to the flow of the vocal line and they have a wide range of volume that never distorts the single-sound effect of the singing.

Byrd's *Four-part Mass* was ideally flexible, the male-alto line an indispensable asset, tenors and basses absolutely on fire to the meaning of the texts, matching the purity of the upper voices, totally committed. Ralph Roseingrave's *Te Deum* sparkled with vitality.....'

At first the choir consisted of eighteen voices, a number which was in the course of time gradually increased to twenty-eight. The Priory Singers rapidly established themselves on the musical scene, their repertoire including music of all periods and their programmes frequently featuring less familiar works as well as music written for them by local composers. They made their first television appearance in December 1986 in a programme entitled, *Love came down,* which had been recorded by Ulster Television (UTV) in St Patrick's Parish Church, Jordanstown. From then on they were frequent broadcasters on both radio and television (BBC and RTÉ). In June 1987 The Priory Singers were one of the choirs invited to participate with such celebrity soloists as Carroll Baker, Gloria Gaynor and George Hamilton IV in *Sing Out*, a series of public concerts recorded by UTV in the Ulster Hall for transmission throughout the ITV network over the summer months. The Singers' performance of my arrangement of the spiritual, *Steal away*, made specially for the series, was selected for inclusion on the commercial LP issued subsequently.

After one of the television *Songs of Praise* programmes in which The Priory Singers took part, we received a letter from a lonely Scottish gentleman whose primary interest had not been the sound of the choir. He was evidently on the lookout for a lady with whom to share his life in retirement and his comfortable little flat in Corstorphine, on the outskirts of Edinburgh. He enclosed a photograph of himself and said that he would be very pleased to hear from any of the more mature female members of the choir who might care to take the matter further. This caused great hilarity among the men.

Radio broadcasts in 1987 included a performance of *A Short Requiem* by Walford Davies recorded in St Mary's Parish Church, Belfast with Donald Davison playing the organ. This so impressed Barry Rose, the producer of the BBC Radio 3 Choral Evensong series, that he offered us a live broadcast on 31 August of the following year for which I chose music largely of Irish provenance. The canticles were sung to Charles Woods's *Collegium Regale* setting in F for double choir and the anthem was

Thomas Bateson's *Holy, Lord God Almighty* for seven voices (SSAATTB) which may have been his exercise for the MusB degree of Trinity College, Dublin, said to have been conferred in 1612. The introit, composed for the occasion by Keith Rogers, was *Give me Understanding,* my setting of the Preces and Responses was used and the psalms for the 30th evening were sung to chants by Alcock, Stanford, Bertalot and Donald Davison who accompanied the service. Donald's setting of Psalm 150, with its colourful free organ accompaniment, was a wonderful expression of the exultant spirit of this great song of praise. The final hymn was 'I bind unto myself today,' sung to the tunes *St Patrick's Breastplate* and *Gartan* which together form the thematic basis of the last movement of Stanford's *Sonata Celtica.* Donald Davison played this movement at the end of the service exploiting to the full the tonal resources of the splendid Harrison organ in Belfast Cathedral from where the broadcast came. Incidentally, the important duty of cantor was undertaken by the Revd Paul Coulton, the Vicar Choral at the Cathedral and also a member of The Priory Singers. Paul was consecrated Bishop of Cork in 1999.

In addition to broadcasts like the above, I was sometimes invited to contribute to local BBC magazine programmes such as *Music Around.* On one occasion in July 1988 I deputised for the Revd Canon Noel Battye, the regular presenter of the Sunday request programme, *Sounds Sacred,* when he was on holiday.

I recall three USOC events which took place during my two-year presidency of the Society (1986 - 87). The first of these was the visit in October 1986 of Dr Donald Hunt, the distinguished Organist and Master of the Choristers at Worcester Cathedral. Dr Hunt, who was the principal guest at the Society's annual dinner, gave an excellent illustrated lecture, entitled 'Elgar of Worcester', the following afternoon.

The second event was a service of dedication for members of the Society in Belfast Cathedral in January 1987 at which the preacher was the Revd Harold Miller, the Dean of Residences at

Harry as President of the USOC (1986-87)

From left: Donald Davison, Harry, Donald Hunt (Organist of Worcester Cathedral),
Andrew Padmore (Organist of Belfast Cathedral), Billy Adair and Charles McCauley
at the USOC annual dinner in October 1986

Queen's University, who was consecrated Bishop of Down and Dromore
in 1997. In the course of his inspiring and thought-provoking sermon
he emphasised the importance and responsibility of the special ministry
which church musicians exercise week by week. I have often wondered
why such an act of dedication did not take place more regularly in view of
its spiritual significance.

The third of these events, organised in collaboration with the USOC,
was an RCO Members' Day held at Queen's University on Saturday 26
September 1987. There were sessions on preparing for the practical and
written examinations for the ARCO diploma and short recitals of pieces
from the current examination syllabus by Evan John and Desmond
Hunter, University Organists at Queen's and the University of Ulster
respectively. The event concluded with an RCO Symposium at which Dr
Donald Davison acted as chairman of a panel consisting of Messrs. Harry
Bramma and Barry Lyndon, respectively RCO Honorary Treasurer and
Clerk, Dr Philip Cranmer, and me.

By 1988, after being in existence for less than two years, The Priory
Singers' standing was such that the choir was receiving invitations to
take part in prestigious events like the Festival of Early Music at Queen's
University and the major Belfast Festival, both held annually. In April, at
the former, we presented a programme of music by Purcell accompanied

by a string ensemble with Norman Finlay playing some of the organ voluntaries. At the latter in November, the choir sang, *inter alia*, a selection from Brahms's *Liebeslieder Op. 52*, Debussy's *Trois Chansons de Charles d'Orléans* and folk-song arrangements by Havelock Nelson. The Priory Singers made regular appearances at both festivals in later years.

In 1988 I was contacted by the Revd Raymond Hoey, then Chairman of the Armagh Church Choir Union (ACCU) and later Archdeacon of Armagh, to ask if I would be prepared to give a series of eight monthly lessons in basic organ-playing in the Diocese, in an effort to meet the increasing need for church organists. This tuition would supplement a course which had already been in operation for several years, namely the Archbishop Gregg Memorial Organ Scholarship. The tutor was the Armagh Cathedral Organist, Martin White, and a limited number of scholarships, funded from the Archbishop Gregg Memorial Endowment, were awarded each year.

My series of lessons, in reality a pilot scheme, attracted sufficient interest to justify the setting up of a second course, the students' fees, in this case, being subsidised by the Diocesan Board of Education. With the kind co-operation of rectors and select vestries, individual one-hour lessons were given fortnightly from 1989 to eight students on Saturdays at various parish churches throughout the Diocese. Although I found this schedule at times rather tiring, I was glad to be in a position to help the cause of church music in this way. When I retired from this commitment in 2000, Archdeacon Hoey paid me this very generous tribute:

'I wish to place on record my own personal thanks and the thanks of the Diocese of Armagh for the wonderful contribution which Dr Grindle made to this aspect of the musical life of the diocese over so long a period. His expertise, patience, friendliness and outstanding teaching gifts inspired and encouraged many students to further their interest in organ-playing, something which is absolutely vital to the continuation of excellence in church music.'

While the aim was to give the students the technical grounding necessary to enable them to accompany a simple service, the progress of some was marked by success in the organ examinations of the Associated Board. Archdeacon Hoey's wife, Joyce and his daughter, Shauna, who shared the post of Organist at Bessbrook Parish Church, were among the first cohort of students. Shauna, an accomplished keyboard and French horn player, was, at nineteen, the first Irish candidate to be awarded the RSCM's Young Organist's Certificate. While studying music at Queen's University, she was a member of my Priory Singers. In 2000, having gained the Advanced Diploma in Horn Performance at Trinity College of Music, London with distinction, Shauna joined the staff of the London music publishing firm, Josef Weinberger Ltd, where she is now Manager of the Music Hire Department. Since 2002 she has been Organist of St Alphage's, Burnt Oak, Edgware where she enjoys playing the church's highly-regarded new organ built by B C Shepherd and Sons in 2003, incorporating Father Willis pipes from 1857. The Priory Singers were delighted to sing at Shauna's wedding to Colin White in Armagh Cathedral in August 2008.

Shauna Hoey being presented with the RSCM's Young Organist's Certificate by Archbishop Robin Eames in 1996, with Archdeacon Hoey (left) and Harry

Whereas all of the organs which I came across in the course of my teaching travels in the Armagh Diocese were perfectly adequate for our purposes, the large two-manual instrument at St Aidan's Parish Church, Kilmore was altogether exceptional. Originally built in 1865 by the leading English firm, William Hill & Son, for Trinity Church, Lower Gardiner Street, Dublin, it is one of the comparatively few examples of Hill's work to survive in anything like their original condition. This organ was removed from Dublin to Kilmore in 1919. Later two of the Hill stops were replaced by three others and an electric blower was added although it appears that the old hand-blowing system still worked well in 1979. It was not until 2001 that a long-overdue complete restoration of this notable instrument was expertly carried out by the Wells-Kennedy Partnership of Lisburn. As a result of this the organ has been awarded by The British Institute of Organ Studies a certificate which states that it is now 'listed in the Institute's Register of Historic Pipe Organs as being an instrument of importance to the national heritage and one deserving careful preservation for the benefit of future generations'.

As well as giving regular organ lessons in the Armagh Diocese I occasionally conducted workshops for choirs affiliated to the ACCU. From time to time I also gave talks to ACCU organist-members on choir-training, repertoire, etc. In 1999 Earl Moffitt, who had succeeded Archdeacon Hoey as Chairman of the ACCU, achieved a cherished objective with the publication of *The Armagh Service Book*, a collection, edited by me, which includes items for the principal church festivals with the exception of Christmas for which there is a large and varied repertoire. Three of the items were composed by Martin White, the Organist of Armagh Cathedral and the remainder, including a setting of the Communion Service, are by the editor. This is music specifically for the sort of choir which is, unfortunately, to be found increasingly in churches today i.e. deficient in male membership with few, if any, tenors. Much of the writing is for unison voices, with passages of three-part harmony - S, A and Men. Warmly welcomed in the Diocese of Armagh, the book has commended itself to organists in other parts of the country who have purchased sets of copies of it for their choir libraries.

I have often been telephoned by despairing clergy seeking advice as to how they might go about filling the vacant organist posts in their churches. When the late Canon Desmond McCreery, the Rector of Bangor Parish Church, rang me one day in the late 1980s, I said to him, in the course of our conversation, that the Church of Ireland would have to do something about this intractable problem. I was asked to join the committee which was set up in the Diocese of Down and Dromore some time later to discuss the matter and to make recommendations to the Diocesan Synod. With the long-established Archbishop Gregg Organ Scholarship Scheme in the Armagh Diocese as a model, plans were drawn up for a course which would embrace the Dioceses of Connor and Down and Dromore. This would be administered by a board of management drawn from both Dioceses. I was to serve as a member of this board for the next fifteen years. Unfortunately, as we had expected might be the case, each diocese could offer us only modest financial assistance and it was evident that a large amount of capital would have to be found if our plans were to be implemented. Our faith was being put to the test but we were about to discover that miracles do still happen.

Providentially, some months earlier I had received a letter from a lady who, having derived great satisfaction from singing in choirs throughout her life, wished to make some provision for the maintenance of the choral aspect of parish church worship and the improvement of its standard. To this end she wished to set up a trust on which she invited me to serve. I had willingly pledged her my support. It occurred to me that this lady might perhaps be prepared to make a contribution towards the funding which we were seeking, and my fellow committee-members agreed that I should pay her a visit. I informed her about our efforts to address the dire shortage of organists whose duties in most churches include the recruitment and training of a choir. I assured her that help with choir-training would be an essential element of the course which was being planned. She promised that she would contact us after she had consulted her financial adviser. Her response was extremely generous and far beyond our expectations. As a result we now had the large capital sum necessary to secure the future of our scheme which continues to enable students to undertake a vitally important role in the service of the church. The lady whose benevolence has made this possible wishes her anonymity to be preserved during her lifetime.

In 1990 the Sunday School Society of Ireland published a collection of hymns, songs and prayers, entitled *Sing and Pray*. This was to be used in conjunction with the Society's course, *Growing Together,* and with the primary religious education curriculum of the Board of Education of the Church of Ireland, *Primary R E.* The theological consultant was the former Primate of the Church of Ireland, Bishop George Simms, a noted scholar and authority on early Celtic manuscripts. As music editor, I had to rearrange much of the existing musical material in such a way that no undue technical demands were made on 'average' pianists. I invited a few of my friends to compose some new tunes where these were required. Of those which I myself wrote, one called *Cairnburn*, after the area in East Belfast where I live, was included in *Church Hymnal,* 5th edition (2000).

Some months after the publication of *Sing and Pray*, Heather and I spent a very pleasant afternoon at Castle Gardens Primary School in Newtownards, where Heather had once been a pupil and after which I had named another of my hymn-tunes. The purpose of our visit was to present a copy of the full music edition of *Sing and Pray* to the Principal, Mr J E Bunting. Heather shared with the children some of her memories of her schooldays at Castle Gardens and I told them a little about my work as editor of *Sing and Pray.* Then, with the help of the senior school choir who had already learnt it, I taught the tune to the rest of the children. Later the combined chorus thanked us in song.

Primary school choirs from Dublin and Belfast contributed performances of a representative selection of items from *Sing and Pray* to an audio-cassette recording which teachers have found to be a very useful additional resource. It would seem that *Sing and Pray* has travelled far beyond these shores. A few years later I received a request from an official in the Roman Catholic Church in Latvia for permission to include fourteen hymns from the collection in an anthology to be published for use in that country.

In May 1990 *Irish Church Praise (ICP)*, an authorized supplement to the 1960 edition of the *Church Hymnal*, was published. This varied collection of 146 hymns, which includes both old and new material, takes particular account of modern trends in public worship. The Priory Singers were one of four choirs to contribute to a set of two audio- cassette recordings of a selection of items from *ICP*, also issued in 1990, to familiarise members of the Church of Ireland with the wide range of hymns and songs which it contains.

A rare opportunity to give a concert in collaboration with The Dublin Consort of Viols was warmly welcomed by The Priory Singers. This took place in the Harty Room at Queen's University on 28 April 1990 during the Festival of Early Music. Our programme, entirely devoted to the music of Gibbons, included two of the great verse-anthems, *This is the Record of John* and the less familiar *See, see the Word is incarnate*. This programme formed the first half of a further concert with The Dublin Consort of Viols in June 1990 at Christ Church Cathedral, Dublin, the second half being given over largely to the music of Purcell, with the Consort and Choir combining in the beautiful *Evening Hymn* (sung by unison sopranos) and the extended verse-anthem, *My beloved spake*.

On Trinity Sunday, 10 June 1990 I had been at Christ Church Cathedral for the celebration of its Patronal Festival, giving an address at Evensong on 'Music at Christ Church down the centuries'. The complete text of this was published in the October issue of the Cathedral Newsletter. Peter Sweeney kindly arranged for his excellent choir to sing both my introit, *Let my Prayer come up* and my setting of the *Preces and Responses* in the course of the service.

In May 1990 I read a paper on *The Roseingraves: An Anglo-Irish Family of Church Musicians* at a meeting of the Irish Chapter of the Royal Musical Association. This was held in the Department of Music at St Patrick's College, Maynooth under the chairmanship of Professor Gerard Gillen. Altogether five scholars shared the fruits of their research in various areas with the members of the audience who, at the end of each presentation, had the opportunity to engage in discussion with the speaker.

After an interval of about thirty-five years it was with great pleasure that I returned on the evening of Sunday 3 June 1990 to Shore Street Presbyterian Church, Donaghadee where my career as a church musician had begun. The Organist of the church, Dr George Beale, a colleague on the staff of Stranmillis College, had invited me to act as guest organist at the service at which the church's new organ, an Allen System 600 Computer instrument, was dedicated. In place of the sermon I gave a short recital and enjoyed accompanying again the hearty singing of the congregation.

Another return visit in 1990 was to Bangor Parish Church to give a recital in the annual summer series on Sunday evenings. The Priory Singers contributed to the series during the summers of the following two years.

At Stranmillis College John McDowell, after many years' committed service, decided in 1991 to take early retirement and, with his departure, the post of Head of the Music Department was abolished. This was consistent with the current policy of gradually reducing the numbers of both staff and students in an attempt to maintain the College's viability as the demand for teachers decreased. Whereas the Music Department had a staff of five in 1975, by 1991 this had been reduced to two. I was appointed to the position of Senior Lecturer in Charge of Music with effect from 1 September 1991. Because I had been a Senior Lecturer since January 1976, this appointment could scarcely have been regarded as promotion for there was no increase in salary to take account of my many additional duties including a growing amount of administration. It was not until September 1994 that I was granted a Principal Lecturership.

My very able colleague, Alex McKee, and I initially shared the teaching-load with Alex accepting responsibility for Professional Studies in Music, i.e. courses for non-specialist students. Later we were glad to have the part-time assistance of two very experienced, retired teachers, Mrs Freda Swann and Mr Tom Morwood. Alex and I endeavoured to maintain the Department's extra-curricular activities. I continued to take weekly rehearsals of the College Choir while Alex worked wonders with the mixed instrumental group, mostly woodwind and brass, with which he was now faced. His special arrangements of jazz numbers, with parts written to suit the capabilities of the individual players, delighted audiences at our concerts.

In 1991 the news that my busy career was to be the subject of a television documentary programme, to be shown on UTV in October of that year, came as something of a surprise, albeit a very pleasant one. The producer, John Anderson, went to great pains to ensure that the picture which he presented was as complete as possible. To this end a camera-crew was my constant companion, or so it seemed, over a period of time. Footage was taken of me lecturing at Stranmillis College, giving a lesson to one of my organ pupils, taking rehearsals, conducting a concert, playing the organ in various churches, etc. Our family was filmed at our local parish church where I read a lesson during Matins and Heather and our two daughters were shown with their Sunday School classes. There is no doubt that my mother, then in her late eighties, was one of the film's 'stars.' Not at all inhibited by the presence of a television camera and personnel, she reminisced quite freely, recounting how my brother and I, when small children, frequently chose 'Church' as the theme for our 'let's-pretend' games, dressing up as the rector and organist with towels serving as academic hoods.

The first public performance on a brand-new organ is always an important and eagerly-anticipated event. It was singularly appropriate that the inauguration of the magnificent, new four-manual organ built by Kenneth Jones in the National Concert Hall should take place during the year that Dublin held the title of European City of Culture. At the Gala Opening Concert on Saturday 28 September 1991 the famous English recitalist, Peter Hurford, played music by Purcell, Bach, Mozart, Mendelssohn and Schumann. The second half consisted of a performance of the well-known Organ Symphony by Saint-Saëns in which the soloist, with the National Symphony Orchestra conducted by Proinnsías Ó Duinn, was Professor Gerard Gillen who, as Organ Adviser to the Board of the National Concert Hall, had had oversight of the entire building project. The concert was broadcast simultaneously on radio and television. Previously I had recorded, at the RTÉ studios, a talk which was transmitted during the concert interval. Entitled, *The Greatest Organist in the World*, this talk explained why Saint-Saëns was so highly rated during his life-time.

Harry with the Rt Hon. Michael Foot MP at the Swift Seminar at Celbridge Abbey in July 1991

The year 1991 also marked the octocentenary of the foundation of St Patrick's Cathedral, Dublin. The impressive programme of celebratory events included the launch of the first three titles in a special series of monographs about the history of the building and its place in the life of the city. As the author of *The Organ and Music of St Patrick's Cathedral*, I was invited to the press reception at the Swift Seminar at Celbridge Abbey on Thursday 11 July at which the Rt Hon. Michael Foot MP, the former leader of the Labour Party at Wesrminster and a noted author and journalist, launched the series.

The Quatercentenary of Trinity College, Dublin was celebrated in 1992 with an ambitious and wide-ranging programme of events which had begun in October 1991. The Priory Singers and I were very pleased to be asked by Dr Brian Boydell to give a concert on 28 March in the College Chapel. Of the sixteen composers represented in our programme, twelve had close connections with the College and five of them had held the Chair of Music. They were Thomas Bateson, Daniel, Ralph and Thomas Roseingrave, Richard Woodward (Junior), Sir Robert P Stewart, Joseph Robinson, Sir Percy Buck, George H P Hewson, Sydney Greig, Charles Kitson, A J Potter, Joseph Groocock, Brian Boydell and Eric Sweeney. The accomplished Assistant Organist of Christ Church Cathedral, Trevor Crowe, a graduate of Trinity in both Engineering and Music, played our accompaniments as well as the solo organ music.

In December 1992 at a concert in Belfast Cathedral in which The Priory Singers were joined by the Belfast Baroque Consort, we gave the first performance in Northern Ireland of Thomas Roseingrave's cantata, *Arise, shine, for Thy Light is come.* This was introduced by Dr Brian Boydell. The programme also included Mozart's *Symphony No 13 in F (K112),* Bach's Cantata No 140, *Wachet auf!* and motets by Palestrina and Monteverdi.

In April 1992 Keith Rogers's Terpsichore Early Music Ensemble combined with The Priory Singers to give a farewell concert in St Martin's Parish Church, Ballymacarrett for Keith who, with his wife, Kathryn, was shortly to leave Belfast for London. During the twenty-five years that he had spent in Northern Ireland, Keith had made a significant contribution to the musical life of the province as a teacher, composer, performer and maker of early instruments. Our programme, which was essentially an affectionate tribute to the many facets of Keith's musical personality, concluded fittingly with his setting of words from Psalm 118, *Give Thanks to the Lord,* the organ accompaniment being played by his gifted protégé, Jonathan Rea. Jonathan, then a sixth-former at Regent House School, went on to read Music at Girton College, Cambridge where, as it happened, the Director of Studies was the distinguished Ulster-born musician, Martin Ennis. Jonathan later returned to Northern Ireland to teach at Bangor Grammar School where he is now Director of Music.

On Sunday 18 October 1992 the centenary of the birth of Herbert Howells was marked in Anglican cathedrals and parish churches everywhere by performances of his music. I was invited to give an address on the composer at the Eucharist at Belfast Cathedral that morning when Howells's *Collegium Regale* setting of the Office was sung.

In 1993 The Priory Singers collaborated with The Terpsichore Recorder Consort, directed now by Rosemary Smyth, in a concert of music by

Byrd who had been born four hundred and fifty years earlier. The Singers also presented a programme of Byrd's music in St Canice's Cathedral, Kilkenny to open the 1993 Kilkenny Arts Festival in August. In June a performance by The Priory Singers of Byrd's *Five-part Mass* had been broadcast on Radio Ulster.

The actual date of Byrd's birthday is 28th November. On the evening of 27th November at 11.00p.m., the Singers gave another performance of this Mass at the conclusion of the 1993 Belfast Festival at Queen's. This revived an old Festival tradition of late-night musical valedictions held in the entrance foyer of the main University building and to which admission was free. With the choir located in a gallery above the audience standing in the foyer below, the singing benefited from the wonderful, cathedral-like resonance.

The Priory Singers and I undertook our first residency together at an English Cathedral when we went to Hereford in August 1993 to sing the services for a week during the Cathedral Choir's summer vacation. It was fortunate that the Assistant Organist, Geraint Bowen, was available to accompany the choir, his sensitivity and familiarity with both the organ and building enabling him to maintain a perfect balance at all times. On weekdays, when the psalms appointed for each evening were required to be sung, much rehearsal time had to be given over to the preparation of what could occasionally amount to fifty or more verses. The final Sunday was a particularly busy day, with the Eucharist at 10.00a.m., followed by Matins at 11.30a.m. and Evensong at 3.30p.m. Nevertheless, the Singers were agreed that the week had been thoroughly enjoyable both musically and socially and they voted unanimously for a repeat of the experience at another English Cathedral in 1995.

Thanks to John Anderson, the co-owner of Modern Records, a Belfast company, The Priory Singers had the opportunity to make their first CD in 1993. It was decided that a selection of twenty favourite hymns would have sufficient popular appeal to guarantee that it would sell well and this proved to be the case. A number of the hymns appeared in arrangements by local musicians with descants, faux-bourdons and free accompaniments. The CD was taken up by local radio presenters who frequently played excerpts from it on their programmes.

Because my brother had been a victim of cancer at an early age, I have always had the utmost admiration for those who devote their lives to the care of the terminally ill. Therefore, when my friend, Pat MacKean, asked me if I would conduct a performance of Handel's *Messiah* in Belfast Cathedral in October 1993 as the local contribution to the 'Voices for Hospices' national fund-raising project, I readily agreed. The chorus was made up of between two and three hundred singers from a wide area including members of twenty-six choirs. The orchestra was the Belfast Baroque Consort. All participants, of course, gave their services and a large sum was raised for a very worthy cause.

Both of our daughters, Hannah and Rachel, are musical. When Hannah was nine she was awarded one of the highest marks in the British Isles in the Trinity College of Music Grade Four Recorder examination. Perhaps if she had received more encouragement at school she might have gone on to fulfil that promise. Rachel, who began learning the violin at primary school, eventually took her place in the City of Belfast Youth Orchestra. At Methodist College, Belfast she was prepared to sing tenor in order to become a member of the élite Chamber Choir. It was with pleasure and not a little pride, I must admit, that I accompanied her when she took part in a lunch-time recital in 1993 at the school and when she did her A-level practical examination the following year. She was determined that her A-level composition would be entirely her own work since she said that her peers assumed that she would seek her father's help with it. Her attractive piece for clarinet and piano was one of two compositions selected for inclusion in a programme broadcast from the school.

Rachel was a member of The Priory Singers during the mid-1990s when she was studying law at Queen's. In later years, after she had gone to live and work in London, she would sometimes join us when we were in residence at one of the English cathedrals.

The major family event in 1994 was Hannah's wedding to Paul Nelson on 7 July in St Mark's Parish Church, Dundela. The ceremony was conducted by the Rector, Archdeacon James Moore, who had been a curate at Bangor Parish Church when I was appointed Organist there in 1962. He was consecrated Bishop of Connor in 1995. Our good friend, Billy Adair, played the organ for the wedding service to allow me to carry out my duties as the father of the bride. The occasion was blessed with beautiful weather and Heather and I were delighted to entertain our guests at the Culloden Hotel at Cultra.

On the musical front, The Priory Singers gave a concert in June 1994 in Belfast Cathedral to mark the quatercentenary of the death of Palestrina. The music sung on this occasion included the *Missa Papae Marcelli*, arguably the finest of his one hundred and five mass settings, the *Stabat Mater* and four of the motets. David Drinkell, who was then the Cathedral Organist and a member of The Priory Singers, opened the programme with a performance of Bach's majestic *Prelude and Fugue in B minor (BWV 544)*.

The Singers gave another performance of the Palestrina Mass on 26 November when they returned to the entrance hall of the University to give a short late-night recital at the conclusion of the 32nd annual Belfast Festival. The following is an extract from Ciaran McKeown's review in the *Belfast Newsletter*: 'This marvellous ensemble was pretty nearly pitch-perfect as its collective voice soared into the splendid Lanyon vault, and the effect was to create a sense of worship: one had the feeling of thanksgiving to the Spirit who inspires all true art.'

In March 1995 The Priory Singers were one of eight local choirs which participated in a live two-and-a-half-hour broadcast from Belfast Cathedral which began and ended with performances of Tallis's famous forty-part motet, *Spem in alium,* conducted by Paul Goodwin. In between, each choir sang a group of two or three pieces under its own conductor. Although, in the performances of the Tallis, there had been the slight loss of pitch which is almost inevitable when such large forces attempt to sing this exacting work in such a resonant acoustic, all of those who took part were grateful for what had been an exciting and rewarding musical experience.

The tercentenary of Purcell's death was duly celebrated in April 1995 with The Priory Singers giving a concert with orchestra in Hillsborough Parish Church of a varied selection of his church music. On Saturday 17 June at Down Cathedral the USOC presented a programme entitled 'A Musical Celebration of Celtic Mysticism' in which organ and vocal solos and choral items were interspersed with readings. The choral music was sung by The Priory Singers who performed anthems by Brian Boydell and Havelock Nelson, a new setting of the *Te Deum* by Keith Rogers and a specially commissioned work by Philip Hammond. The text of *The Boyhood of Christ* is a seventh century Irish poem translated by Thomas Kinsella and Philip's imaginative response to it captures its changing moods to perfection with skilfully varied textures, rhythms and tonality.

Born in Belfast in 1951, Philip Hammond was educated at Campbell College and Queen's University. Until his retirement in 2009, he was Arts Development Director at the Arts Council of Northern Ireland. In Irish musical circles he is highly regarded as a pianist, critic and broadcaster. As a composer he has been commissioned by many leading international artists and ensembles to write for a variety of media. His music is played frequently by the Ulster Orchestra. In 2003 Philip Hammond was awarded the degree of Doctor of Music by Queen's University, Belfast.

The Priory Singers were in residence at Exeter Cathedral 14-20 August 1995 and I was personally delighted to meet the Cathedral Organist, Lucien Nethsingha, whose work I had long admired. Lucian, who was at that time officially on holiday, showed a keen interest in The Singers, attending every service and sometimes staying for a chat afterwards. He was so impressed by the playing of our organist, Nigel McClintock, whom he described as 'a natural,' that he offered him a recital at Exeter Cathedral at a later date. Lucian was also impressed by the singing of the choir and when he learned that I intended to resign as its conductor at the end of the year due to pressure of work, he tried very hard to dissuade me from doing so.

After a visit to Dun Laoghaire on 3 September 1995 to give a recital in the annual summer series at St Michael's Church, The Priory Singers and I began rehearsals for our final concert together at Belfast Cathedral on 9 November. This attracted a considerable amount of media coverage including interviews on both radio and television. The programme, which was introduced by John Anderson, the well-known local musician and broadcaster, consisted of a wide range of choral items selected by members of the choir and organ solos played by Nigel McClintock who also acted as our accompanist. The large and very responsive audience gave the choir a standing ovation at the end of the concert.

At Heather's suggestion, an inheritance was used to meet most of the cost of a practice-organ which was installed in our drawing-room in 1996. Having spent a large part of my life playing organs in the near-arctic temperatures which prevail in most churches especially during the winter months, I found it very pleasant to be able to practise in the comfort of my own home. Built by my friend Philip Prosser, a member of The Priory Singers, the organ has been seen and heard on television a number of times.

On Friday 13 July 1984, the beautiful Palladian dining-hall at Trinity College, Dublin was very badly damaged in a major fire. Fortunately, no one was injured and heroic efforts were made to salvage pictures, fittings and furnishings. The painstaking restoration work was the subject of a television film documentary made in the course of the following year. At the invitation of Professor Hormoz Farhat, Dr Brian Boydell's successor at Trinity, I

Practice organ by Philip Prosser at 37 Cairnburn Crescent, Belfast

recorded on the organ in the Chapel at TCD a programme of voluntaries by Ralph Roseingrave and Thomas Carter, two eighteenth-century Dublin composers. This music was used as the film's soundtrack.

During the years 1995 to 1997 I was the examiner for the Archbishop's Certificate in Church Music which was awarded to those who had successfully undertaken a course of training in organ-playing and choir-directing provided by the Dublin and Glendalough Diocesan Church Music Committee. Much thought had clearly been given to the compilation of the course's comprehensive syllabus and to the marking system, with the criteria set out in impressive detail. As one of those charged with the devising of a syllabus and marking system for the course run by the Connor and Down and Dromore Diocesan Organ Scholarship Board, I must confess that I was greatly influenced by the work of my southern counterparts.

The UTV School Choir of the Year Competition, which was launched in 1996 and was held annually until 2005, proved to be a very important event in the musical calendar. In the early years of the competition the panel of adjudicators, consisting of Irene Sandford, the well-known Ulster soprano, Leonard Pugh and me, visited various regional centres for the preliminary rounds with the finals taking place in Belfast. Later, as the competition developed, the number of adjudicators was increased and all of the rounds took place at venues in the city. As well as bringing some outstanding choirs to the attention of a wider public, this extremely well-organised competition could justifiably claim to be, at least to some extent, responsible for an improvement in the general standard of choral singing in the province's schools.

The winner of the Primary School Section of the first UTV Competition was the Choir of Strandtown Primary School conducted by Valerie Ireland who, during the thirty-two years that she was in charge of music at the school, maintained consistently high standards. In later years Valerie served as a member of the adjudicating panel. Two other members of The Priory Singers have conducted winning choirs in the Grammar School Section of this competition. These were Ruth McCartney (Methody) and Philip Bolton (Inst).

In 1997 my mother died in her ninety-third year. She was devoted to the Church and was actively involved for most of her life in various aspects of its work. As a mother she would have been considered to be rather strict but her earnest desire was that her children should make the most of their abilities and that they should be, above all, good citizens. In middle age she succeeded her dear friend, Miss Jeannie Hannah, as Superintendent of the Church Street Mission in Bangor. She found fulfilment in this leadership role, conducting meetings, engaging speakers and concerning herself with the welfare of the mostly elderly ladies who made up the Mission's membership. There is no doubt that my mother owed her longevity to my younger sister, Norma, who looked after her while pursuing a busy academic career. Mum spent her latter days happily in an excellent residential home in Newtownards run by Mrs Norma Reid who saw her care of those in the twilight of life as her Christian vocation.

By the late 1990s, with staff and student numbers at Stranmillis College lower than they had been for a very long time, morale among the members of staff was not high and the prospect of early retirement was becoming increasingly attractive. Because a further two years' service would have made little difference to my pension, which would be considerably short of the maximum because of my not having been a full-time teacher for the whole of my working life, I decided to resign from the College in 1998. At the end of the summer term, before I departed, my colleague, Alex McKee and I organised a competition for primary school choirs with the willing help of the Music students. This was the Music Department's contribution to the College's seventy-fifth anniversary celebrations and it was a great success.

In retirement I have not been idle. I continued to act as an organ tutor in the Armagh Diocese until June 2000, I accepted some private pupils particularly for harmony and counterpoint and, happily, I was now free to undertake most of the interesting engagements which came my way from time to time.

Having been urged, since my retirement, by former members of The Priory Singers to reconstitute the choir, I agreed to do so in 2000 and, although there were some changes in personnel, we simply took up again from where we had left off. A new departure for the Singers was *Carols by Candlelight* which we presented for the first time at Hillsborough Parish Church in December 2000. This proved to be so popular that it became an annual fixture although, when this location ceased to be available to us from 2004, we transferred the event to St John's, Orangefield and later to St Molua's Parish Church, Stormont. Carols by local composers including Alison Cadden, Philip Bolton and Philip Prosser, all of them members of the choir, figured prominently in our programmes. In 2006 our 20th Anniversary Carol Competition was won by Richard Woods from Armagh with a setting of *The Angel Gabriel*.

Further residencies during August at English Cathedrals included Hereford again in 2001 and Lincoln in 2003. Our organist for both of these was Jonathan Hardy. Jonathan who had passed the ARCO diploma examinations when he was in the lower sixth at Methody, was organ scholar at Magdalen College, Oxford 2001-2004, graduating with a 'First' in Music. He was also awarded the FRCO diploma in 2004.

At Gloucester in 2005, at Bath Abbey in 2006 and Chichester in 2007 our accompanist was Christopher Boodle, a former organ scholar at New College, Oxford and later Assistant Organist at Belfast Cathedral. Towards the end of the week at Chichester Christopher was regrettably taken ill and had to withdraw. Fortunately, Mark Wardell, the highly gifted Assistant Organist at the Cathedral was available to play for us on the Friday and Sunday. Two of the Singers, Jonny Ireland and Robert Thompson, who are organists, kindly shared the accompanying duties on the Saturday.

It became traditional during Priory Singers' cathedral visits for the members of the choir to produce a humorous diary of the week in the form of a psalm, usually cobbled together at odd times in local hostelries, for singing to an Anglican chant at the end of our stay. With the advent of Alison Cadden, we had our very own resident poetess, capable of producing, apparently without effort, verse to suit any occasion. As I approached Lincoln Cathedral on our final afternoon to take the pre-Evensong rehearsal, Alison's latest masterpiece, *Harry Grindle had a Choir,* sung to the tune of *Old Macdonald had a Farm,* was sounding out over the close from the song-room high up in the Cathedral building. This work was even accorded a special mention by the Precentor when he thanked the Singers in the course of the service. He regretted that he had not heard a complete performance.

Alison's version of *Glorious things of thee are spoken* (Tune: *Austria*), written during the Singers' visit to Chichester in 2007, is printed below. Although in places the meaning may appear obscure to the uninitiated, most readers with an interest in church music should find the verses entertaining:

Glorious things of thee are spoken,
Harry, founder of our choir,
Thou, whose word is never broken,
Can, alone our lips inspire.
Every Tewseday, in Dundeela,
Thou art there with file in hand:
Sops and Altos, Tenors, Basses-
All arrive at thy command.

First, some gentle exercises-
Lips and teeth, and tip of tongue;
Scales in stretto, then in canon,
All pitch-perfect, sweetly sung.
Then a new one: Aristotle,

When he spied a bird of prey-
Poor old chap! He lost his bottle-
Hope it wasn't Chardonnay....

Next, the music for Chi-chester:
Psalms and hymns and songs of praise,
Anthems, masses and responses
Keep us busy all our days.
No time left for socialising-
Only time to sing or sleep.
Sight-seeing, shopping, swimming:
Life in general - all can keep.

See the streams of runny noses:
Basses stayed up half the night,
Playing poker, disco-dancing-
Gave the Altos quite a fright!
Sops and Tenors smile so smugly-
They would not behave like so:
They were all in bed by seven-
Beauty sleep is all they know.

Blest inhabitants of Priory,
We through Harry members are.
Let the world take note and listen:
Dr Grindle is a star!
Fading is our final residence-
This the cry within the choir:
Harry, please remain our President-
We will not let you retire!

A J C

07.08.07

During the period 2000-2008 The Priory Singers recorded in Belfast Cathedral three CDs, all of them being issued by Priory Records, the well-known English company. The first of these, with Donald Davison as our accompanist, was *Beside the Waters of Comfort (The glorious Psalms of David)* (2003). This selection of nineteen psalms, sung to Anglican chants, eleven of which I had written, was warmly welcomed. 'If you want to sing/play/direct/compose Anglican chants, this disc would serve as an admirable model.' (*Church Music Quarterly*, December 2005).

Let Christians all with joyful Mirth (Christmas music from Northern Ireland), with Philip Stopford, the current Director of Music at Belfast Cathedral, playing the organ, highlighted the work of composers who were either born or have at some time been based in Northern Ireland. 'Words and music combine to excite the senses...I cannot recommend this disc highly enough...' (*Soundboard,* October 2006).

John Barnard, himself the composer of such superb hymn-tunes as *Guiting Power* ('Christ triumphant, ever reigning') greeted our third CD enthusiastically in the *Bulletin of the Hymn Society.* With such a large number of recordings of hymns already available, it was important that this CD, *Hymns of Love, Hope and Joy,* should be distinctive and Mr Barnard thought that it was. As well as several well-known hymns in new arrangements, there are a number of new tunes two of which are mine. One of these, *Stranmillis,* which had been a prize-winner in the St Paul's Cathedral Millennium Hymn Competition in 1999, was subsequently included in the new edition of the St Paul's Cathedral Hymnal.

In June 2002 I was driving to Limerick to conduct organ examinations at the Limerick School of Music. On the way through the village of Tyrrellspass, I noticed two high-powered sports cars and a motor-cycle parked at the side of the road. The motor-cyclist and the occupants of the cars, who were rather shady-looking characters, were evidently up to something, as I was soon to find out. When I had gone a short distance out along the road to Limerick, there was a loud roar behind me as these three vehicles, now involved in a race along the middle of the road between the lines of traffic, approached at a very high speed. Cars were sent flying in all directions and mine came to rest with its rear bumper wedged between the horizontal beams of the vehicular restraint on the other side of the road and with its bonnet flattened. By the grace of God there was not a single crack in the car's windscreen. Another car finished up on its roof further along the road. It was nothing short of a miracle, the Gardai said, that someone had not been killed. One man, who had been badly hurt, had to be cut from his car. I was exceedingly fortunate to escape with nothing more than a whiplash injury although I was, naturally, very shaken. Nevertheless, the next day I examined the students at the Limerick School of Music and returned by train to Belfast. My car, which I had been due to trade in the following week, was declared a write-off. A visit to London with Heather to attend a garden-party at Buckingham Palace on 16 July helped to put what had been an horrific experience out of my mind, at least, temporarily.

The wedding of our younger daughter, Rachel, to Ewen Kerr on 25 September 2004 provided me with the challenge and opportunity to compose some occasional music. She entered the Chapel of Unity at

Methodist College to *Fanfare for the Bride* and came down the aisle with her husband to the accompaniment of *Carillon,* a toccata based on certain changes with which, as a bell-ringer, she would have been familiar. Phillip Elliott, the accomplished Organist of Hillsborough Parish Church, took this and the other new music in his stride.

Priory Singers' concerts during this period included one at Armagh Cathedral in June 2002 in aid of an appeal for funds to secure the future of the Cathedral's musical establishment. The organist on this occasion was Martin White who the previous month had retired after thirty-four years' faithful service at the Cathedral. The choral music, all by Irish composers, included Stanford's monumental setting of *Magnificat (Op.164) for eight-part chorus.* We were very pleased to be invited to contribute to the series celebrating the centenary of Belfast Cathedral in November 2004. In June 2005 a programme of choral and orchestral music by Italian composers was given for the Dante Alighieri Society of Northern Ireland in Belfast Cathedral and in June 2006, the 20th anniversary of the foundation of The Priory Singers was marked with a concert introduced by John Anderson in St Molua's Parish Church (Purcell and Vivaldi's *Gloria).*

When the time came for me to take my leave of The Priory Singers on

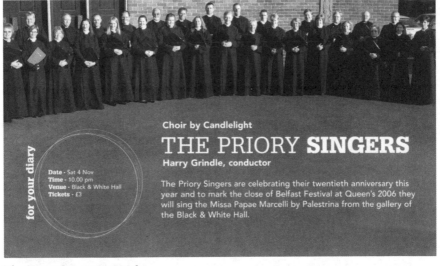

Choir by Candlelight

THE PRIORY **SINGERS**

Harry Grindle, conductor

for your diary

Date - Sat 4 Nov
Time - 10.00 pm
Venue - Black & White Hall
Tickets - £3

The Priory Singers are celebrating their twentieth anniversary this year and to mark the close of Belfast Festival at Queen's 2006 they will sing the Missa Papae Marcelli by Palestrina from the gallery of the Black & White Hall.

The Priory Singers in 2006

Sunday 15 June 2008, I knew that it had to be in the context of Evensong at Bangor Abbey where I had set out on my musical pilgrimage some sixty-five years earlier. Apart from Howells's Gloucester setting of the canticles all of the music was by composers closely associated with the Abbey over the years. The address was given by Bishop Edward Darling who had been the General Editor of both *Irish Church Praise* (1990) and *Church Hymnal*, 5th edition (2000) and Co-editor with Dr Donald Davison of the *Companion to CH5*. The current President of the Hymn Society of Great Britain and Ireland, Bishop Darling was awarded an Honorary Fellowship of the Guild of Church Musicians in 2006 . The lessons were read by my wife, Heather, and the Rector of the Abbey, Canon Ronnie Nesbitt. The collection was for the Henrietta Byrne Memorial Fund for Young Church Musicians.

It had not been an easy decision finally to sever my connection with The Priory Singers with whom it had been a privilege to make music over many years and in many places. They are a very special group of people who share a commitment to the pursuit of high standards and who enjoy one another's company. It was with great pleasure that I learned that Nigel McClintock had been appointed to succeed me as Director. Nigel's mother, Maeve, and I had been in the same form at Regent House School and his brother, Aubrey had been one of my choristers at Belfast Cathedral. Nigel, who had himself been a chorister at the Cathedral later, studied at the RCM. He was in charge of the music successively at St George's Parish Church, Belfast and then at Croydon Parish Church before his appointment as Director of Music at St Peter's Roman Catholic Cathedral, Belfast in 2008. I am sure that he and The Priory Singers will form a very successful partnership.

While the satisfaction that one experiences in the course of a life-time's music-making is in itself amply rewarding, it is, nevertheless, gratifying when one's work is considered worthy of official recognition. I was thrilled to be one of eight people to be conferred with a Lambeth degree, in my case a Doctorate in Music, by the Archbishop of Canterbury, Dr Rowan Williams, in 2005. In 2008 I was among those chosen to receive the Royal Maundy from HM the Queen at Armagh Cathedral, and I was awarded an MBE in the

Harry with Archbishop Rowan Williams at Lambeth Palace, 6 June 2005 *(Image courtesy of Lambeth Palace)*

Harry with his sisters, Margaret (right) and Norma, July 2009

New Year Honours 2009.

For Heather and me the year 2008 was particularly significant because during it we celebrated our fortieth wedding anniversary. Our two dear daughters, Hannah and Rachel, both now married, have brought us much joy and their children, Rory, Scott and Ruth have, naturally, a special place in the affections of their grandparents. In retirement, Heather and I continue to pursue our interests in art, music and various other subjects while enjoying the company of our friends. We have been greatly blessed. Deo gratias!

Harry and Heather with their daughters, Hannah (left) and Rachel at Buckingham Palace, June 2009 *(Photo: Charles Green, Edgware, Middlesex)*

Name Index

Acton, Charles 106, 121, 133, 146
Adair, Jeremy 165
Adair, William (Billy) 55, 114, 182, 195
Agnew, Tom 126, 178
Allaway, James 116
Allen, Albert 28
Allen, Pascal 137
Allister, Jean 137
Almeida, Antonio de 96
Alwyn, Kenneth 111
Amadeus String Quartet 48
Anderson, Adrian 168
Anderson, John 191, 194, 197, 203
Anderson, Rob 57
Andrews, H K 33
Angus, Alan 38, 56
Antwerp, Cathedral 87
Archbishop Gregg Memorial Organ
Scholarship 186
Archbishop's Certificate in Church
Music 198
Armagh, Cathedral 187, 203, 205
Armagh Church Choir Union 186
Armstrong, Douglas 93, 154
Armstrong, Norma 106
Armstrong, Sir Thomas 105
Arnold, Denis 25
Arts Council of Northern Ireland 93,
117-8
Atkinson, Agnes Jean see Grindle,
Agnes Jean
Atkinson, David (Davy) (uncle) 2, 8
Atkinson, Joseph (Joe) (uncle) 2, 8
Atkinson, Margaret (grandmother) 3
Atkinson, Revd Donald 38, 41, 47, 48
Atkinson, Robert (Bob) (uncle) 2
Atkinson, Samuel (Sam) (uncle) 2, 7
Atkinson, William James (grandfather)
2
Auterson, 'Jake' 12, 13-4

Baguley, Michael 144
Baker, Carroll 183
Balligan, St Andrew's Church 95
Ballyholme, Methodist Church 103
Ballymena
    County Hall 135
    St Louis Grammar School 119
    Town Hall 111
Ballynahinch, Magheradroll Parish
Church 96
Ballywalter, Holy Trinity Parish
Church 95
Ballywalter Park 94, 95
Bangor
    Bangor Abbey 8, 10, 27, 43,
    57, 59, 112, 152, 178, 203-4
    Bangor Golf Club 52, 60
    Bangor Harmonic Society 58
    Bangor Musical Festival 15, 32,
    64, 167
    Bangor Parish Church (St
    Comgall's) 8, 11, 17, 36, 48, 51-5,
    57-60, 64, 109, 167, 188, 191, 195
    Hamilton Road Presbyterian
    Church 123, 135
    Trinity Public Elementary School
    4, 6
Barber, Ian 56, 64
Bardsley, Rt Revd Cuthbert 139
Barker, Philip 14-6
Barlow, Alan 46
Barnard, John 202
Barnes, John 129
Barror, Ethne 105
Bath Abbey 200
Battersby, Rick 123
Battye, Revd Noel 184
BBC
    Choral Evensong 89-90, 98, 112,
    115, 123-4, 137, 144, 157, 183-4
    Friday Night is Music Night 111

Let the Peoples Sing 109, 164, 170
Music Around 184
Music for You 111
Northern Ireland 94, 106, 123, 140, 141
Northern Ireland Orchestra 63, 78, 82, 94, 111, 141, 153
Radio Ulster 153, 168, 182, 194
Sing we at Pleasure 112
Songs of Praise 137, 140-1, 183
Sounding Voices 139-40
Sunday Gallery 129
Symphony Orchestra 46, 64-5
Beale, George 190
Beattie, Mavis 64
Belfast
    Ashleigh House school 136
    Bank Buildings 83, 112
    Belfast Cathedral (St Anne's) 63-4, 67-80, 82, 86, 87-8, 91, 94, 108-9, 113, 116, 123, 130, 133-4, 137-40, 144, 146-58, 165, 167, 169, 184, 193, 194, 196, 197, 200, 201-4
    Belfast Central Library 75
    Belfast Musical Festival 33-4
    Belmont Presbyterian Church 138
    Campbell College 38, 56, 61, 73, 122, 129
    Chapel of the Resurrection 99
    Festival at Queen's 57, 81-2, 93, 95-6, 185, 194, 196
    Fisherwick Presbyterian Church 95, 166-7, 177
    Grosvenor High School 95
    Harty Room 93, 165, 176, 190
    Methodist College 101, 195, 203
    Modern Records 194
    Park Parade Secondary School 30-1
    Queen's University 20, 23-6, 30-1, 57, 83, 92, 94, 95, 103-4, 113, 166, 172, 185
    Rotary Club 75
    School of Music 138
    Sir William Whitla Hall 57, 82, 172-3
    St Anne's Parish Church 67-8
    St Bartholomew's Parish Church 95, 168, 177
    St Enoch's Presbyterian Church 125-6
    St James's Parish Church 55, 98
    St John's Orangefield 199
    St John's Parish Church Malone 134
    St Joseph's College 163
    St Mark's Parish Church Dundela 168, 205
    St Martin's Parish Church 195
    St Mary's College 163-4, 177
    St Mary's Parish Church 100, 106, 112, 122, 177, 183
    St Molua's Parish Church 178, 182, 199, 203
    Stranmillis University College 92, 144, 152, 163-5, 168, 172, 176, 177, 191, 199
    Tughan-Crane's Music Shop 96
    Ulster Hall 81, 86, 105-6, 111, 116, 183
    Union Theological College 172
    Wellington Hall 104, 137
    Willowfield Parish Church 27-9, 30, 31, 33-4, 36, 55, 95
Belfast Baroque Consort 147, 193, 195
Belfast Masonic Charities 78
Belfast Philharmonic Society 86
Bell, Christopher 158
Bell, Daphne 164
Bell, Derek 93, 112
Bell, Revd John 55
Bell, Stephen 158
Berriman, Canon Gordon 123
Bertalot, John 105, 108
Birmingham, Solihull School 127
Blackburn Bach Choir 105
Blower, Geoffrey 168

Boal, John 85, 91
Bolton, Philip 198, 199
Boodle, Christopher 200
Booth, George 77
Boucher, E W 125
Boulard, Valerie 111
Boult, Sir Adrian 34, 119
Bourke, Very Revd Frank 180
Bowen, Geraint 194
Bowen, Kenneth 86
Boyd, Alan 126, 129, 159, 168, 182
Boyd, Hugh Alexander 175-6
Boydell, Brian 174-5, 193, 196, 197
Bramma, Harry 185
Bream, Julian 48
Brennan, Captain C J 2, 48, 61-2, 69-70, 89, 132, 182
Brook, John 57
Brown, Murray 167
Browne, Ernest 12
Bryant, David 122
Bunting, J E 189
Burrowes, Alfred 147, 156, 182
Burrowes, Norma 51, 60, 137-8, 146-7
Butler, Bishop Arthur 130, 134
Byrne, Henrietta see Moran, Henrietta
Byron, Sr Paul 119

Cadden, Alison 199, 200
Cairns, Revd Donald 84, 125, 145
Cambridge
    King's College 45
    St John's College 45
Carnalea Municipal Golf Course 59
Carols for Choirs 84, 91
Carrowdore, Parish Church 55
Castleconnell, All Saints Parish Church 181
Cathedral Consort 84-5, 92-4, 97, 99, 104-6, 111-2, 115-7, 132, 147, 170
Cathedral Singers 147, 152, 156
Chaundy, Edred 9, 20-2, 182
Chichester, Cathedral 200
Chilver, Sir Henry 163

Chorzempa, Daniel 153
Church Hymnal 9, 189, 190
Church Music International Festival 180-1
Churchill, Sir Winston 78
City of Belfast Orchestra 81, 105
City of Belfast Youth Orchestra 154, 195
Claney, Brenda 92, 103, 132
Claney, Gordon 132
Clark, Christine 5
Clark, Frederick (Fred) (brother-in-law) 5
Clark, Jonathan 45
Clements, Joseph 13
Clinton, Gordon 89
Clooney, L'Derry, All Saints' Parish Church 57
Collings, Revd Neil 151
Collins, Mervyn 159
Collins, Rosemary 122
Comissiona, Sergiu 105
Connor and Down and Dromore Diocesan Organ Scholarship 198
Cosma, Edgar 106, 124
Coulton, Revd (later Bishop) Paul 184
Craig, Canon Graham 132
Cranmer, Philip 25-6, 34, 80, 83, 91, 94-5, 103, 111, 137-8, 147, 185
Crawley, Ivor 76
Creighton, James 101
Crimmins, Seamus 181
Crockart, Andrew 178
Croker, June 120
Cromie, Beaty 120
Crooks, Isabel 181
Crooks, Revd (later Dean) Samuel Bennett 69, 74, 77, 82, 88, 96, 108-9, 110-1, 113, 114, 123, 126, 127, 129, 133, 137, 138, 139, 141, 152-3, 179, 181
Crowe, Trevor 202
Cullington, Donald 182

Dakers, Lionel 141

Dante Alighieri Society of Northern Ireland 203
Darke, Harold 15
Darling, Bishop Edward 204
Davidson, Thomas 96
Davies, Stella 40
Davison, Donald 64, 95, 112, 115, 122, 134, 171, 183-4, 185, 201, 204
Day, Edgar 137
Deane, Uel 137
Dearnley, Christopher 106
Denton, Carys 56
Devon, Dartington Hall 48
Devonshire and Dorset Regiment Band 80, 90
Donaghadee, Shore Street Presbyterian Church 20, 26-7, 178, 190-1
Dorset, Canford School 34
Douglas, Audrey 166
Douglas, Barry 101
Douglas, Joseph 10
Douglas IoM, Finch Hill Congregational Church 86
Downpatrick, Down Cathedral 112, 178, 196
Downe House Summer School of Music 34
Drennan, Jim 178
Drew, Sir Thomas 66
Drinkell, David 195
Dromore Diocesan Choral Festival 96-7
Drumbeg, Parish Church 135
Dublin
    Arts Festival 145
    Christ Church Cathedral 180, 190
    Christ Church, Leeson Park 106
    National Concert Hall 192
    New Irish Recording Company 132
    St Louis Convent 119, 121
    St Patrick's Cathedral 140, 145, 175, 192
    Trinity College 64, 121, 169, 172, 174, 193, 197
Dublin Consort of Viols 190
'Duke Special' 48
Dun Laoghaire, St Michael's RC Church 172, 197
Dunleath, Lord 91, 94-5, 99, 101
Dunmurry, Kilmakee Presbyterian Church 177
Dunne, Veronica 82
Dykes Bower, Stephen 42

Eames, Revd (later Archbishop) Robin 58-0, 64, 181
Egan, Fr Tom 136
Elliott, Phillip 203
Elliott, Revd (later Bishop) R C H 17
Ellis, Revd Robin 59
Emery, Ernest 11-2, 17-8, 19, 29, 36, 50-1, 53, 54, 58, 60, 64
Emery, Trevor 60
Emmerson, Michael 93
Enniskillen, St Macartin's Cathedral 77-8
Everard, George 99
Exeter, Cathedral 196

Farhat, Hormoz 197
Farrell, Timothy 131
Fee, Howard 98
Fee, Maisie 96-7
Feehan, Fanny 145
Feldenkreis, Mosche 118-9
Festival of Early Music 185, 190
Finan, Sr Mary 119
Finchley Choral Society 46
Finlay, Norman 147, 186
Fitzgerald, Ciaran 180
Fivemiletown Choral Society 78
Fleet, Edgar 82
Fleming, Michael 45
Fletcher, Eric 41-2
Foot, Rt Hon Michael 192

Fox, Douglas 57
Francis, Alun 129
Frazer, Revd John 27-8
Freestone, Ellen 44, 168
Freestone, Frank 44, 45, 168
Freestone, Paul 44, 47
Friends of Belfast Cathedral 88
Friern Barnet, St John's Parish Church
40, 41, 46
Frost, Robert 1477
Fürst, Janos 105-6, 116, 118

Galliver, David 25
Galloway, Anthony 180
Galway, James 106
Galway, Redemptorist College, Mervue
135
Gamble, Jack 179, 181
Gamble, Jean 179
Gavin, Eileen 106, 137
Gaynor, Gloria 183
Geoghegan, Stephen 114, 140
Germani, Fernando 153
Gibson, Peter 92
Gilford, Diocesan Choral Festival 97
Gillen, Gerard 120-1, 150, 172, 190,
192
Glock, Sir William 48
Gloucester, Cathedral 200
Godin, Henri 23-4, 31
Goodwin, Paul 196
Gordon, Brian 159
Graham, David 101
Graham, Frieda 115
Graham, Huston 15-7, 64, 72, 75, 80,
85, 92, 98
Grand Opera Society of Northern
Ireland 33, 93
Gray, Edwin 124, 130, 140, 141, 146,
150, 158, 167, 178
Gray, Harold 111, 116
Gray-Wilson, Norma 111
Greaves, Algernon 151-2
Greer, David 172

Greevy, Bernadette 140, 145, 147
Griffin, Very Revd Victor 140
Grindle, Agnes Jean (mother) 1, 2-3, 4,
6, 19, 74, 192, 198-9
Grindle, Annie (aunt) 1
Grindle, Charles (Charlie) (uncle) 1, 4
Grindle, David (brother) 4, 39
Grindle, George (cousin) 1
Grindle, Hannah (daughter) 102, 126,
143, 195, 205
Grindle, Harry Edward (father) 1, 3-4,
5-6, 9, 13, 18, 102, 152
Grindle, Heather (wife) 25, 92, 97,
102-3, 110, 117, 126-7, 131, 136, 143,
167-8, 176-7, 189, 191, 195, 202, 204,
25
Grindle, Margaret (sister) 4-5, 8
Grindle, Norma (sister) 4, 5, 31, 103,
178, 199
Grindle, Rachel (daughter) 143, 195,
202, 205
Groocock, Joseph 169-70, 193
Gross, William 40
Guest, George 45

Hale, Paul 108
Hamill, Stephen 100-1
Hamilton, Canon James 9
Hamilton, George IV 183
Hamilton Harty Memorial Recital 25
Hammond, Philip 196
Hampstead, Parish Church, 44
Hancock, Gerre 64
Hannah, Jeannie 198
Hardy, Jonathan 199
Harris, Peter 136
Harvey, Revd Brian (Canon
theologian) 77, 99
Haslett, Stewart 72, 135, 160
Hawridge, Douglas 42
Hay, E Norman 9-10, 80, 182
Heberden, Ernest 125
Henrietta Byrne Memorial Fund 204
Henry, Paul 129

Henry, Victor 83, 112, 114, 115, 117, 125, 129
Hereford, Cathedral 194, 199
Hickman, Aubrey 27
Hillery, Patrick 180
Hillsborough, Parish Church 196, 199
Hinckley, Peter 30
Hinds, Eric 82, 141
HM the Queen 205-6
Hoey, Joyce 186
Hoey, Paul 157
Hoey, Revd (later Archdeacon) Raymond 186
Hoey, Shauna 186-7
Holland, Thomas (Tommy) 30-31
Holmes, May 14, 20
Holmes, Roy 92
Holst, Imogen 48
Holt, Hazel 135
Holywood, Musical Festival 128
Howells, Herbert 43, 157-8, 173, 193
Huddleston, Rt Revd Trevor 114
Humphries, Revd David 177
Hunt, Donald 184
Hunter, Brian 84, 131
Hunter, Desmond 150, 185
Hunter, Peter 122, 160
Hunter, Rosemary 122
Hurford, Peter 192
Hurst, George 34

Incorporated Association of Organists 57, 106
Institute of Irish Studies 181
Ireland, Jonny 200
Ireland, Valerie 126, 166, 168, 198
Irish Church Music Association 135
Irish Church Praise 171, 190, 204
Irish Guards Band 111
Irvine, Revd Herbert 103

Jackson, Francis 85
James, Henry 149
James, Kenneth 149

Jasper, Canon Ronald 131
Jenkins, Christopher 160-1
John, Evan 25, 57, 111, 116, 149, 185
Johnson, Robert 120
Johnston, Anne 74-5
Johnston, David 124, 144
Johnston, Esdale (Jono) 126
Johnston, Maureen 74-5
Jones, Bertram 16-7
Jones, Caroline 167
Jones, Sir Harry and Lady 151
Jordanstown, St Patrick's Parish Church 183
Joubert, John 139

Kay, Brian 132
Kedge, Bernard 112
Keefe, Bernard 48
Keenan, Charles 164, 165
Kerr, Revd Cecil 95, 103
Kerr, Ewan 202-3
Kerr, Ruth (granddaughter) 205
Keys, Ivor 20
Kilkenny, St Canice's Cathedral 194
Killaloe, St Flannan's Cathedral 180
Kilmore, St Aidan's Parish Church 187
Kimberley, Alan 91
King, Cyril 126
King's Singers 153
Knight, Gerald 56, 65, 90, 141

Langridge, Philip 111
Lee, David 106
Lee, Pan Hon 155-6
Lee, Ronald 95
Leggatt, Donald 73, 108, 112, 117, 122
Leinster Society of Organists and Choirmasters 57, 80, 134
Lennon, Clifford 166
Limerick
  School of Music 202
  St Mary's Cathedral 180
Lincoln, Cathedral 200
Lindsay, H F Selwood 92, 132

Lindsay, Revd Joseph 63-4
Lindsay Singers 105, 112
Linenhall Choir 135
Loane, Barry 92
Loane, Carolyn (Lindi) 103
Loane, Heather see Grindle, Heather
London
    All Saints', Margaret Street 45-6
    Buckingham Palace 202
    Friern Barnet Grammar School
    38-48, 168
    St Edward's House 131
    St Paul's Cathedral 45, 64, 129-
    30, 132, 144
    St Paul's, Portman Square 41
    Trinity College of Music 125, 176,
    195
    Ulster Office 151
    Westminster Abbey 38, 45, 64,
    108, 131, 141, 151-2
    Westminster Cathedral 151
Lovett, Terence 63, 82, 94
Lyndon, Barry 185
Lyttle, John 55

Mack, Brian 105
MacKean, Pat 194
Mackey, Hugh 161
Maguire, Margaret 141
Maguire, Maurice 101
Maitland, Alan 133
Malcolm, George 48
Markevich, Igor 118-9
Marshall, Bob 10
Marshall, Canon O V 134
Martin, Roger 161-2
Massey, Roy 89
Maxwell, Ian 100, 122
Maynooth, St Patrick's College 190
McCarrison, Leslie 55
McCartney, Ruth 198
McCay, William 101
McClintock, Aubrey 161, 204
McClintock, Maeve 204

McClintock, Nigel 196, 197, 204
McConnell, David 106
McCoubrey, Larry 123
McCready Singers 82
McCreery, Canon Desmond 188
McDonald, James 12, 31
McDonald, William 178
McDowell, John 164, 165-6, 191
McGuffin, Michael 125
McKee, Alex 191, 199
McKee, Joe 182
McKeown, Ciaran 196
McMahon, Gladys 8
Megraw, R A 178
Middleton, James 114
Miles, Maurice 86, 105
Miller, Revd (later Bishop) Harold
184-5
Minchinson, John 116
Mitchell, Alasdair 135
Mitchell, Rt Revd F J 60
Moffitt, Earl 188
Monaghan, St Macartan's RC
Cathedral 120
Monte Carlo International Summer
Course for Orchestral Conductors 118
Moore, Archdeacon (later Bishop)
James 195
Moran, Edwin 32
Moran, Henrietta 32, 36, 92, 103, 123
Moran, Isabel 32, 105, 115
Moran, Stephen 32
Mortimer, Very Revd Sterling 181
Morwood, Tom 191
Muggeridge, Malcolm 141
Murray, Ann 121

National Symphony Orchestra of
Ireland 192
Neale, Doris 144
Nelson, Havelock 33, 78, 82, 83, 92,
106, 112, 115, 149, 141, 153, 168, 186,
196
Nelson, Paul 195

Nelson, Rory (grandson) 205
Nelson, Scott (grandson) 205
Nesbitt, Canon Ronnie 204
Nethsingha, Lucien 196-7
New Irish Chamber Orchestra 145
Newmarch, Frederick (Fred) 40, 41
New Year Honours 205
Newtownards
 Castle Gardens Primary School
 189
 Methodist Church 103
 Regent House Grammar School 4,
 12-5, 18-9, 31, 92, 204
 Strean Presbyterian Church 168
Nichol, Isaac 67
Nichol, Simon 48
Nielsen, Henning Lundt 29
Nies-Berger, Edouard 29
Nolan, Revd John (Vicar Choral) 75,
77, 126
North-East Ulster Schools' Symphony
Orchestra 137

Ó Dálaigh, Cearbhall 145
Ó Duinn Proinnsías 192
O'Hare, Brendan 122
O'Hare, Michael 122
O'Rawe, Gerard 156
Olin Chamber Orchestra 82
Oxford Music Bulletin 84
Oxford University Press 181

Page, Joan 54
Parker, Wesley 179
Parsons, Frank 11-12, 15, 16, 22
Partridge, Ian 78
Patterson, Revd Ruth 177-8
Patterson, Revd Tom 27, 178
Peacocke, Very Revd (later Bishop)
Cuthbert 64, 74, 109-10
Peeters, Flor 55, 87, 135, 156
Pelan, Margaret 24
Percival, Alan 105

Portrush, Ballywillan Presbyterian
Church 168
Portstewart, Agherton Parish Church
123
Potter, A J (Archie) 33, 121, 193
Powell, E H 89, 137
Powell, Revd Frederick J 92, 132, 137,
182
Preston, Simon 64, 76, 95
Price, Margaret 86
Prieur, André 145
Priory Records 201
Priory Singers 182-3, 185-6, 187, 190,
191, 193-4, 195-7, 198, 199, 200, 201,
203-4
Prosser, Philip 197, 199
Pugh, Leonard 154, 198

Queen's University Singers 94
Quin, Archdeacon (later Bishop)
George 36, 48, 51-2, 59, 60, 64, 109
Quin, Nora 51, 59

Radio Éireann 77, 94
Radio Telefís Éireann 134, 145-6, 183
Rainey, Ellen 124, 133
Ramsay, Keith 40, 41, 49
Ramsey, Basil 133
Rathcol 92, 138, 147
Raynor Cook, Brian 153
Rea, Jonathan 193
Regan, Sheila 130
Reid, Norma 199
Reynolds, Raymond 103
Richards, Michael 164, 165
Rittwegger, Leon 87
Roberton, Kenneth 32
Robinson, Eric 111
Rodway, Ashleigh 124
Rogers, Kathryn 193
Rogers, Keith 92, 114, 132, 141, 147,
156, 184, 193, 196
Rose, Barry 183
Roseingrave, Daniel 182, 193

Roseingrave, Ralph 182, 193, 198
Roseingrave, Thomas 193
Rosen, Hans Waldemar 94
Rowan, James 28
Royal Artillery (Woolwich) Band 147-8
Royal Liverpool Philharmonic
Orchestra 81
Royal Maundy 204-5
Royal College of Organists 42-4, 56-7,
65, 185
Royal School of Church Music 56-7,
65, 97, 108, 116, 141, 167-8

Salvation Army Lurgan Citadel Band
140
Sandford, Irene 141, 198
Sargent, Sir Malcolm 64-5, 76
Schweitzer, Albert 29
Scoular, Clive 130, 151
Segal, Judith 145
Shallway Foundation 134
Shaw, Watkins 182
Sheridan, Mary 120
Shimmin, Eleanor 86
Sidwell, Martindale 44
Simpson, Robert 12-3
Sing and Pray 189
Sligo, St John's Cathedral 181
Smart, David 40-1, 49
Smart, Lena 63
Smith, Anthony 78
Smith, Jack 84, 85, 129
Smyth, Roderick 162
Smyth, Rosemary 193-4
Somerville-Large, Bill 133
St Comgall's Singers 55
St Louis Order 102, 119-20
Steinitz, Paul 48
Stevenson, Margaret 179
Stolow, Meyer 116
Stoneley, Ernest 54
Stopford, Philip 202
Strange, David 80
Stranmillis Brass Ensemble 166

Stranmillis College Orchestra 166
Stranmillis Singers 164, 165, 166, 167,
168, 177
Strasbourg, University 29
Studholme, Marion 111
Studio Symphony Orchestra 82
Susskind, Walter 96
Swallow, Michael 95, 99
Swann, Freda 191
Sweeney, Eric 121, 193
Sweeney, Peter 180-1, 190

Taylor, Paul 1151, 116, 135
Teare, Edward 112
Temperley, Nicholas 181
Terpsichore Early Music Ensemble
193-4
Thiman, Eric 34, 42-3
Thomas, Marjorie 42, 47
Thomas, Revd Philip 42
Thompson, Robert 200
Thompson, William 166
Trory, Geoffrey 168
Tuam
    St Jarlath's College Hall 139
    St Mary's CoI Cathedral 139
Turner, T S (Tim) 20, 76, 101-2

Ulster Church Music Centre 171-2
Ulster College of Music 125
Ulster Opera 95-6
Ulster Orchestra 86, 95, 105-6, 111,
115-6, 118, 124, 129, 135, 141, 155
Ulster Singers 82, 83, 115, 135
Ulster Society of Organists and
Choirmasters 22, 29, 57-8, 63,80, 85,
95, 125, 134, 168, 172, 178, 182, 184-5
Urwin, Ian 129, 141
UTV 191
UTV Love came down 183
UTV School Choir of the Year 198
UTV Sing Out 183

Van Straubenzee, William 131-2

Verney, Sir Harry 90
Victoria Male Voice Choir 31-2
Vincent, James 176
Vine, John 34, 182

Walker, Brian 181
Walker, Norman 98
Wardell, Mark 200
Warren, Raymond 91, 92, 113, 153
Warrenpoint, Feis 171
Waugh, Thomas 19
White, Colin 187

White, Martin 116, 186, 188, 203
Wilcox, Alan 86
Willcocks, Sir David 34, 45, 105, 154-5, 173
Williams, Archbishop Rowan 204
Williams, John 47
Willoughby, Cyril 124, 144
Wilson, Gordon 72
Wood, Harry 69
Woods, Richard 199

Young, Jack 64, 80, 87-8, 142